Statistical
Misconceptions

Statistical Misconceptions

Schuyler W. Huck
University of Tennessee – Knoxville

Routledge
Taylor & Francis Group
New York   London

Psychology Press
Taylor & Francis Group
270 Madison Avenue
New York, NY 10016

Psychology Press
Taylor & Francis Group
27 Church Road
Hove, East Sussex BN3 2FA

Library of Congress Cataloging-in-Publication Data

Huck, Schuyler W.
    Statistical misconceptions / Schuyler W. Huck.
        p. cm.
        ISBN 978-0-8058-5902-7 (hardback) -- ISBN 978-0-8058-5904-1 (pbk.)
        1. Psychometrics. I. Title.

    BF39.H83 2008
    150.72'7--dc22   2008019136

**Visit the Taylor & Francis Web site at
http://www.taylorandfrancis.com**

**and the Psychology Press Web site at
http://www.psypress.com**

DEDICATION

This book is dedicated to three groups of individuals: those who have overcome one or more of their statistical misconceptions, those who will (at some point in the future) follow in the footsteps of those in the first group, and those whose life's work includes helping others to cast aside false beliefs about statistics.

BRIEF CONTENTS

CONTENTS

9   *t*-Tests Involving One or Two Means   195

10   ANOVA and ANCOVA   209

11   Practical Significance, Power, and Effect Size   225

12   Regression   243

Appendix A: Citations for Material Referenced in the Preface   263

PREFACE

Misconception, n. The action or an act of misconceiving or misunderstanding something. Now chiefly: a view or opinion that is false or inaccurate because [it is] based on faulty thinking or understanding. (Oxford English Dictionary, 2008)

People have misconceptions about many things. For example, it is commonly (but incorrectly) thought that the moon's orbit around our planet takes 28 days, that Napoleon Bonaparte was short, that humid air is more dense than dry air, that the normal body temperature of humans is 98.6° Fahrenheit, and that the Earth was considered to be flat by most people when Columbus began his voyage in 1492. People also have misconceptions about statistics.

This book and its companion Web site have been written to help people identify and then discard the major statistical misconceptions that have infiltrated the way they think about data. In a very real sense, therefore, this text is designed primarily to help people *undo* the statistical misconceptions that they already have. A secondary goal is to sharpen readers' way of thinking so they are less likely to acquire, in the future, new misconceptions that have not as yet infected their notions about statistics.

This Book's Statistical Misconceptions: What They Are (and What They Aren't)

As used here, the term *statistical misconception* refers to any of several widely held but incorrect notions about statistical concepts, about procedures for analyzing data and about the meaning of results produced by such analyses. To illustrate, many people think that (1) normal curves are bell shaped, (2) a correlation coefficient should never be used to address questions of causality, and (3) the level of significance dictates the probability of a Type I error. Some people, of course, have only one or two (rather than all three) of these misconceptions, and a few individuals realize that all three of those beliefs are false.

This book's target audience is made up of people who have had or currently have some exposure to statistical content in high school, and/ or college, most likely because a statistics course or sequence was or is a required part of their curriculum. The individuals in this group had or have something other than statistics as their academic major, and no career as a statistician was or is being considered. Although this book has been written primarily for current and past students, instructors and independent researchers may also benefit from examining the various misconceptions included here.

It should be noted that the statistical misconceptions discussed in this book are not small items of new content not covered in the readers' prior course work. Rather, the misconceptions focus on the mainstream concepts and relationships contained in the statistics courses and textbooks encountered by those in the target audience. The table of contents ought to make it clear that this book's content deals with familiar rather than exotic topics.

Evidence Regarding the Existence/Persistence of Statistical Misconceptions

Convincing evidence exists to defend the claim that many statistical misconceptions function to interfere with statistical decisions and the proper interpretation of data-based findings. This evidence comes in a variety of forms and from a variety of countries. For example, consider the following (with reference citations provided in Appendix A):

- A computer package called *StatPlay* has been developed by Geoff Cummings and Neil Thomason in Australia. The central goal of this program was and is "to overcome misconceptions about fundamental statistical concepts."

- At a recent meeting of the International Conference for Teaching Statistics, a researcher from Belgium (Herman Callaert) presented a paper entitled "Understanding Statistical Misconceptions." His final sentence is telling: "In order to design instructional interventions created specifically to eliminate students' misconceptions, a deeper understanding of those misconceptions is certainly needed."

- An article appeared recently in the *International Journal of Mathematics Education in Science and Technology* entitled "Errors and Difficulties in Understanding Elementary Statistical Concepts." In it, the team of researchers (led by Carmen Bantanero from Spain) discuss a host of specific statistical misconceptions in a variety of content areas (e.g., measures of spread, correlation, sampling, and hypothesis testing).

- Erica Morris, from England, has developed a computer-assisted program called *Link*; its goal is "to address students' misconceptions in correlation in the context of psychological studies."

- In a report entitled "A Deep Structure Model of Students' Statistical Misconceptions," researcher Zemira Mevarech from Israel points out that a particular set of misconceptions, situated in the minds of college students, "is so deeply ingrained in a student's underlying knowledge base that mere exposure to a more advanced course in statistics is not sufficient to overcome those misconceptions."

- A team of researchers from Taiwan and Canada (led by Tzu-Chien Liu) recently conducted a study to see if cognitive style is related to the effectiveness of computer multimedia in reducing statistical misconceptions. Results showed that "imagers" benefited more from the multimedia exercises than did "verbalizers."

- Joan Garfield, a stellar researcher from the United States, has devoted her career to statistical education. In her report entitled "How Students Learn Statistics," she points out that "several research studies in statistics as well as in other disciplines show that students' misconceptions are often strong and resilient—they are slow to change, even when students are confronted with evidence that their beliefs are incorrect."

The Origin of Statistical Misconceptions

Given that statistical misconceptions exist, it is natural to ask the question, Where do they come from? It is clear that this question has two answers. Some misconceptions, most assuredly, are grounded in human intuition that sometimes leads a person to think that something is true when it isn't. Other misconceptions, unfortunately, are generated by incorrect or incomplete statements about statistics that are found in books, seen on the Internet, and presented orally in classrooms. In a very real sense, certain statistical misconceptions are caused not by *internal* forces (such as one's intuition); instead, they are generated by *external* conditions (such as statements uttered or written by one's mentors).

Undoing Statistical Misconceptions

As indicated earlier, this book has been written to help people identify and then discard the major statistical misconceptions that have infiltrated the way they think about statistics. To accomplish this goal, each misconception is discussed in a standard five-part format. First, a one- or two-sentence description of the misconception is presented. Next, one or more quoted passages—taken from books, journal articles, convention papers, or Web sites—are presented that (1) illustrate the misconception in action or (2) discuss the prevalence of the misconception. In the third portion of each misconception's write-up, the author indicates why it is dangerous to have the misconception. This is followed by a presentation of the proper thoughts one should have about the topic being considered.

The fifth and final element of each misconception considered in this book is a guided exercise involving an interactive Internet activity. By actually playing with these online exercises (called Java applets), the reader will have a chance to grasp firmly the core meaning of certain statistical concepts, to test his or her predictions as to how a change in one statistical variable will influence a different variable, and to see that certain intuitive thoughts about statistics are not valid. It should be noted that these applets were selected carefully to help achieve this book's goal of undoing the statistical misconceptions. Each misconception was first identified and described; then, literally hundreds of Internet Web sites were examined in an effort to find the best applet for each misconception.

Content, Structure, and Recommendations for Use

This book contains a discussion of 52 different statistical misconceptions. These misconceptions are grouped according to content, with the book's 12 chapters coinciding with the topics typically taught in introductory and intermediate statistics courses:

1.   Descriptive statistics

2.   Distributional shape

3.   Bivariate correlation

4.   Reliability and validity

5.   Probability

6.   Sampling

7.   Estimation

8.   Hypothesis testing

9.   *t* tests on one or two means

10.   ANOVA and ANCOVA

11.   Practical significance, power, and effect size

12.   Regression

As indicated earlier, each of this book's 52 write-ups has five elements. These sections answer five questions concerning each misconception: (1) What is the misconception? (2) Does anyone have this misconception? (3) Why is it dangerous to have this misconception? (4) How should one think correctly about the statistical concept under consideration? (5) Is there an interactive, Internet-based Java applet available for helping people overcome this particular misconception?

The most efficient and beneficial way to use this book involves a three-step approach to each misconception. First, read the brief description of the misconception (as well as the quoted passages that immediately follow that description). If you know for certain that you do *not* have that particular misconception, move on to a different part of the book. On the other hand, if you realize that the misconception is floating around inside your head, read the next two sections: "Why This Misconception Is Dangerous" and "Undoing the Misconception." After reading those two sections, consider the simple questions asked in the final section, "Internet Assignment." Depending on how you answer those questions, you may or may not decide that it is worth your time to visit this book's companion Web site so you can link up to an online, interactive Java applet that sheds light on the misconception under consideration.

The Evidence Offered to Show That the Misconceptions Exist

For each of the 52 misconceptions, one or more quoted passages appear under the heading "Evidence That This Misconception Exists." In those cases where someone's misconception is revealed by his or her written statement, such passages constitute clear evidence that the misconception exists. On the other hand, in those cases where the quoted material points to the *prevalence* of the misconception, I acknowledge that the alleged evidence is qualitatively different (from the first kind of documentation) and is not as strong. The quoted passages pointing to the prevalence of misconceptions, at their core, are simply opinions. However, I consider such opinions to be credible because they are aligned with the statements I have seen or heard students and colleagues make during my four decades of work as a college professor.

I have positioned the reference citations for all "Evidence" quotations in Appendix B, rather than following the common practice of putting such citations on the pages containing the quotations. My sole motivation in presenting the quoted passages that reveal improper thinking is to document the existence of such thoughts—and I have no desire to publicly ridicule or humiliate the individuals who made these statements. Accordingly, I have purposefully separated names from quotations.

Over the years, I, too, have possessed many statistical misconceptions. Upon noting my faulty thinking, my friends, teachers, and anonymous reviewers have helped me to eliminate my misconceptions and thereby to think more clearly about statistics. With appreciation for the way those formal and informal mentors responded to *my* misconceptions, I felt obliged to position the reference material for all "Evidence" quotations in Appendix B.

Companion Web Site

This book's companion Web site has been created to provide readers with computer-based, interactive opportunities to help them overcome this book's statistical misconceptions. This Web site is located at http://www.psypress.com/statistical-misconceptions, and it contains two things for each of the book's misconceptions:

- A link to an interactive Java applet available on the Internet

- Detailed directions (prepared by this book's author) on how to use the Java applet

Because the interactive Internet assignments are so powerful in illuminating the proper way to think about statistical concepts, you are strongly encouraged to engage in these activities. In other words, be inclined to use the book's companion Web site as a stepping stone to a variety of online Java applets that are fun to use and helpful to people as they try to overcome their misconceptions. Even if you think that the fourth element of any misconception discussion ("Undoing the Misconception") is fully successful in replacing any of your original bad thoughts with good ones, you still may find it worthwhile to look at the Java applet that has been paired with that particular misconception. For one thing, your knowledge of that applet will allow you to describe it (and recommend its use) to someone else you encounter who needs help in eradicating the misconception. You also may discover that the applet allows you to gain new knowledge completely unrelated to the particular misconception with which the applet is paired.

This book's Internet assignments were field tested by graduate students in a variety of different disciplines. These individuals were asked to provide hard-nosed feedback regarding the usefulness of these interactive activities. This feedback was incredibly positive. Over and over again, the graduate students stated that the interactive online activities allowed them to gain, for the first time, a deep understanding of statistical concepts. What these graduate students said about the Java applets supports the view that interactive opportunities are not just important, but essential to overcoming statistical misconceptions.

Acknowledgments

Although I willingly take full responsibility for any errors that have inadvertently crept into the final version of this book, I want to acknowledge the contributions made by others to the creation and refinement of this work.

First, I thank my instructors. Throughout my formal education, my teachers have encouraged me to think clearly, to be precise, and to look for exceptions to the rule. After completing my PhD, my instructors became the authors of books I adopted for the courses I taught, the anonymous reviewers who evaluated manuscripts I submitted to peer reviewed journals, and the many presenters and discussants who have spoken at professional meetings. Over the course of nearly four decades, these individuals have made me aware of many misconceptions that had infected my own brain.

Next, I thank my students. During class sessions and phone conversions, in e-mail messages sent to my inbox and notes left on my office door, and within the context of impromptu hallway and parking lot conversations, students have asked and stated things that revealed many misunderstandings of statistical concepts and relationships. To a large degree, those expressed misconceptions made it apparent that this book might help learners. A second set of students need to be thanked. A small group of top-flight graduate students (Michelle Anderson, Allie Brown, Olivia Halic, and Brian Strahine) reviewed my writing and offered sound advice regarding grammar, clarity of expression, and organization. Two PhD students in particular—Hongwei Yang and Lila Holt—need to be singled out for their extensive and thorough assistance with this book project. Hongwei made several contributions of a highly technical nature; he argued successfully that certain topics should be included while others (already written) should be omitted, and he helped locate evidence to show that this book's misconceptions truly do exist. Lila was immensely helpful in preparing the book's many figures and the companion Web site.

I also express appreciation to the reviewers who examined the initial prospectus and an early draft of the book's manuscript: Nancy Leech (University of Colorado at Denver), Richard Lomax (Ohio State University), Scott Maxwell (University of Notre Dame), Joseph S. Rossi (University of Rhode Island), and Erik Turkheimer (University of Virginia). I am indebted to these individuals for the important contributions they made to this project. Their comments helped shape the final form of each misconception's write-up, their attention to detail revealed mistakes I had made in presenting technical information, and their general support for this book project helped me to stay motivated from start to finish.

Finally, I thank Debra Riegert and Lane Akers. Debra is my editor at Taylor & Francis. Her knowledge of the field, her commitment to quality, her ability to get highly competent reviewers to read portions of the manuscript, and her patience with me (when I missed deadlines) made Debra a pure joy to work with. Without question, I could not have had a better editor than Debra Riegert! Lane Akers is a long-term friend from the publishing field. I have respected Lane for nearly 40 years, and I want to thank him for providing initial support for this project.

Schuyler W. Huck

CHAPTER 1

Descriptive Statistics

There is evidence that, despite best efforts, many students and also some teachers and researchers have persistent statistical misconceptions.*

The trouble with statistics is that they are often counter-intuitive. What seems like a common sense answer to a question is often wrong.†

* Thomason, N., Brown, T., Maillardet, R., Finch, S., and Cumming, G. *StatPlay and the challenges of statistics education across many disciplines.* Retrieved December 19, 2006, from http://www.infodiv.unimelb.edu.au/telars/mettle/ditam/1997/case_studies/Thomason.html.

† Ben-Ami, D. (2003). Close encounters with aliens and other fallacies. *Morningstar* (UK). Retrieved October 1, 2007, from http://www.morningstar.co.uk/UK/Funds/article.aspx?lang=en-GB&articleID=24118&categoryID=14.

☐ 1.1 Measures of Central Tendency

The Misconception

There are three different measures of central tendency: the mean, the median, and the mode.

Evidence That This Misconception Exists*

The first of the following statements comes from a recent peer-reviewed article in the medical field. The second statement comes from a book dealing with quality control. The third statement comes from an online U.S. government document.

1. *The central tendency is the tendency of the observations to accumulate at a particular value or in a particular category. The three ways of describing this phenomenon are mean, median, and mode.*

2. *There are three measures of central tendency: mean, median, and mode.*

3. *There are three kinds of average: the mean, the median, and the mode.*

Why This Misconception Is Dangerous

Various measures of central tendency have been invented because the proper notion of the "average" score can vary from study to study. Depending on the kind of data collected, the degree of skewness in the data, and the possible existence of outliers, it may be that the most appropriate measure of central tendency is found by doing something *other than* (1) dividing the sum of the scores by the number of scores (to get the mean), (2) calculating the midpoint in the distribution (to get the median), or (3) determining the most frequently observed score (to get the mode).

---

* Appendix B contains references for all quoted material presented in this section.

If you are familiar with only the arithmetic mean, the median, and the mode, you'll find yourself guilty of trying to "cram a square peg into a round hole" if a situation calls for one of the lesser known measures of central tendency. A popular little puzzle question makes this point:

> If a car travels at a constant rate of 40 miles per hour between points A and B but then makes the return trip at a constant rate of 60 miles per hour, what is the car's average speed?

Here, as in certain situations involving real data, one of the lesser known averages is called for.

Undoing the Misconception

It is best to think of the various kinds of central tendency indices as falling into three categories based on the computational procedures one uses to summarize the data. One category deals with means, with techniques put into this category if scores are added together and then divided by the number of scores that are summed. The second category involves different kinds of medians, with various techniques grouped here if the goal is to find some sort of midpoint. The third category contains different kinds of modes, with these techniques focused on the frequency with which scores appear in the data.

In the first category (means), we obviously find the arithmetic mean. However, other entries in this category include the geometric mean, harmonic mean, trimmed mean, winsorized mean, midmean, and quadratic mean.*

- The *geometric mean* is equal to $\sqrt[N]{(X_1)(X_2)...(X_N)}$. For example, the geometric mean of 2, 3, and 36 is equal to $\sqrt[3]{(2)(3)(36)}$, which is 6.

- The *harmonic mean* is equal to N divided by $\sum_{i=1}^{N} 1/X_i$. For example, the harmonic mean of 2, 4, and 4 is equal to $3/[(1/2)+(1/4)+(1/4)]$, which is 3.

- The *trimmed mean* is the arithmetic average of the scores that remain after discarding the highest and lowest pth percent of the data. For

---

* The trimmed mean and the midmean are sometimes referred to as *truncated means*; the quadratic mean is sometimes referred to as the *root mean square* and is abbreviated as *RMS*.

example, the trimmed mean might be computed as the arithmetic mean of the middle 80% of the scores.

- The *winsorized mean* is the arithmetic average of all N scores after replacing the highest and lowest pth percent of the scores with the highest and lowest observed scores located on the "edges" of the middle section of scores. For example, the winsorized mean of the scores 1, 2, 4, 6, 8, and 21 might involve replacing the 1 with a 2 and the 21 with an 8, thus making the winsorized mean equal to 5.

- The *midmean* is the arithmetic mean of the middle 50% of the scores. For example, the midmean of the 12 scores 2, 3, 4, 6, 6, 6, 8, 8, 8, 9, 13, and 30 is 7.

- The *quadratic mean* is equal to $\sqrt{(1/N)\sum_{i=1}^{N} X_i^2}$. For example, the quadratic mean of 1, 1, 7, and 7 is 5.

In the second category (medians), we of course find the traditional median (which is equivalent to Q_2, the 50th percentile). Three other kinds of central tendency also belong in this category: midrange, midhinge, and trimean.*

- The *midrange* is the halfway point between the high and low scores. With 12 scores equal to 2, 3, 4, 6, 6, 6, 8, 8, 8, 9, 13, and 30, the midrange is equal to 16.

- The *midhinge* is the halfway point between Q_1 (the 25th percentile point) and Q_3 (the 75th percentile point). Thus, with eight scores equal to 3, 3, 5, 6, 8, 8, 10, and 14, the midhinge is equal to 6.5.

- The *trimean* is equal to $(Q_1 + 2Q_2 + Q_3)/4$, where Q_1, Q_2, and Q_3 are the lower, middle, and upper quartile points, respectively. For example, the trimean for the 12 scores 2, 3, 4, 6, 6, 6, 8, 8, 8, 9, 13, and 30 – [5 + 2(7) + 8.5]/4 = 6.875.

---

[a] Despite its name, the trimean is far more like a median than a mean. That's because it is based on only three points in the distribution of scores, Q_1, Q_2, and Q_3. Granted, the trimean is equal to the arithmetic mean of the three quartile points after weighting Q_2 twice as heavily as Q_1 and Q_3. However, it is possible that none of the quartile points will have a numerical value equal to any observed score in the distribution. Thus, the trimean (like the median) is based on an ordering of the scores rather than a consideration of all scores' numerical values.

The third category of central tendency indices involves modes. Here, we find the traditional notion of the mode: the most frequently occurring score in the data set. In addition, three additional kinds of modes exist: minor mode, crude mode, and refined mode.

- The *minor mode* is the most frequently occurring score in the smaller of the 2 "humps" of a bimodal distribution. Thus, the minor mode is equal to 3 for the data displayed in Figure 1.1.1.*

- The *crude mode* is simply the midpoint of the modal interval in a grouped frequency distribution. For example, the crude mode for the data in Table 1.1.1 is equal to 17, the midpoint of the interval containing 10 of the 31 scores.

- The *refined mode* also deals with a grouped frequency distribution.† The refined mode adjusts the crude mode by considering the frequencies of the intervals adjacent to the modal interval. It is computed as

$$L + \frac{i\left(f_{mo} - f_b\right)}{\left(f_{mo} - f_b\right) + \left(f_{mo} - f_a\right)}$$

where L = the lower limit of the modal interval, i = the interval width, f_{mo} = the frequency in the modal interval, f_b = the frequency in the interval immediately below the modal interval, and f_a = the frequency in the interval immediately above the modal interval. For the frequency distribution, the refined mode is equal to 15.5.

Internet Assignment

Would you like to see how different measures of central tendency produce radically different numerical values for the "average" score, even when they are based on the same data? Would you like to do this in a fast manner using an Internet-based, interactive Java applet that lets you control the size of each score and the number of scores in the group?

---

* Note that the minor mode is *not* equal to the second most frequently observed score.
† The refined mode is discussed on pp. 21–22 of Weisberg, H. F. (1992). *Central tendency and variability*. Thousand Oaks, CA: Sage.

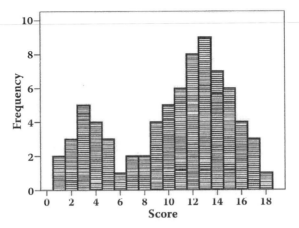

FIGURE 1.1.1 Major and minor modes in a bimodal distribution.

TABLE 1.1.1. A Frequency Distribution Summarizing 31 Scores

Interval	Frequency
35–39	2
30–34	2
25–29	3
20–24	2
15–19	10
10–14	8
5–9	3
0–4	1

If you would like to see some proof that different measures of central tendency can yield highly different results, visit this book's companion Web site (http://www.psypress.com/statistical-misconceptions). Once there, open the folder for Chapter 1 and click on the link called "Measures of Central Tendency." After doing this, you will find detailed instructions (prepared by this book's author) on how to use the Java applet. Doing this interactive "assignment" is guaranteed to get your brain thinking about measures of central tendency.

☐ 1.2 The Mean of Means

The Misconception

If one large group is made up of two subgroups (e.g., males and females), and if the mean score for each subgroup is available on a variable of interest, then the mean for the full group can be computed as the mean of the two subgroup means.

Evidence That This Misconception Exists*

The first of the following statements comes from a journal called *Teaching Statistics*, while the second statement comes from a journal focused on mathematics teacher education. (In the second statement, note the finding that only 21% of the college students correctly computed the mean of means.)

1. *Previous research ... found that many students who attempted to combine means of two groups of different sizes into an overall mean of the pooled group did not weight the two given means and computed their uniformly weighted (arithmetic) mean, even though the different group sizes were explicitly given.*

2. *The [research] participants were 263 undergraduate students [who] had studied mathematics for 5 years at high school level.... Twenty-one percent correctly solved the weighted means problem. The remaining students used a variety of incorrect approaches when attempting the problem. The predominant approach used by 25% of the students involved adding the original means and dividing the sum by the number of quantities added (n = 2). Participants did not take into account that the values presented were means, and solved the problem as if asked to find the mean of two values.*

Why This Misconception Is Dangerous

It is easy to compute the mean of subgroup means, especially when the large group is composed of just two subgroups. Moreover, doing this

---

* Appendix B contains the reference for the quoted material presented in this section.

seems logical (at first glance, at least). Each subgroup mean is based on all scores in a portion of the whole, and all subgroups added together make up the whole; therefore, the mean of the subgroup means—because it is based on all original scores—would seem to be a fast and accurate way to compute the mean for the full group.

Although it might seem logical to compute the mean of subgroup means, doing this can lead to a highly inaccurate result that misrepresents the full group. In those special situations where (1) a full group is made up of different subgroups and (2) each subgroup itself is composed of even smaller parts that are common across subgroups (such as male and female workers within each of several different departments of a business), the strategy of computing the mean of means not only can produce a finding that misrepresents the full group, but also can generate conclusions that misrepresent (and possibly "reverse") the relative status of the smaller parts that make up the subgroups.

In situations where there are two or more homogeneous subgroups (i.e., subgroups that are not made up of smaller parts), the computation of the mean of the subgroup means can produce a result that does not adequately describe any of the subgroup data—even if the subgroups are the same size! In some situations, it simply makes no sense to combine subgroups into a single larger group. To do so may yield a statistical result that does not represent adequately the data in *any* of the subgroups.

Undoing the Misconception

Table 1.2.1 contains some fictitious data concerning salaries paid to the male and female faculty members who work in two academic disciplines—engineering and social work—in a university.* The mean salary is presented for both males and females in each discipline.

First, you need to be aware that the mean salary of the 100 faculty members in engineering is $101,000 (not $105,000); likewise, the mean salary for the 40 faculty members in social work is $43,000 (not $42,000). Also note that the females' mean salary within each discipline is higher than the mean salary for males; however, when the two disciplines are combined, the mean for males ($94,000) is higher than the mean for females ($60,500).

---

* These data come from Carol Livingstone's PowerPoint presentation, *Gender equity studies: The good, the bad, and the ugly*. Retrieved December 12, 2006, from http://www.dmi.uiuc. edu/reg/AAUPUIS.PPT.

TABLE 1.2.1. Mean Data on Salaries

Gender	Index	Engineering	Social Work
Males	N	90	10
	Mean salary	$100,000	$40,000
Females	N	10	30
	Mean salary	$110,000	$44,000

The mean of subgroup means leads to the correct numerical value only if the subgroups are the same size. If subgroups vary in size, the mean for the combined group must be computed as a *weighted* mean. For example, the mean salary for all 100 males in the previous example should be computed as

$$\frac{N_1(\bar{X}_1) + N_2(\bar{X}_2)}{N_1 + N_2} = \frac{90(\$100,000) + 10(\$40,000)}{90 + 10} = \$94,000$$

As this example shows, the difference between two means at one "level of aggregation" can be the reverse of what it is when data are looked at in a more (or less) comprehensive manner. Thus, what's true of the whole may not be true of the parts, and vice versa.

Internet Assignment

Is the human brain able to function like a high-speed computer and determine the numerical value of the weighted mean? Probably not, if the subgroup means involve decimals or the subgroup sizes are not easy to handle in one's head. But what if (1) each N is a multiple of 10 not larger than 40 and (2) each subgroup mean is a multiple of 5 between 10 and 40? Those restrictions ought to make it easier to compute the weight mean. So, under those two restrictions, could *your* brain act fast and correctly guess what the weighted mean is equal to?

If you would like to challenge yourself with a little weighted mean puzzle, visit this book's companion Web site (http://www.psypress.com/statistical-misconceptions). Once there, open the folder for Chapter 1 and click on the link called "The Mean of Means." This will take you to an Internet-based interactive Java applet that computes the weighted mean. For each of two sets of data (prepared by this book's author), you will be asked to guess what the weighted mean is before the Java applet gives you the answer. The first data set is easy to deal with, and your quick guess will be correct. But what about the second data set? Will you be able to guess the weighted mean for those scores too?

☐ 1.3 The Mode's Location

The Misconception

For any distribution of scores that's illustrated with a histogram or a smooth curve, the mode is located at the top of the tallest bar (in a histogram) or at the apex of the highest, or perhaps only, "hump" (in any picture that uses a curved line to show the distribution).

Evidence That This Misconception Exists*

The first of the following statements comes from a statistics book aimed at geographers, the second statement comes from a book dealing with dental public health, and the third statement comes from a PowerPoint slide presentation in a college-level statistics course. (In these passages, note that the mode is referred to as *a peak*, as *the highest point* on the curve, and as the *top of the curve*)

1. *How many different peaks are there? Obviously, if there is only one peak, there is one typical value. Such a peak is called a mode, and a distribution with one mode is said to be unimodal....*

2. *The mode is the highest point of the curve; the median is the value that divides the area under the curve in half.*

3. *Mode: Most frequent score (top of the curve).*

Why This Misconception Is Dangerous

The danger of this misconception is that it functions as a barrier to the proper interpretation of pictorial representations of distributional shapes. If a person misconstrues the location of the mode (by thinking it is on the curve rather than on the baseline), he or she is likely to think incorrectly about other picture-related statistical concepts. For example, critical regions for certain test procedures (such as t, F, and χ^2) will be thought of,

---

* Appendix B contains references for all quoted material presented in this section.

incorrectly, as two-dimensional tail *areas* of the theoretical distributions. Similarly, those who cannot correctly position the mode in a picture are likely to mistakenly think that those who earn a given stanine score on a test are located *inside* a narrow, vertical "slice" of the distribution (rather than *on* the baseline under that section of the distribution).

Undoing the Misconception

In any picture of a score distribution, the mode is located on the horizontal straight line that has bars or a smooth line positioned above it. The mode is positioned, on this line, directly *beneath* the tallest bar or highest hump. To locate the mode, you first look high off the baseline in search of the tallest bar or the point where the curved line is at its highest point. Next, you drop your gaze—following an invisible plumb line—to the baseline to find the score value on that line that's directly under the tallest bar or the curve's highest point.*

In a positively skewed distribution, the mode's numerical value is smaller than the numerical values of the median and the mean. This fact makes sense so long as one realizes that the mode is a point on the baseline. Those who think that the mode is equivalent to the highest point above the baseline will mistakenly think that the mode is larger than the median and mean in distributions that are skewed to the right.

Internet Assignment

Are you at all uncertain as to where the mode belongs in a pictorial summary of a set of scores? Do you have a few minutes to play with an Internet-based Java applet that computes the modal score and shows where it is located in a histogram whose shape you can change?

If you would like to see where the mode is located in graphs that summarize distributions of real or hypothetical data, visit this book's companion Web site (http://www.psypress.com/statistical-misconceptions). Once there, open the folder for Chapter 1 and click on the link called "The Mode's Location." After doing this, you will find detailed instructions (prepared by this book's author) on how to use the Java applet. For any distribution that you create, the mode will be computed and its proper location in the graph shown.

---

* In a normal distribution, the mode is equivalent to a z-score of 0.

☐ 1.4 The Standard Deviation

The Misconception

The standard deviation indicates the average (i.e., mean) numerical discrepancy between individual scores and the mean score.

Evidence That This Misconception Exists*

The first of the following statements comes from a recently published dictionary of statistics. The second statement comes from an online document entitled *Antarctic Explorers*.

1. *Standard deviation (SD): quite a difficult concept to understand because of its nonintuitive nature. Possibly the easiest while still accurate way to regard it is as the average amount by which scores in a set of scores differ from the mean of that set of scores.*

2. *The standard deviation is the average of the deviation of the measurements from the mean.*

Why This Misconception Is Dangerous

The definition given above is for the average deviation, not the standard deviation. Although both of these indices of dispersion focus on the deviation scores, they are different from each other both conceptually and computationally.

The standard deviation (*SD*) and the average deviation (*AD*) are conceptually different in how they approach the notion of "spread." For example, the point from which deviations are taken is arbitrary with the average deviation; that point can be the arithmetic mean, the median, or any other value. With the standard deviation, however, deviation scores are always measured as distances from the mean. The average deviation and the standard deviation also differ with respect to the intended weight given to extreme scores (i.e., scores that lie far away from the data

---

* Appendix B contains references for the quoted material presented in this section.

set's center). Such scores are intended to impact the value of *SD* more than the value of *AD*.

The standard deviation and the average deviation also differ computationally. For most sets of data wherein at least two scores differ, $SD \neq AD$. Thus, to confuse the average deviation with the standard deviation can lead to inaccuracies in statistical results that use the standard deviation (along with other "ingredients") in more complicated formulas designed to accomplish other objectives. For example, an individual's *z*-score after taking a test indicates how far that individual's score lies above or below the group mean, relative to the variability of the group's scores. If the average deviation (rather than the standard deviation) is used to measure a person's standing in the group, the result will not likely match up with the person's actual *z*-score.

Undoing the Misconception

The fact that the standard deviation is not the average value of the deviation scores is made clear by the formula for the standard deviation:

$$SD = \sqrt{\sum_{i=1}^{N}\left(X_i - \bar{X}\right)^2 / N}$$

where X_i represents the *i*th score in the group, $\bar{X}$ represents the arithmetic mean, and N represents the number of scores in the group.* For these 10 scores—0, 1, 2, 3, 4, 4, 5, 7, 11, and 13—$SD = 4$. The average deviation for these same data (with deviations taken from the arithmetic mean) is equal to 3. To get these values for *SD* and *AD*, Table 1.4.1 was initially prepared† and then the summary data in the right column were used to compute

$$SD = \sqrt{\frac{160}{10}} \quad \text{and} \quad AD = \frac{30}{10}$$

With most sets of scores, the standard deviation will be larger than the average deviation from the mean. For the data we just examined,

---

* If the group of scores is considered to be a sample, the denominator under the radical sign must be changed from N to $n - 1$.

† In computing the average deviation, the algebraic sign of the deviation scores is disregarded. Because such deviations are computed as absolute values, all scores in the bottom row of the chart are positive.

TABLE 1.4.1. Initial Calculations Involved in Computing SD and AD for 10 Scores

		X_1	X_2	X_3	X_4	X_5	X_6	X_7	X_8	X_9	X_{10}	Σ
X_i	=	1	1	2	2	2	2	3	4	9	14	40
$(X_i-\bar{X})^2$	=	9	9	4	4	4	4	1	0	25	100	160
$X_i-\bar{X}$	=	3	3	2	2	2	2	1	0	5	10	30

the standard deviation was 1.33 times as large as the average deviation. In a normal distribution, the standard deviation is about 1.25 times as large as the average deviation. There are a few situations where the standard deviation turns out equal to the average deviation, but it is never the case that the average deviation is larger than the standard deviation.

Internet Assignment

Do you have a good "feel" for what the standard deviation is and how it differs from the average deviation? If not, you might benefit from spending a few minutes playing with an Internet-based interactive Java applet that can be used to show how these two statistical concepts differ.

To convince yourself (in a fun way) that the standard deviation is conceptually different from the average deviation, visit this book's companion Web site (http://www.psypress.com/statistical-misconceptions). Once there, open the folder for Chapter 1 and click on the link called "The Standard Deviation." After doing this, you will find detailed instructions (prepared by this book's author) on how to use the Java applet, along with three questions (prepared by this book's author) that are very likely to help you understand what a standard deviation really is.

☐ Recommended Reading

Dalenius, T. (1965). The mode—A neglected statistical parameter. *Journal of Royal Statistical Society, Series A, 128*(1), 110–117.

Delmas, R., & Liu, Y. (2005). Exploring students' conceptions of the standard deviation. *Statistics Education Research Journal, 4*(1), 55–82.

Gonzales, V. A., & Ottenbacher, K. J. (2001). Measures of central tendency in rehabilitation research: What do they mean? *American Journal of Physical Medicine & Rehabilitation, 80*(2), 141–146.

Interpreting results: Mean, geometric mean and median. (n.d.). Retrieved November 1, 2007, from http://www.graphpad.com/help/Prism5/prism5help.html?stat_means_medians_and_more.htm.

Langford, E. (2006). Quartiles in elementary statistics. *Journal of Statistics Education, 14*(3). Retrieved November 2, 2007, from www.amstat.org/publications/jse/v14n3/langford.html.

Lee, C., Zeleke, A., & Wachtel, H. (2002). *Where do students get lost: The concept of variation?* Paper presented at the International Conference on Teaching Statistics, Durban, South Africa.

Makar, K., & Confrey, J. (2005). "Variation-talk": Articulating meaning in statistics. *Statistics Education Research Journal, 4*(1), 27–54.

Pollatsek, A., Lima, S., & Well, A. D. (1981). Concept or computation: Students' understanding of the mean. *Educational Studies in Mathematics, 12*(2), 191–204.

Reading, C., & Shaughnessy, J. M. (2004). Reasoning about variation. In D. Ben-Zvi & J. Garfield (Eds.), *The challenge of developing statistical literacy, reasoning and thinking* (pp. 201–226). Dordrecht, The Netherlands: Kluwer Academic Publishers.

Simpson's paradox—When big data sets go bad. (n.d.). Retrieved April 27, 2007, from http://www.intuitor.com/statistics/SimpsonsParadox.html.

Streiner, D. L. (2000). Do you see what I mean? Indices of central tendency. *Canadian Journal of Psychiatry, 45*(9), 833–836.

Distributional Shape

Scientists have been known to fool themselves with statistics due to lack of knowledge of probability theory and lack of standardisation of their tests.*

---

* *Misuse of statistics.* Retrieved January 13, 2007, from http://www.en.wikipedia.org/wiki/Misuse_of_statistics.

☐ 2.1 The Shape of the Normal Curve

The Misconception

The normal curve is bell shaped. When drawn, therefore, the normal curve should resemble the side view of a bell, as illustrated in Figure 2.1.1.

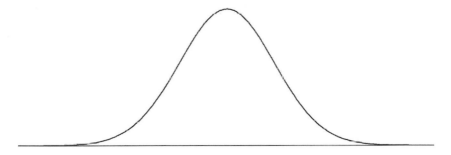

FIGURE 2.1.1 A normal curve.

Evidence That This Misconception Exists*

The first of the following statements comes from a book dealing with psychology, the second statement comes from a book dealing with bio-statistics, and the third statement comes from an online document for educational researchers.

1. *A normal curve is bell-shaped, with a large number of scores in the middle, tapering to very few extremely high or low scores.*

2. *The normal curve has the shape of a bell.*

3. *The normal curve refers to a frequency distribution in which the graph of scores resembles a bell—hence, the famous bell-shaped curve.*

---

* Appendix B contains references for all quoted material presented in this section.

Why This Misconception Is Dangerous

Normality is an underlying assumption of many statistical procedures used by applied researchers. For example, a *t*-test comparing two sample means is based on the presumption that the scores in each of the two populations are normally distributed. Other statistical tests also are based on the presumption that the populations being sampled are normal.

If a researcher checks the normality assumption by visually inspecting each sample's data (for example, by looking at a frequency distribution or a histogram), that researcher might incorrectly think that the data are nonnormal because the distribution appears to be too tall and skinny or too flat and squatty. As a result of this misdiagnosis, the researcher might unnecessarily abandon his or her initial plan to use a parametric statistical test in favor of a different procedure, perhaps one that is thought to be distribution-free.

Undoing the Misconception

The shape of a normal curve is influenced by two things: (1) the distance between the baseline and the curve's apex, and (2) the length, on the baseline, that's set equal to one standard deviation.* The *arbitrary* values chosen for these distances by the person drawing the normal curve determine the appearance of the resulting picture. For example, if the first of these distances is made large while the second is made small, the resulting normal curve will be tall and narrow compared with the frequently seen bell-shaped version of the normal curve.

Consider the two curves shown in Figure 2.1.2. Each is a normal curve even though the one on the left looks too tall and "skinny," whereas the one on the right looks to be too short and "squatty."

A formula dictates the height of every point on the normal curve as compared with the height of the curve's tallest point. One formula (of many) for the normal curve is

$$f(x) = \frac{1}{\sigma\sqrt{2\pi}} e^{-\frac{1}{2}\left(\frac{x-\mu}{\sigma}\right)^2}$$

---

* Many books indicate that the two defining properties of a normal curve are the mean and the standard deviation. Although this is true, the mean does not influence the *shape* of the curve. Instead, μ influences only the place where the curve is centered on the baseline.

FIGURE 2.1.2 Two normal curves.

If we know how far, in a horizontal direction, a point on the curve lies away from the curve's vertical "midline," then that point's vertical distance off the baseline is fixed by the normal curve's formula. That's the case for *every* point on the curve. Nevertheless, the shape of the normal curve can be manipulated by changing the curve's maximum height and/or the baseline distance that's set equal to one standard deviation away from the mean.

It should be noted that any finite data set cannot "follow" the normal curve exactly. That's because a normal curve's two "tails" extend out to positive and negative infinity. The curved line that forms a normal curve gets closer and closer to the baseline as the curved line moves further and further away from its middle section; however, the curved line never actually touches the abscissa.* Thus, if we have the heights of 100,000 people who are attending a football game, those heights may resemble (i.e., approximate) a normal distribution; however, it's impossible for those measurements to form a perfect normal curve simply because there will always be a highest and a lowest score in any finite group of measurements.

Internet Assignment

Would you like to see a normal curve change its shape right before your eyes? Moreover, would you like to be the one who causes it to deviate from the bell-shaped curve that typically comes to mind when we hear or see the words *normal curve*? If so, spend a few minutes playing with an Internet-based interactive Java applet that puts you in control of the normal curve's shape.

To see some things about the normal curve that you may not have ever seen before, visit this book's companion Web site (http://www. psypress.com/statistical-misconceptions). Once there, open the folder for

---

* The term *abscissa* is simply the technical label for the horizontal axis in a two-dimensional graph.

Chapter 2 and click on the link called "The Shape of the Normal Curve." After doing this, you will find detailed instructions (prepared by this book's author) on how to use the Java applet. Those instructions will show you how to create some very non-bell-shaped normal curves!

☐ 2.2 Skewed Distributions and Measures of Central Tendency

The Misconception

If a set of scores forms a positively skewed distribution, the numerical values of the arithmetic mean, median, and mode will turn out such that mean > median > mode. On the other hand, if a distribution of scores is negatively skewed, mean < median < mode.

Evidence That This Misconception Exists*

This first of the following statements comes from a recently published book dealing with statistics. The second statement comes from an online document dealing with measures of central tendency. (Note the word *always* that appears in each of these passages.)

1. *[T]he mode, median, and mean do not coincide in skewed distributions, although their relative positions remain constant—moving away from the "peak" and toward the "tail," the order is always from mode, to median, to mean.*

2. *In any skewed distribution (i.e., positive or negative) the median will always fall in-between the mean and the mode.*

Why This Misconception Is Dangerous

In summarizing data for technical reports, many researchers provide no hint as to the possible skewness of their data. More often than not, the research report contains no numerical index of skewness and no verbal description (e.g., "the data were positively skewed") based on a visual inspection of the data.

Many readers of these reports think they can determine if and how data are skewed, so long as multiple measures of central tendency are included in the research report. Such guesswork can backfire because computers now permit the direction and magnitude of skewness to be

---

* Appendix B contains references for the quoted material presented in this section.

assessed more accurately than was the case years ago when only crude formulas were available. Those crude formulas led to "rules of thumb" that supposedly allowed one to assess skewness via measures of central tendency. Unfortunately, the application of those rules can make one think that data are skewed left when they are actually skewed right (or vice versa).

Undoing the Misconception

Pictures of skewed distributions typically show a systematic decrease in score frequency as one moves, in either direction, away from the modal score. An example of this kind of picture is shown on the left side of Figure 2.2.1. In skewed distributions such as this, the arithmetic mean, median, and mode will assume numerical values that cause mean > median > mode (in positively skewed distributions) or mean < median < mode (in negatively skewed distributions).

The distribution on the right side of Figure 2.2.1 is also positively skewed. However, the frequencies of scores do not taper off in a systematic fashion as one moves up or down the scale from the modal score of 5. In distributions such as this (which are not uncommon), the numerical values of the arithmetic mean, the median, and the mode may not follow the rules of thumb that are commonly taught. The data shown on the right side of Figure 2.2.1 illustrate this possibility. Even though the data are positively skewed, the mean is the smallest of these three measures of central tendency, whereas the mode is the largest.*

Distributional shape is an important attribute of data, regardless of whether scores are analyzed descriptively or inferentially. Because the degree of skewness can be summarized by means of a single number, and because computers have no difficul ty providing such measures (or estimates) of skewness, those who prepare research reports should include a numerical index of skewness every time they provide measures of central tendency and variability.† If researchers did this, no one would

---

* For the 100 scores that produced the figure on the right side of Figure 2.2.1, the mean, median, and mode are equal to 4.28, 4.50, and 5.00, respectively.

† Although many different formulas have been developed to measure skewness, two are quite popular for measuring what is technically referred to as the *third moment around the mean*. If one has access to population data, skewness is defined as $\Sigma(X_i-\mu)^3/N\sigma^3$. If one is using sample data to estimate skewness in a population, skewness is defined as $n\Sigma(X_i-\bar{X})^3/[(n-1)(n-2)s^3]$.

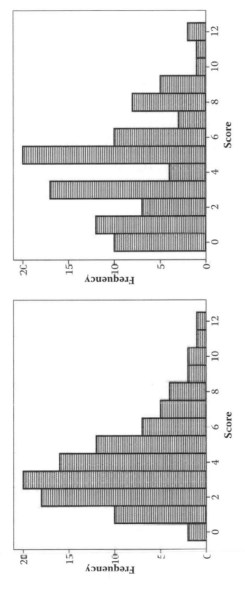

FIGURE 2.2.1 Two skewed distributions.

be forced to make a guess as to the direction and degree of skewness based on reported measures of central tendency.

Internet Assignment

Would you like to see some data that are skewed but inconsistent with the common thought that the median lies between the mode and the mean? Would you like to be the one who enters the data into an Internet-based interactive Java applet that will compute these three "average" scores (along with a measure of skewness)? If so, it's easy to do these things.

To expand your knowledge concerning the mean, median, and mode, visit this book's companion Web site (http://www.psypress.com/ statistical-misconceptions). Once there, open the folder for Chapter 2 and click on the link called "Skewed Distributions and Measures of Central Tendency." After doing this, you will find detailed instructions (prepared by this book's author) on how to enter a set of 12 scores into the Java applet. You will find an important question (also prepared by this book's author) concerning the descriptive statistics that will be provided after the applet analyzes the data. This question concerns the alignment—or perhaps it would be better to say *mis*alignment—between the type of skewness in the data, on the one hand, and the relative positions of the mean, median, and mode, on the other.

☐ 2.3 Standard Scores and Normality

The Misconception

Standard scores, such as z-scores and T-scores, are normally distributed.*

Evidence That This Misconception Exists[†]

This first of the following statements comes from a peer-reviewed journal in public health. The second statement comes from a book dealing with language disorders. The third statement comes from materials distributed in conjunction with a conference for medical residents sponsored by the American Academy of Physical Medicine and Rehabilitation.

1. *Z-scores are normally distributed and allow the use of parametric statistics.*

2. *Because standard scores are normally distributed, they can be interpreted in terms of known properties of the normal distribution, especially expectations concerning how expected or unexpected a particular score is.*

3. *The normal curve is the basis for standard scores (e.g., T-scores, z-scores).*

Why This Misconception Is Dangerous

If data are normally distributed, certain things are known about the group and individual scores in the group. For example, the three most frequently used measures of central tendency—the arithmetic mean, median, and mode—all have the same numerical value in a normal distribution. Moreover, if a distribution is normal, we can determine a person's percentile if we know his or her z-score or T-score. Thus, a normal distribution allows us to say that a z-score of $+.25$ corresponds

---

* A raw score, X, is converted into a z-score via the formula $z = \frac{X - \mu}{\sigma}$, where μ and σ are the group's mean and standard deviation, respectively. A T-score equals $10z + 50$.

† Appendix B contains references for all quoted material presented in this section.

to a percentile of 60, and a *T*-score of 40 corresponds to a percentile of 16.

It is dangerous to think that standard scores, such as *z* and *T*, form a normal distribution because (1) they don't have to and (2) they often won't.

If you mistakenly presume that a set of standard scores are normally distributed (when they're not), your conversion of *z*-scores (or *T*-scores) into percentiles can lead to great inaccuracies. You might think that a person with a large, positive *z*-score is positioned in the top fourth of the group, when that person actually holds a low standing. Or, you might think that a person with a *T*-score of 50 scored at the median, when in fact this person may have a percentile that's far above (or below) the group's middle score.

Undoing the Misconception

Whatever nonnormality exists in the raw scores will be transferred directly to *z*-scores and *T*-scores. Thus, if a set of raw scores has a mild, negative skew, the set of *z*-scores (or *T*-scores) based on the raw scores will have a mild, negative skew. If a set of raw scores is "overly peaked" (compared to a normal distribution), converting the raw scores to *z*-scores (or *T*-scores) will not bring about normality; the standard scores will be just as overly peaked as the original raw scores.

Consider the histogram displayed in Figure 2.3.1. For the 100 scores used to create this histogram, the mean is equal to 4 while the standard deviation is equal to 2.46. Clearly, this distribution of scores is positively skewed.

If the raw scores used to create the histogram in Figure 2.3.1 are converted to *z*-scores, two things will happen. First, the entire distribution is shifted to the left until the third-tallest bar is positioned directly over the score of 0. Second, each bar's horizontal distance from the third-tallest bar is decreased so as to be about 41% as far "out" as it was originally.* For example, the bar in Figure 2.3.1 that's above the score of 8 ends up being only 1.63 points—rather than 4 points—to the right of the new score position, 0, of the third-tallest bar. In a similar fashion, the bar that originally was located over 1 (and thus 3 raw score points below the group mean) gets repositioned over a new score of –1.22. Figure 2.3.2 shows the result of converting the raw scores into *z*-scores. If you compare

---

* The number 41 comes from rounding off the fraction 1/σ and then turning the result into a percentage.

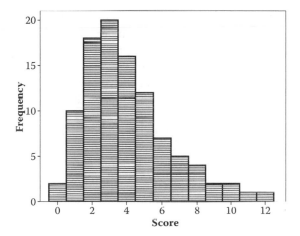

FIGURE 2.3.1 Histogram for 100 raw scores.

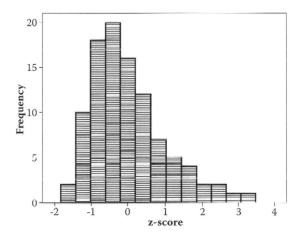

FIGURE 2.3.2 Histogram for the z-score equivalents of the data in Figure 2.3.1.

Figure 2.3.2 with Figure 2.3.1, you should be able to see that the shapes of the two distributions are identical.

After the original distribution is shifted horizontally (to cause the new mean to be 0), the multiplication of scores by the fraction $1/\sigma$ creates an "accordion" effect on the bars of the histogram. If σ is larger than 1 (as in the example we've been considering), the bars of the histogram move closer together, just like the vertical panels of an accordion move closer together if the ends of the accordion are pushed toward each other.

On the other hand, the histogram's bars become more spread out if σ is smaller than 1, just like the effect of pulling the ends of an accordion further away from each other. However, this accordion effect has no influence whatsoever on the height of any bar. This is why a conversion of raw scores into z-scores does not affect the distribution's shape.

If raw scores are converted into T-scores rather than z-scores, the situation is the same: no change in the shape of the distribution. In this case, the distribution is first shifted up or down the score continuum until the revised mean is equal to 50. Then, every score is multiplied by the fraction $10/\sigma$. The "accordion effect" here causes the standard deviation of the new scores to become equal to 10, regardless of the variability of the original raw scores.

Internet Assignment

Would you like to see some "proof" that nonnormality remains intact when raw scores are transformed into z-scores? Would you like to see that this is true for T-scores as well? If so, an Internet-based interactive Java applet can be used to generate the evidence you seek.

As a first step, visit this book's companion Web site (http://www. psypress.com/statistical-misconceptions). Once there, open the folder for Chapter 2 and click on the link called "Standard Scores and Normality." After doing this, you will find detailed instructions (prepared by this book's author) on how to enter a small set of raw scores into the Java applet and how to get the applet to compute indices of skewness and kurtosis for those scores. Then, you'll do the same thing using the z-score and T-score counterparts of the raw scores. You should find it interesting to compare the skewness and kurtosis indices across the three analyses.

☐ 2.4 Rectangular Distributions and Kurtosis

The Misconception

Being flat, any rectangular distribution (such as the one in Figure 2.4.1) is maximally platykurtic.*

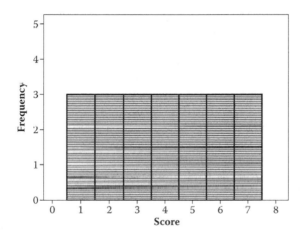

FIGURE 2.4.1 Histogram for 21 scores.

Evidence That This Misconception Exists†

The first of the following statements comes from an electronic handbook of statistics. The second statement comes from a master's thesis. (Note the word *extreme* in each passage.)

1. *Kurtosis is a measure of whether the data are peaked or flat relative to a normal distribution. That is, data sets with high kurtosis tend to have a distinct peak near the mean, decline rather rapidly, and have heavy tails. Data sets with low kurtosis tend to have a flat top near the mean rather than a sharp peak. A uniform distribution would be the extreme case.*

2. *A uniform distribution would be the extreme platykurtic case.*

---

* When describing distributional shape, the term *uniform* means the same thing as *rectangular*.

† Appendix B contains references for all quoted material presented in this section.

Why This Misconception Is Dangerous

In his comprehensive treatise on kurtosis, Lawrence DeCarlo argues that applied researchers should consider and report measures of kurtosis for their data.* One reason for this admonition is the fact that deviations from normality in the form of positive or negative kurtosis can disrupt the functioning of various statistical tests. For example, kurtosis can affect tests on means, variances, and covariances.

If measures of kurtosis become as commonplace as measures of central tendency, variability, and skewness in researchers' efforts to summarize groups of data, it is important that those who compute measures of kurtosis (and those who see them in research reports) understand what kurtosis measures measure. Unfortunately, kurtosis is not the easiest concept to pin down.

The concept of kurtosis is often thought to deal with the "peakedness" of a distribution. Compared to a normal distribution (which is said to have a moderate peak), distributions that have taller peaks are referred to as being *leptokurtic,* while those with smaller peaks are referred to as being *platykurtic.* Regarding the second of these terms, authors and instructors often suggest that the word *flat* (which rhymes with the first syllable of *platykurtic*) is a good mnemonic device for remembering that platykurtic distributions tend to be flatter than normal.

There are degrees to which a distribution can deviate from normality in terms of peakedness. A platykurtic distribution, for instance, might be slightly less peaked than a normal distribution, moderately less peaked than normal, or totally lacking in any peak. One is tempted to think that any perfectly rectangular distribution, being ultraflat in its shape, would be maximally platykurtic. However, this is not the case.

Undoing the Misconception

Kurtosis is usually defined as

$$\frac{\sum (X_i - \mu)^4}{N\sigma^4}$$

---

* DeCarlo, L. T. (1999). On the meaning and use of kurtosis. *Psychological Methods*, 2(3), 292–307.

which conceptually reduces to the mean of the z-scores, each of which is raised to the fourth power. This formula yields a kurtosis value of 3 for a normal distribution. Values larger than 3 describe leptokurtic distributions, while values smaller than 3 describe platykurtic distributions.*

As indicated by the formula in the previous paragraph, kurtosis is influenced by the variability of the data. This fact leads to two surprising characteristics of kurtosis. First, not all rectangular distributions have the same amount of kurtosis. Second, certain distributions that are not rectangular are more platykurtic than are rectangular distributions!

If we restrict our thoughts to rectangular distributions for discrete variables, the degree of kurtosis (Ku) in the data can be computed easily.[†] In this situation,

$$Ku = 3 - \frac{6\left\{\left(H - L + 1\right)^2 + 1\right\}}{5\left(H - L\right)\left(H - L + 2\right)}$$

where H and L represent the high and low scores, respectively. If we apply this formula to the data in Figure 2.4.1, $H = 7$, $L = 1$, and the kurtosis for the 21 scores is equal to 1.75.

Consider now what happens to the kurtosis of the rectangular distribution in Figure 2.4.1 if we change the range of scores. Suppose the 21 scores had turned out such that there were seven scores of 1, seven scores of 2, and seven scores of 3. For these data, the index of kurtosis is equal to 1.5. Or, imagine that the rectangular distribution involves 210 scores that extend from 1 to 70. Here, kurtosis turns out to be equal to 1.8.

The different values for kurtosis that we've considered (1.75, 1.5, and 1.8) may seem fairly similar. However, it must be remembered that the data in each situation formed a perfectly flat distribution. Although these differences appear to be small, they illustrate the fact that measures of kurtosis are influenced not just by the degree to which a distribution is peaked or flat. Kurtosis also is influenced by the amount of variability in the data.

The second surprising feature of kurtosis is that rectangular distributions, which are flat, are not maximally platykurtic. Bimodal

---

* Some people like to subtract 3 from the formula presented in this paragraph so that a normal distribution has a kurtosis value of 0.

† A discrete variable has only a finite number of values along a continuum. The number of children per family, for example, is such a variable because a family's "score" can be 0 or 1 or 2 or some other whole number. However, no family could have 1.273 children. (With *continuous* variables, such as the height or weight of people, any of an infinite number of values is possible.)

distributions can yield lower kurtosis values than rectangular distributions, even in those situations where the number of scores and score variability are held constant.

Internet Assignment

Would you like to see some "proof" that kurtosis is not at a maximum when a distribution is flat? Would you prefer the proof to be connected to some small sets of real scores? If so, spend a few minutes playing with a particular Internet-based interactive Java applet.

To see the concept of kurtosis in action, visit this book's companion Web site (http://www.psypress.com/statistical-misconceptions). Once there, open the folder for Chapter 2 and click on the link called "Rectangular Distributions and Kurtosis." After doing this, you will find detailed instructions (prepared by this book's author) on how to enter three small sets of scores into the Java applet. Just prior to the time the Java applet does the statistical analysis, you will be asked to make a guess as to which of the three data sets is most platykurtic. After seeing the numerical indices of kurtosis for the three sets, you may feel as if your initial guess was lucky or smart—or that it was ill-founded!

☐ Recommended Reading

Basu, S., & Dasgupta, A. (1997). The mean, median, and mode of unimodal distributions: A characterization. *Theory of Probability and Its Applications, 41*(2), 210–223.

Bower, K. M. (n.d.). Some misconceptions about the normal distribution. In *Statistical methods for quality improvement podcasts.* Retrieved March 23, 2007, from http://www.podcastdirectory.com/podcasts/7454.

David, H. A. (2005). Tables related to the normal distribution: A short history. *American Statistician, 59*(4), 309–311.

Gould, S. J. (1985). The median isn't the message. *Discover, 6,* 40–42.

Hippel, P. T. von. (2005). Mean, median, and skew: Correcting a textbook rule. *Journal of Statistics Education, 13*(2). Retrieved November 10, 2004, from www.amstat.org/publications/jse/v13n2/vonhippel.html.

Malgady, R. G. (2007). How skewed are psychological data? A standardized index of effect size. *Journal of General Psychology, 134*(3), 355–359.

National Institute of Standards and Technology. (n.d.). Measures of skewness and kurtosis. In *Engineering statistics handbook* (chap. 1.3.5.11). Retrieved November 2, 2007, from http://www.itl.nist.gov/div898/handbook/eda/section3/eda35b.htm.

Normal distribution. (n.d.). Retrieved June 7, 2007, from http://www.stat.wvu.edu/SRS/Modules/Normal/normal.html.

Rhiel, G. S. (2006). Coefficient of variation calculated from the range for skewed distributions. *Psychological Reports, 98,* 72–78.

Stahl, S. (2006). The evolution of the normal distribution. *Mathematics Magazine, 79*(2), 96–113.

Wuensch, K. L. (2007). *Skewness, kurtosis, and the normal curve.* Retrieved November 2, 2007, from http://core.ecu.edu/psyc/wuenschk/d.

CHAPTER 3

Bivariate Correlation

Within psychology pedagogical research, there has been somewhat of a focus on statistical misconceptions that impede students' acquisition of statistical concepts [revealing] that students can hold confusions and misconceptions about even seemingly straightforward mathematical concepts such as correlation [and that] misconceptions are prevalent, persistent and often resistant to traditional forms of instruction....*

---

* Zinkiewicz, L., Hammond, N., & Trapp, A. *Applying psychology disciplinary knowledge to psychology teaching and learning.* Retrieved December 16, 2006, from www.psychology.heacademy.ac.uk/docs/pdf/p20030321_r2p.pdf.

☐ 3.1 Correlation Coefficients

The Misconception

Correlation coefficients range in value from −1.00 to +1.00.

Evidence That This Misconception Exists*

The first of the following statements comes from a book in psychology. The second statement comes from a recent government document disseminated by the State of Western Australia. The third statement comes from an online book dealing with human genetics. (Note the word *always* that appears in the first two passages.)

1. *If calculated properly, correlation coefficients always range between +1.00 and −1.00.*

2. *Correlation always has a value between −1.0 and 1.0.*

3. *Mathematically, a correlation coefficient can range from −1.0 to 1.0.*

Why This Misconception Is Dangerous

Certain statistical summaries are interpretable only if we know the range of possible values for the summary. For example, a percentage will land on a continuum that extends from 0 to 100. Likewise, a stanine score will be a whole number somewhere between 1 and 9, and a probability will turn out equal to some value between 0 and 1.0. If we did not know these maximum high and low values, interpreting a percentage, stanine, or probability would be impossible. In a very real sense, those highest and lowest possible values provide a frame of reference that makes it possible to interpret those statistical summaries.

What is the parallel frame of reference for correlation coefficients? Under certain conditions, some correlational procedures produce correlation coefficients that must land on a continuum that extends from −1.0

---

* Appendix B contains references for all quoted material presented in this section.

to +1.0. Note, however, that the previous sentence began with the phrase "under certain conditions." If the needed conditions do not exist, those correlational procedures will have a truncated continuum of possible values. Certain other correlational procedures yield coefficients that never can be negative.

If a person thinks that correlation coefficients always end up on a continuum that extends from −1.00 to +1.00, he or she will be unable to judge accurately the relationship strength. What looks to be moderate may actually be strong. Worse yet, a correlation that makes a relationship look weak and meaningless may actually be as high as it can possibly be!

Undoing the Misconception

Let's consider each of several correlational procedures and ask the simple question: What is the range of possible values for the correlation coefficient? As you will see, certain kinds of correlation have a range of possible values extending from −1.00 to +1.00 *only under special circumstances*. Other kinds of correlation yield coefficients *on only a segment of this continuum*.

- Pearson's r can assume values between −1.00 and +1.00 only if the data on the two variables being correlated have the same distributional shape. For example, if the X values are positively skewed while the Y values are negatively skewed (or vice versa), r cannot turn out equal +1.00 or −1.00.

- Spearman's rank-order correlation, ρ, can assume values anywhere between −1.00 and +1.00, presuming that no ties exist within the data on either variable or that each variable has ties, but in the same location. If both variables have ties with the tied ranks being different on one variable than those on the other variable, ρ cannot equal either +1.00 or −1.00.

- The phi correlation, ϕ, can assume a value of ±1.0 only if the two dichotomous variables each have the same percentage of 1s. If one variable has 90% 1s while the other variable has only 10% 1s, the maximum possible value of ϕ is only 0.11!

- The contingency coefficient, C, has a range of possible values that extends from 0 to $\sqrt{k-1/k}$, where k stands for the number of categories in the variable that has the smaller number of categories. For 2 × 2 tables, the highest possible value of C is 0.71.

- Cramer's V has a continuum of possible values that extends from 0 to +1.0.

- Cohen's kappa, κ, a measure of interjudge agreement, is equal to +1.0 in the case of perfect agreement and 0 in the case of "chance agreement."* However, κ can assume negative values (that are *not* bounded by −1.00) and its maximum value is less than +1.00 if the marginal probabilities are asymmetric.

Internet Assignment

Would you see some proof that Pearson's r does not always range from +1.0 to −1.00? Would you like this evidence to come from some paired data that you create in an effort to maximize r? If so, a simple yet challenging little exercise awaits you.

To see the little exercise that this book's author has developed, visit this book's companion Web site (http://www.psypress.com/statistical-misconceptions). Once there, open the folder for Chapter 3 and click on the link called "Correlation Coefficients." After doing this, you will be given some data and a set of detailed instructions on how to enter these scores into an Internet-based interactive Java applet that will compute Pearson's r. You are likely to have some fun with this little activity, and you may discover a thing or two about Pearson's r in the process.

---

* Suppose you and a friend each take a well-shuffled deck of cards and then simultaneously turn cards over, one at a time, from each deck. Further suppose that a match is said to exist if the two cards are both face cards or if both cards are not face cards. If you did this, you'd see lots of matches over the 52 times you each turn over a card. To be more specific, simply by chance, you'd likely observe about 3 matches that involve face cards and about 30 matches that involve cards others than the Jack, Queen, or King. Because kappa "adjusts" for expected chance agreement, kappa would be low (.08) if you had 36 matches, even though you'd be matching nearly 70% of the time.

☐ 3.2 Correlation and Causality

The Misconception

The correlation between two variables, X and Y, never reveals anything about a possible causal relationship between the two variables. Simply stated: correlation ≠ cause.

Evidence That This Misconception Exists*

The following statements come from three different online blogs.

1. *Correlation NEVER implies causation!*

2. *The fact that correlation never implies causation, which may be lost on many people, is extremely important.*

3. *In the words of my college psychology professor, correlation never, never, never, never, never, never, never, never, never, never, never, never, never, never, never, never, equals causation. NEVER!*

Why This Misconception Is Dangerous

The oft-heard admonition against inferring cause from correlation is dangerous for two reasons. First, this warning implies that causal arguments are legitimate or not depending on the kind of statistical tool(s) used to analyze data. That notion of what's needed to illuminate causal forces totally disregards the importance of research design. Statistical procedures can be helpful in studies that investigate cause; however, researchers concerned with causality must take care to reduce or eliminate alternative hypotheses for any causal connections suggested by their data.

The warning that correlation ≠ cause is also dangerous because it functions to keep the logical and mathematical equivalence of certain statistical procedures hidden from view. Data can sometimes be analyzed in different ways and yet produce the exact same results. It's important

---

* Appendix B contains references for all quoted material presented in this section.

for researchers (and for the readers of their research reports) to know about these equivalencies. Otherwise, they will think that different analyses are accomplishing different objectives, when in fact those different analyses are doing exactly the same thing.

Undoing the Misconception

To show that correlation *can* speak to the issue of causality, let's consider a hypothetical medical investigation. This study involves a new drug that's being tested to see if it can relieve headache pain. We'll first consider the setup of the study. Then, we'll look at two different ways the study's data could be analyzed so as to justify a cause-and-effect claim.

Suppose we randomly assign 100 people with headaches to two groups, a treatment group ($n = 50$) and a placebo group ($n = 50$). Those in the first of these groups are given a pill that contains a new drug that supposedly reduces headache pain, while those in the placebo group are given a look-alike pill that contains no medicine. Let's further assume that this is a double-blind clinical trial, that we ask people to rate their headache pain on a 0-to-20 scale one hour after taking their pills, that we statistically compare the mean ratings of the two groups, and that there are no plausible reasons why the means of the two groups might be different (or similar), other than the possibility that the "active" pills do (or don't) have a differential impact compared to the placebo pills.

Many researchers would choose to analyze the data from this headache study with an independent-samples *t*-test. So, let's imagine that this is how the data are treated statistically. Let's also imagine that the *t*-test's result is statistically significant, with the rated headache pain being lower, on average, for those who took the active pills than for those who took the placebo pill. Given that the *t*-test showed a statistically significant difference between the means of the two groups, the researchers legitimately could make the claim that the drug in the active pills most likely had a causal impact on the headache ratings.

What's important to realize is that the data of this hypothetical study could be examined using a correlation coefficient. If this had been done, the *X* variable would correspond to group membership (with a 1 or 2 assigned to each person to indicate whether an active pill or a placebo pill was swallowed), while the *Y* variable would correspond to headache pain level, as indicated by the self-ratings collected one hour after the pills were taken. Stated differently, *X* would be the independent variable while *Y* would be the dependent variable. Table 3.2.1 shows what the data for this study might look like.

TABLE 3.2.1. Data From the Hypothetical Headache Study

Participant	Group[a]	Headache Rating
Person 1	1	7
Person 2	2	11
Person 3	1	5
Person 4	2	9
.	.	.
.	.	.
.	.	.
Person 100	2	14

[a] 1 refers to active pill group; 2 refers to placebo pill group.

Had the results from this hypothetical study been correlated, they would have been identical to the results of the t-test.* In other words, if the t-test indicated that a statistically significant difference existed between the two sample means, then the correlation would be statistically significant as well. (Similarly, if the t-test turned out to be nonsignificant, so too would the test of the correlation coefficient yield a nonsignificant result.)

The t-test and the test of the correlation coefficient would produce identical results because these two statistical procedures are mathematically equivalent. This equivalence shows up in the data-based p-level that's examined to see if the independent variable (active versus placebo pill) has a statistically significant connection to the dependent variable (headache pain one hour after taking the pill). Whether the data are analyzed via an independent-samples t-test or a test on r, the p-level is the same.

---

* The resulting correlation could be referred to as Pearson's r or as the point-biserial correlation, r_{pb}. Both yield identical results, for the formula used to obtain r_{pb} is nothing more than a simplification of r in the situation where one of the two variables is dichotomous.

Later, in Chapter 8, we will consider misconceptions concerning *p*-levels. Those misconceptions notwithstanding, it is still the case that our hypothetical study would yield the same *p* regardless of whether the two group means are compared or the headache ratings are correlated with group membership. The first of these statistical procedures would produce findings considered by researchers to address the causal impact of the new drug on headache relief. Because the correlational analysis is identical to the *t*-test (and because the study involved a manipulated independent variable and no plausible threats to internal validity*), we are justified here in saying that the correlation coefficient, *r*, speaks to the issue of cause and effect.

Internet Assignment

Would you like to see some convincing evidence that a correlation coefficient *can* speak to the issue of cause and effect? Would you like the evidence to be connected to a small set of raw scores that you can analyze using an Internet-based interactive Java applet? If so, you can easily generate and examine such evidence.

To locate the scores you will be analyzing, visit this book's companion Web site (http://www.psypress.com/statistical-misconceptions). Once there, open the folder for Chapter 3 and click on the link called "Correlation and Causality." There you will find the data along with detailed instructions (prepared by this book's author) on how to enter a small set of raw scores into an online Java applet and how to get the applet to analyze the data in two different ways. You will also be given a link to that Java applet. The results provided by these two analyses you perform may surprise you!

---

* A study's internal validity is considered to be high if no confounding variables exist that might make (1) inert treatments appear to be potent or (2) potent treatments appear to be inert. When random assignment is used to form comparison groups, many (but not all) potential threats to internal validity vanish.

☐ 3.3 The Effect of a Single Outlier
on Pearson's *r*

The Misconception

A single outlier cannot greatly influence the value of Pearson's *r*, especially if *N* is large.

Evidence That This Misconception Exists*

The first of the following statements comes from an online case study called Sex Discrimination Problem, in which data on newly hired employees were examined to see whether their beginning salaries were related to other variables, such as age, educational level, and prior experience. One employee with an exceptionally high starting salary was identified as an outlier but was not removed from the sample when Pearson's correlation was used to measure the relationships among the study's variables, presumably because it was just a single outlier out of 93 cases. The second statement is a response option in a multiple-choice question from a practice exam in a college-level math course.

1. *[T]here is only one outlier.*

2. *A single outlier has no effect.*

Why This Misconception Is Dangerous

Pearson's product-moment correlation is used in a wide variety of disciplines to answer many important research questions. For example, evidence from *r* is used to determine the reliability and validity of data, to assess the relationship strength between two dependent variables, and to ascertain the predictive worth of independent variables in regression analyses. Although there are many other kinds of bivariate correlation

---

* Appendix B contains references for all quoted material presented in this section.

(e.g., Spearman's rho and Cramer's V), it's a fact that Pearson's r is used more than any other procedure to correlate data on two variables.

A single data point that exists as an "exception to the rule" can cause r to be a highly distorted summary of the relationship among the remaining $N - 1$ data points. This is true even if N is large. Unfortunately, the information contained in published research reports suggests that most applied researchers compute r without conducting a visual or statistical check to see if any outliers are present. When no such check is made, Pearson's r can misrepresent both the nature and strength of the relationship being measured.

Undoing the Misconception

In statistics, the law of large numbers says that the numerical value of a sample statistic will likely be a better approximation of the population parameter to the extent that the sample is large.* It would be a *misapplication* of this law to think that a single outlier's ability to distort r is diminished as N increases. Archimedes supposedly said that he could move the world if you gave him a long enough lever and the freedom to stand far away from our celestial planet. In a similar fashion, give me the freedom to position a single new data point anywhere I wish, and I can change the sign of r, the strength of r, or both.

Consider the two sets of data shown in Figure 3.3.1. They are identical except that one additional point has been added to the scatter diagram on the right. What effect did that single data point have? It changed r from 0.00 to +.81! That single data point would have caused r to be −.81 if its X value had been 32 rather than 100. Clearly, a single data point can cause a weak relationship to look strong, if we fail to detect it as an outlier.

It should be noted that a single outlier can have just the opposite effect. That is, an outlier can cause a high correlation to become weak. Consider Figure 3.3.2. These two sets of data are identical except that one additional point has been added to the scatter diagram on the right. What effect did that single data point have? It changed r from +1.00 to 0.00! Clearly, a single outlier can cause r to mask a strong relationship that exists in the data.

Can a single outlier make a difference when there are lots of other scores? Yes! Consider Figure 3.3.3. In the left scatter diagram, it may look like there are only four data points. However, each of those four dots

---

* The law of large numbers was established in the late 1600s by Jakob Bernoulli, a Swiss mathematician.

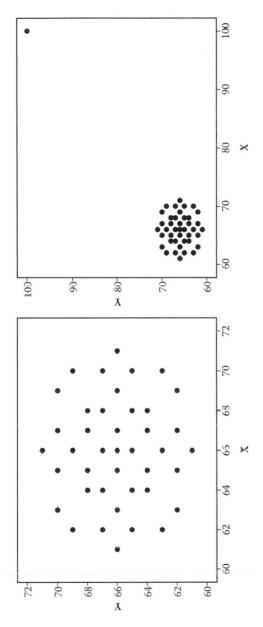

FIGURE 3.3.1 A single outlier causes $r = 0$ to become $r = +.81$.

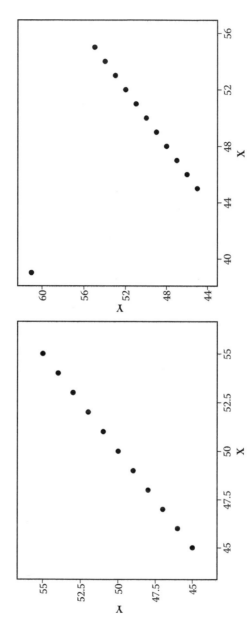

FIGURE 3.3.2 A single outlier causes $r = +1.00$ to become $r = 0.00$.

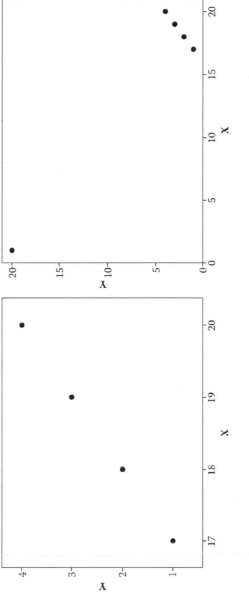

FIGURE 3.3.3 A single outlier (with 200 other data points) causes $r = +1.00$ to become $r = -.10$.

represents 50 data points that are piled on top of each other. Thus, that scatter diagram actually contains 200 data points. Clearly, the correlation for those 200 scores is +1.00. The right side of Figure 3.3.3 contains those same 200 data points plus a single outlier positioned at $X = 1$, $Y = 20$. That single outlier causes r to change from +1.00 to −.10!

Internet Assignment

Would you like to see some convincing evidence that a single outlier can greatly affect the numerical value of Pearson's? Would you like the evidence to be connected to a small set of data points that you position into the scatter diagram of an Internet-based interactive Java applet? If so, spend a few minutes doing this Internet assignment.

Your initial task is to visit this book's companion Web site (http://www.psypress.com/statistical-misconceptions). Once there, open the folder for Chapter 3 and click on the link called "The Effect of a Single Outlier on Pearson's r." There you will find detailed instructions (prepared by this book's author) on how to use the interactive Java applet. After learning how the applet works, you will perform a simple task that will demonstrate the power of a single outlier. If you are good at performing this task, you should be able to demonstrate that a single outlier can change r's numerical value (when rounded to two decimal places) from +1.00 to −1.00.

☐ 3.4 Relationship Strength and *r*

The Misconception

If the data on two variables having similar distributional shapes are correlated using Pearson's *r*, the resulting correlation coefficient can land
anywhere on a continuum that extends from 0.00 to ±1.00; therefore,
an *r* of +.50 (or −.50) indicates that the measured relationship is half as
strong as it possibly could be.

Evidence That This Misconception Exists*

The first of the following statements comes from a published document
designed to help people interpret the output provided by SAS, a widely
used statistical package. The second statement comes from a research
project conducted by three students at the University of Michigan.

1. *You interpret the size of a correlation coefficient to determine the strength of
   the relationship between the two variables. Generally speaking, the larger
   the size of coefficient (in absolute value), the stronger the relationship....
   Below is an informal guide for interpreting the approximate strength of the
   relationship between two variables, based on the absolute value of the [cor-
   relation] coefficient:*

   ±1.00 = Perfect correlation
   ±.80 = Strong correlation
   ±.50 = Moderate correlation
   ±.20 = Weak correlation
   .00 = No correlation

2. *All of the attitude variables had significant but generally low correlations
   with activism behavior; those who were more comfortable being associated
   with the environmental movement had a moderate correlation (r = .51).*

---

* Appendix B contains references for all quoted material presented in this section.

Why This Misconception Is Dangerous

Pearson's correlation is used in most fields of study to answer questions concerning bivariate relationships. In certain studies, a computed r functions as the end product of the statistical analysis. In other investigations, correlation coefficients serve as the primary "ingredients" of a more complicated statistical procedure (e.g., factor analysis or multiple regression). Simply stated, Pearson's r is arguably the most frequently used statistical measure, beyond the mean and standard deviation.

It is important for r to be interpreted properly by those in two groups: those who conduct empirical investigations and those who are consumers of research reports. Interpreting r correctly is important because a variety of "high-stakes" decisions—such as which college applicants should be accepted, how much money (of a government's budget) should be allocated to education, and how much alcohol should be consumed—cannot be made wisely without considering the relationship between variables. Unfortunately, many people think r reflects directly the amount of relationship strength contained in the data. And, if one r is twice as large as a different r, they think that the first relationship is twice as strong as the second relationship.

Undoing the Misconception

In most situations, the coefficient of determination, r^2, is a better measure of relationship strength than the correlation coefficient, r. This is because the square of r indicates the proportion of variability in one of the two variables that is explained by (i.e., associated with) variability in the other variable. For example, if the correlation between a college entrance exam—perhaps the SAT or ACT—and college grade point average (GPA) is equal to .50, then r^2 is equal to .25, meaning that 25% of the variability in college GPA is associated with scores on the college entrance exam.

As indicated in Table 3.4.1, the value of r^2 is always lower than the value of r (except for the situation where $r = \pm1.00$ or $r = 0.00$). Moreover, the chart shows that the value of r must be slightly larger than .70 in order for 50% of the variability in one variable to be explained by variability in the other variable.

TABLE 3.4.1. Relationship Between r and r^2

$|r|$	r^2	$|r|$	r^2
1.00	1.00	.40	.16
.90	.81	.30	.09
.80	.64	.20	.04
.70	.49	.10	.01
.60	.36	.00	.00
.50	.25		

Internet Assignment

Would you like to gain a better understanding of why r must be squared in order to determine how much variability in one variable is associated with variability in the other variable? Would you like to gain this understanding by looking at a scatter diagram (in addition to a formula)? And would you like the scatter diagram to be interactive so you can change the data and then see what happens to r^2? If so, you'll be happy to know that an Internet-based Java applet exists that can do these things.

If you would like to use this Java applet, visit this book's companion Web site (http://www.psypress.com/statistical-misconceptions). Once there, open the folder for Chapter 3 and click on the link called "Relationship Strength and r." There you will find detailed instructions (prepared by this book's author) on how to use the interactive Java applet. After learning how the applet works, you will be challenged to generate a small set of data such that r^2 turns out to be equal to .50. For the data you create, you will be able to look at two scatter diagrams and see the extent to which variability in Y is reduced by considering variability in X. Moreover, you will see the way in which r^2 can be computed by means of a ratio of variances (rather than by a squaring of r).

☐ 3.5 The Meaning of $r = 0$

The Misconception

If Pearson's product–moment correlation, r, turns out equal to 0.00, this indicates that there is no relationship between the X and Y scores used to compute that correlation coefficient.

Evidence That This Misconception Exists*

The first three of the following statements, taken from online documents designed to help people understand correlation, illustrate the point made in the fourth statement, taken from a governmental social research unit in London.

1. *A correlation of zero means there is no relationship between the two variables.*

2. *When no relationship (or zero correlation) is present what we see is that no relationship can be seen between two variables.*

3. *If r = 0, then there is no relationship between the data y and x: we can't make any prediction about how y should change if we vary x.*

4. *Another misconception is that a low correlation coefficient suggests that the relationship between X and Y is weak or low.*

Why This Misconception Is Dangerous

Pearson's r is used far more often than any other correlational procedure to assess the strength and direction of the relationship between two sets of data. Those who compute r (as well as those who see it computed by others) ought to be familiar with r's underlying assumptions. If these assumptions are violated, the numerical value of r can misrepresent the data that have been analyzed. Just as a thermometer cannot be used to measure time, Pearson's r is a tool that is ill-suited for certain tasks.

---

* Appendix B contains references for all quoted material presented in this section.

Based on researchers' written summaries of their empirical investigations, it is clear that Pearson's r is used regularly to measure bivariate relationships without checks being applied to see if the data are appropriate for r. If such checks are not made, it's possible for a set of data—even when no outliers exist—to produce a correlation coefficient that underestimates the strength of the relationship that exists between the X and Y scores. In fact, it's possible for r to be equal to 0.00 even in the presence of an exceedingly strong relationship.

Undoing the Misconception

Pearson's r works well only if the relationship between X and Y is linear. If the relationship between the two variables is curvilinear, the value for r will underestimate the strength of the existing relationship. In certain circumstances, the value of r grossly misrepresents the true relationship that's "in" the data. In fact, the computed value of r can make one think that the data on two variables are uncorrelated when in fact the relationship is as strong as it could be!

Whether or not a relationship is linear usually can be determined by inspecting a scatter diagram. To be linearly related, the X and Y scores do *not* need to produce data points that all lie in a straight line. Rather, it's the "path" of the data points that must be straight. The data in Figure 3.5.1 obviously are not all lined up in a straight line. Despite that fact, the relationship is linear because the path of the dots, when moving from left to right (or right to left) across the scatter diagram, is clearly straight. The path is tilted, but it nonetheless is straight.*

If the relationship between the X and Y scores is not linear, the relationship is said to be *curvilinear*. (The term *nonlinear* is sometimes used to describe a relationship that's not linear.) A simple example of such a relationship is shown in Figure 3.5.2.

If the relationship between X and Y is curvilinear in nature, r will misrepresent the "connection" between the two sets of scores. For example, for the 12 data points displayed in Figure 3.5.2, $r = 0.00$. This product–moment correlation suggests that X and Y are unrelated. However, there actually is an extremely strong relationship between the

---

* The technical definition of linearity involves the means of the Y scores computed separately for each value of X. In Figure 3.5.1, the mean height of the three points above $X = 1$ is 5; the mean height of the three points above $X = 3$ is 6; and so forth. The data displayed in this scatter diagram are linear because these six values of $\bar{Y}$ lie in a straight line.

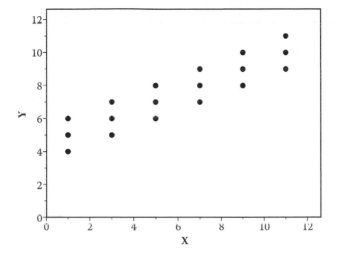

FIGURE 3.5.1 Example of linear data.

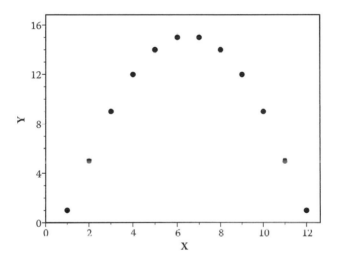

FIGURE 3.5.2 Example of curvilinear data.

X and Y scores. Given any X score, we can predict perfectly what the paired Y score is.

Those who compute Pearson's r for their data should always check to see if a linear relationship exists between the X and Y scores. Moreover, they should report having done this in their research reports. If the relationship shows up as being linear, Pearson's r can be used to assess the relationship between the X and Y data (assuming, of course, that there are no other problems that might make it inappropriate to compute r).

If a preliminary check on the data reveals a curvilinear relationship, two options exist. First, an alternative to r can be used to measure the correlation between X and Y. The correlational measure called eta is used by some researchers who select this first option.* The second option involves transforming the data so as to remove the curvilinearity.†

Internet Assignment

Would you like to see another scatter diagram that displays nonlinear data? Would you like the displayed data to be interactive such that you can change the value of r and then see what happens to the plot of the data? If so, spend a few minutes playing with a particular Java applet that's located on the Internet. To use this Java applet, visit this book's companion Web site (http://www.psypress.com/statistical-misconceptions). Once there, open the folder for Chapter 3 and click on the link called "The Meaning of $r = 0$." There you will find detailed instructions (prepared by this book's author) on how to use the interactive Java applet.

---

* The symbol for eta is η. This is the lowercase version of the seventh letter of the Greek alphabet.
† Taking the natural log of each score often reduces the amount of curvilinearity in a set of data.

☐ Recommended Reading

Asuero, A. G., Sayago, A., & González, A. G. (2006). The correlation coefficient: An overview. *Critical Reviews in Analytical Chemistry, 36*(1), 41–59.

Brett, M. T. (2004). When is a correlation between non-independent variables "spurious"? *OIKOS, 105*(3), 647–656.

Corcy, D. M., Dunlap, W. P., & Burke, M. J. (1998). Averaging correlations: Expected values and bias in combined Pearson *r*s and Fisher's *z* transformations. *Journal of General Psychology, 125*(3), 245–261.

Goodwin, L. D., & Leech, N. L. (2006). Understanding correlation: Factors that affect the size of *r*. *Journal of Experimental Education, 74*(3), 251–266.

Hassler, U., & Thadewald, T. (2003). Nonsensical and biased correlation due to pooling heterogeneous samples. *Journal of the Royal Statistical Society*, Series D: The Statistician, 52(3), 367–379.

Hatfield, J., Faunce, G. J., & Job, R. F. (2006). Avoiding confusion surrounding the phrase "correlation does not imply causation." *Teaching of Psychology, 33*, 49–51.

Lane, D. M. (2004). Transformations. In *Rice virtual lab in statistics*. Retrieved November 2, 2007, from http://www.ruf.rice.edu/~lane/stat_sim/transformations/index.html.

Levin, J. (1972). The occurrence of an increase in correlation by restriction of range. *Psychometrika, 37*(1), 93–97.

Matt, G. E. (2007, Fall). Correlation (r) and correlation squared (r²). In *Correlation, relationships, scatterplots*. Retrieved November 2, 2007, from http://www.sci.sdsu.edu/class/psychology/psy271/Weeks/psy271week07.htm#r2.

McClelland, G. (n.d.). Heterogeneous subsamples of data. In *Fundamental statistics for the behavioral sciences: Seeing statistics* (chap. 9). Retrieved November 2, 2007, from http://www.uvm.edu/~dhowell/fundamentals/SeeingStatisticsAppletsCD/HeteroSubSamp.html.

McClelland, G. (n.d.). Influential observations. In *Fundamental statistics for the behavioral sciences: Seeing statistics* (chap. 9). Retrieved November 2, 2007, from http://www.uvm.edu/~dhowell/fundamentals/SeeingStatisticsAppletsCD/CorrPointRemove.html.

Shih, W. J., & Huang, W. M. (1992). Evaluating correlation with proper bounds. *Biometrics, 48*, 1207–1213.

Zimmerman, D. W., & Williams, R. H. (2000). Restriction of range and correlation in outlier-prone distributions. *Applied Psychological Measurement, 24*, 267–280.

Reliability and Validity

Results of the study showed that even students with formal instruction in statistics [at the undergraduate and graduate levels] continue to demonstrate misconceptions.*

---

* Hirsch, L. S., & O'Donnell, A. M. (2001). Representativeness in statistical reasoning: Identifying and assessing misconceptions. *Journal of Statistics Education, 9,* 1.

□ 4.1 Statistical Indices of Reliability and Validity

The Misconception

Statistical indices of reliability and validity document important psycho-metric properties of a test.

Evidence That This Misconception Exists*

Both of the following statements come from peer-reviewed journals deal-ing with psychiatry. (These passages clearly suggest that the ABLE and SDS instruments are reliable and valid.)

1. *ABLE (Attention, Behavior, Language, and Emotions), a new screening tool, was used to estimate the prevalence and the severity of concerns parents and teachers have about children's school adjustment and evaluate their need for services. Data obtained from parents and teachers of children ran-domly selected from public Pre-K classrooms in 6 states (N = 415) and from a mental health screening of rural and urban children (N = 5,577) support the validity and reliability of ABLE.*

2. *The SDS [Severity of Dependence Scale] is a brief, valid and reliable screen for cannabis dependence among people with psychosis.*

Why This Misconception Is Dangerous

In studies that assess people's knowledge or skills, the test that produces the study's data typically is not created anew, but instead is an existing instrument developed by a previous researcher. In other words, it's often the case that test A is developed by researcher P and then used later by researcher Q. The danger here is not Q's use of P's test; instead, the dan-ger is that Q and those who read Q's research report think that test A, when used in Q's study, has the same psychometric properties as it did when P created it.

---

* Appendix B contains references for all quoted material presented in this section.

By incorrectly thinking that reliability and validity are attributes of a test, a researcher may end up selecting what seems like a good test for his or her study when in fact the selected test produces low-quality data.

Undoing the Misconception

Regardless of how carefully a test has been developed, the test's collection of questions does not have *any* level of reliability or validity. Sitting on a shelf or positioned on the desks of examinees who are working on it, the test cannot correctly be said to have a test–retest reliability of .80 or a predictive validity of .70. Moreover, the previous sentence holds true even if we switch to some other type of reliability (e.g., Cronbach's alpha), switch to some other form of validity (e.g., concurrent), or change the numerical values.*

All of the different kinds of reliability and validity that lead to numerical indices (such as those included in the preceding paragraph) are based on the scores generated by administering a test to a group of examinees. Change the nature of the examinee group and it's not only possible but likely that quantitative assessments of reliability and validity will also change. For this reason, it is imperative that reliability and validity be viewed as residing in the scores that become available after the test is administered, not in the test itself. The test scores should be our focus when we think about reliability and validity, for such scores obviously represent the interaction of test questions with test takers.

Imagine a test that's built to assess the knowledge gained by students who have taken a plane geometry course in high school. Administer that test in a test–retest manner and the correlation among the two sets of scores might turn out to equal .85. Or, use the first set of scores earned by those students to predict how well they will do in a subsequent course in solid geometry, and the correlation here might turn out equal to .75. Now imagine that we administer the same test in plane geometry to a group of fourth-graders. If those younger students guess when responding to the question (as would likely happen), the reliability and validity estimates based on their scores would turn out to be extremely low.

If two groups of examinees are equivalent in terms of age and background, it is still the case that reliability and validity estimates derived from test scores would vary across groups. This could be caused by any

---

* The only exception occurs when we switch our focus of attention to content validity. This kind of validity does, in fact, reside *in* the test itself rather than in the scores produced by an administration of the test.

number of factors. For example, if one of the groups is homogeneous while the other group is heterogeneous, estimates of reliability and validity would likely be higher for the latter group.

Even if two groups of examinees have been drawn randomly from the same population, statistical indices of reliability and validity will vary from group to group. Just as a sample mean varies from sample to sample (with this degree of variability estimated by the standard error of the mean), so too does r—the sample value of a correlation—vary across samples. For this reason, any r-based estimate of reliability or validity ought to be thought of as just that—an estimate. If the test itself possessed these psychometric properties of reliability and validity, no estimate would be needed!

For the reasons just cited, statistically-based estimates of reliability and validity should be considered to be properties of the *scores* earned by the examinees who are tested (rather than as properties of the test itself).

Internet Assignment

Would you like to gain a better understanding of why reliability and validity are characteristics of test scores rather than of tests? Would you like to gain this understanding by looking at (and playing with) the data contained in an Internet-based interactive Java applet? If so, complete this Internet assignment.

To do this assignment, visit this book's companion Web site (http://www.psypress.com/statistical-misconceptions). Once there, open the folder for Chapter 4 and click on the link called "Statistical Indices of Reliability and Validity." There you will find detailed instructions (prepared by this book's author) on how to use the interactive Java applet. You will quickly generate different sets of test scores that vary in reliability, even though the data come from the same test. By doing this, you will prove the point that psychometric assessments of "test quality" actually assess the quality of test scores rather than the test itself.

☐ 4.2 Interrater Reliability

The Misconception

If used with the same set of data, different procedures for estimating interrater reliability yield approximately the same reliability coefficients. Therefore, it doesn't make much of a difference which procedure is used.

Evidence That This Misconception Exists*

The first of the following statements comes from a recent peer-reviewed journal article entitled "Interrater Agreement and Reliability." The second statement comes from an online document dealing with different ways to estimate interrater reliability. (Note the phrases *common measurement misconception* and *widespread practice* that appear in these passages.)

1. *A common measurement misconception or myth is that interrater "reliability" and interrater "agreement" have equivalent meanings (Goodwin & Goodwin, 1999). Although the distinction has been explained by various measurement experts and psychometricians (e.g., Crocker & Algina, 1986; Frick & Semmel, 1978), researchers and practitioners tend to use the terms synonymously.*

2. *[T]he widespread practice of describing interrater reliability as a single, universal concept is at best imprecise, and at worst potentially misleading.*

Why This Misconception Is Dangerous

The choice of the procedure for computing indices of interrater reliability is critically important. Simply put, different procedures define interrater reliability differently, and the numerical index of interrater reliability can vary widely depending on the definition that's used. Thus, a particular method for computing interrater reliability might make it seem that raters were in close agreement with each other when interrater

---

* Appendix B contains references for all quoted material presented in this section.

reliability actually is quite low from a different and more appropriate perspective.

Undoing the Misconception

The measured amount of interrater reliability varies depending on many considerations. Four of these are (1) whether or not chance agreement is taken into consideration, (2) whether or not a dichotomy is imposed on a score continuum, (3) whether or not perfect reliability demands that raters assign identical scores to any given object or person being rated, and (4) whether or not raters are viewed as a random sample from a larger pool of potential raters.

To illustrate how a consideration of chance can affect interrater reliability, suppose two raters evaluate each of 10 applicants for a high-paying scholarship. Further suppose that the criteria used by judges are stringent because only one applicant will be chosen. The data from these two hypothetical judges are shown in Table 4.2.1, with a "1" indicating that the rater thinks the applicant deserves the scholarship, and a "0" indicating a "thumbs down" recommendation.

For these data, the "% agreement" measure of interrater reliability is .80. However, if consistency across the two raters is estimated by means of Cohen's kappa—a measure of interrater reliability that takes into consideration "chance agreements"—the index of reliability is only .375.*

To illustrate how an imposed dichotomy can affect interrater reliability, consider now the situation where ratings along a numerical scale are converted into pass–fail decisions. Suppose two health department officials independently rate the cleanliness of 10 restaurants on a 0-to-100 scale. On this scale, a score of 100 indicates that a restaurant is perfectly clean, whereas a score of 0 indicates that the restaurant is disgustingly filthy. Further suppose the ratings of the 10 restaurants end up as shown in Table 4.2.2.

---

* The logic behind Cohen's kappa is simple. Because each of the raters considered only 2 of the 10 applicants to be qualified for the scholarship, the probability that these raters would rate the same applicants positively, *assuming that their evaluations are randomly assigned to the applicants*, is equal to $.2 \times .2 = .04$. Likewise, the probability that the raters would rate the same applicants negatively is $.8 \times .8 = .64$. Thus, the probability of the raters agreeing by chance is $.04 + .64 = .68$. The raters actually agreed in their evaluations of 8 of the 10 applicants. This proportion of "agreements," .80, is three-eighths of the way between the probability of agreements based on chance, .68, and 1.00, the proportion of agreements there would be if the raters were in full agreement with each other. Three-eighths, when converted into a proportion, is .375.

TABLE 4.2.1. Data From Two Raters Who Rated 10 Applicants

Applicant	Rater X	Rater Y
Bobby	0	0
Donna	1	0
Frank	0	1
Grace	0	0
Harry	0	0
Lynn	1	1
Marty	0	0
Scott	0	0
Terry	0	0
Walt	0	0

TABLE 4.2.2. Cleanliness Ratings of 10 Restaurants

	Restaurants									
Rater	A	B	C	D	E	F	G	H	I	J
Health official 1	91	70	76	62	99	84	82	55	77	88
Health official 2	89	69	79	74	97	82	76	62	81	89

If Pearson's correlation is used to assess the level of interrater reliability, r turns out to be .94, a value that indicates very high consistency between the raters. However, if each restaurant's rating is converted into a pass or fail grade (with a score of 70 required in order to pass the inspection), the correlation of the revised data—using a 1 for pass and a 0 for fail—is only .375, a value that makes the raters appear to be not consistent at all.*

---

* The correlation of .375 comes from computing Pearson's r (or phi) from the pass–fail data. An alternative measure—the tetrachoric correlation—has not been computed, because it has a different purpose than simply describing the correlation in the observed data.

To illustrate how the issue of agreement versus consistency can affect interrater reliability, suppose two movie critics independently evaluate each of 10 movies on a scale that extends from 0 (lousy) to 20 (terrific). The data are shown in Table 4.2.3.

TABLE 4.2.3. Ratings of 10 Movies

Rater	Movies									
	M	N	O	P	Q	R	S	T	U	V
Movie critic 1	16	15	20	17	15	13	18	11	16	19
Movie critic 2	12	10	14	11	9	7	13	9	11	14

If Pearson's r is used to assess the interrater reliability across the two movie critics, the data appear to be quite reliable. That's because $r = .89$. However, if the intraclass correlation is used rather than r, the picture painted is quite different.* That's because $ICC(2,1) = .30$. The difference between these values is due to the fact that r assesses consistency between the raters' ratings, whereas $ICC(2,1)$ assesses the degree to which the raters' ratings are identical.

In Table 4.2.3, it should be obvious that movie critic 1 gave higher scores, on average, than did movie critic 2. In fact, there is a 5-point difference between the two means. This difference between the means does not affect r whatsoever, but it does affect $ICC(2,1)$. If we add 3 points to each score provided by movie critic 2 (thereby decreasing the discrepancy between the two means), r remains equal to .89. The intraclass correlation, however, changes from .30 to .67.[†]

Internet Assignment

Would you like to see an Internet-based interactive Java applet that computes various indices of interrater reliable? Would you like to see whether

---

* There are several different versions of the intraclass correlation that can be computed. The one used here is referred to as $ICC(2,1)$. The numbers in parentheses indicate that this version of ICC is based on model 2 (a two-way mixed ANOVA) with interest in the reliability of ratings that would come, later, from a single rater.

[†] If we add another two points to each score provided by movie critic 2 (thus making the two means identical), both r and $ICC(2,1)$ would equal .89.

the various indices of reliability are similar when all are based on the same set of ratings? If so, complete this Internet assignment.

To do this assignment, first visit this book's companion Web site (http://www.psypress.com/statistical-misconceptions). Once there, open the folder for Chapter 4 and click on the link called "Interrater Reliability." Then, follow the detailed instructions (prepared by this book's author) on how to use the interactive Java applet. You may be surprised by the results produced for the quality ratings given by four raters to each of several beers.

☐ 4.3 Cronbach's Alpha and Unidimensionality

The Misconception

A high value for Cronbach's alpha indicates that a measuring instrument's items are all highly interrelated, thus justifying the claim that the instrument is unidimensional in what it measures.

Evidence That This Misconception Exists*

The first of the following statements comes from a university document designed to help people understand the output of SPSS, a widely used statistical package. This passage comes from the response to an FAQ (i.e., frequently asked question): *What does Cronbach's alpha mean?* The second passage comes from an online document associated with a graduate-level course entitled Quantitative Research in Public Administration. The third statement comes from a newsletter about assessment and evaluation in a state university system.

1. *Cronbach's alpha measures how well a set of items (or variables) measures a single unidimensional latent construct.*

2. *If alpha is greater than or equal to .6, then the items are considered unidimensional and may be combined in an index or scale.*

3. *Alpha is a measure of internal consistency, or how well the items on a test hang together.*

Why This Misconception Is Dangerous

Most tests, personality inventories, and attitude scales contain several items, each of which generates a response from the person being measured. Even though the response format can vary widely, the scoring of such instruments typically involves two steps. First, a determination is made as to how many points a respondent has earned on each

---

* Appendix B contains references for all quoted material presented in this section.

separate item. Then, a total score—for the full instrument or for each of its parts—is calculated by summing the points earned across the various items. This process leads to what is called a "summed score" or a "composite score."

In many situations, the total score arrived at by summing across individual items is meaningful only if those items "hang together" in the sense that they are tied to the same domain or underlying construct. When a set of items does this, those items are said to be unidimensional.

As pointed out by John Hattie in his classic article, unidimensionality is often highly important:

> One of the most critical and basic assumptions of measurement theory is that a set of items forming an instrument all measure just one thing in common. This assumption provides the basis of most mathematical measurement models.*

If an instrument's items are *not* homogeneous in what they measure, then two individuals with the same total score could look alike even though they might be quite different. To illustrate this possibility, suppose half of the items in a measuring instrument are connected to dimension A, while the remaining items in that same instrument are connected to dimension B. If that were the case, a person who earns high scores from the A-focused items but low scores from the B-focused items would end up with the same total score as someone else whose performance on items from the two domains is just the reverse. The difference between these two individuals would be masked by the lack of unidimensionality.

Some people think that Cronbach's alpha assesses unidimensionality. This is a misconception because a multidimensional instrument can yield scores for which the alpha coefficient is high. The clear danger of this misconception is that a measuring instrument's total scores will not be interpreted properly. High (or low) scores may be attributed to one thing when they are actually the result of something else. The problem is analogous to thinking (incorrectly) that people's BMI (i.e., body mass index) scores are determined solely by their weight. That notion would lead one to think, wrongly, that two people with the same BMI scores are the same weight (or that two people with different BMI scores are not equally heavy).†

---

* Hattie, J. (1985). Assessing unidimensionality of tests and items. *Applied Psychological Measurement, 9*(2), 139.

† A person's BMI takes into consideration both height and weight. If these characteristics are measured in inches and pounds, a person's BMI = [weight ÷ height^2] × 703. If height is measured in meters and weight in kilograms, BMI = weight ÷ height^2.

Undoing the Misconception

Cronbach's alpha (α) is connected to the mean bivariate inter-item correlation ($\bar{r}$), as indicated by the following formula:

$$\alpha = \frac{k(\bar{r})}{1+(k-1)\bar{r}}$$

where k represents the number of items in the measuring instrument (or in the section of the instrument for which alpha is being calculated).* Thus, if $\bar{r}$ were equal to .20 in an instrument containing eight items, α would be equal to 8(.20)/(1+(8−1)(.20)), or .667.

Because Cronbach's alpha deals with internal consistency and because α will increase as $\bar{r}$ gets larger (assuming that k remains constant), it might seem that a high value for α necessarily implies that items "hang together" in the sense that they measure the same thing. According to this line of reasoning, a high value for α indicates that the measuring instrument is unidimensional. Unfortunately, this line of reasoning is logically flawed.

In logic, there is something called the "fallacy of affirming the consequent." This fallacy takes place if you first come to know that one thing truly does imply something else, but then make the improper logical leap and conclude that both things must coexist if you know only that the "something else" exists. Stated succinctly in the general form, this fallacy involves thinking: "If P then Q; therefore, if Q then P." If it's raining, you can count on seeing an open umbrella as pedestrians walk through a city. However, you *cannot* count on it raining if you see an open umbrella. (Some people use umbrellas to shield themselves from the sun.)

If a measuring instrument is known to be unidimensional, then proper administration of that instrument necessarily will produce data that generate a high value for Cronbach's alpha. The reverse, however, does not follow. If it is known that an instrument has produced data for which α is high, then that instrument *cannot* correctly be considered to be unidimensional. This is the case because a high value for α will be produced if an instrument contains separate subsets of items with high correlations among items within each subset, but low inter-item correlations across subsets. Such an instrument might have two, three,

---

* This formula is the Spearman-Brown prophesy formula applied to the mean inter-item correlation.

or more dimensions. Thus, having a high value for Cronbach's alpha is a necessary but not sufficient condition for unidimensionality.

An example may help to prove this point. Suppose a seven-item instrument produces the inter-item correlations displayed in Table 4.3.1. These data strongly suggest that the instrument has tapped two dimensions, not one. Items 1 to 3 seem to "hang together," as do items 4 to 7. However, the inter-item correlations across these two portions of the instruments are quite low. Despite the fact that the instrument appears *not* to be unidimensional, $\alpha = .80$.

TABLE 4.3.1. Inter-Item Correlations for a Seven-Item Instrument

Item	Item 1	Item 2	Item 3	Item 4	Item 5	Item 6	Item 7
Item 1	—	.70	.80	.10	.10	.10	.10
Item 2		—	.60	.10	.10	.10	.10
Item 3			—	.10	.10	.10	.10
Item 4				—	.80	.60	.70
Item 5					—	.70	.80
Item 6						—	.60
Item 7							—

Whereas Cronbach's alpha cannot be used to assess the dimensionality of a measuring instrument, other statistical procedures are able to accomplish this objective. Because a concern over dimensionality represents a concern over an instrument's construct validity, the techniques of factor analysis, principal components analysis, and latent trait analysis are often used to answer the question: "How many dimensions are being measured, and what is the nature of it (if there is just one dimension) or them (if there are two or more dimensions)"? These procedures are complex, and a discussion of them is beyond the scope of this text.

Internet Assignment

Would you like to see an Internet-based interactive Java applet that computes Cronbach's alpha? Would you like to see what kind of alpha is produced for data that come from a test that lacks unidimensionality? If so, consider completing this Internet assignment.

This assignment is easy. First, go to this book's companion Web site (http://www.psypress.com/statistical-misconceptions). Once there, open the folder for Chapter 4 and click on the link called "Cronbach's Alpha and Unidimensionality." Then, follow the detailed instructions (prepared by this book's author) on how to use the interactive Java applet. You may be surprised by the computed value of α in light of the inter-item correlations that you'll see.

□ 4.4 Range Restriction and Predictive Validity

The Misconception

If a product–moment correlation coefficient is used to assess predictive validity, range restriction will cause r to underestimate the strength of the relationship between the predictor and criterion variables.

Evidence That This Misconception Exists*

The first of the following statements comes from an online report of the predictive validity of an instrument used to predict students' success during their first year in a veterinary medicine program. The second statement comes from a book on the intelligence testing of minority students. The third statement comes from an online document dealing with correlation.

1. *[C]orrelation coefficients are weakened by range restriction....*

2. *It is well known in statistics that range restriction attenuates (weakens) correlations.*

3. *If one of your variables has an artificially restricted range, then the correlation will be pushed closer to zero.*

Why This Misconception Is Dangerous

The primary statistical tool that's used to document (or better said, to estimate) predictive validity is Pearson's correlation. To the extent that measurements collected today are highly correlated, as indicated by r, with measurements collected in the future (on the same or a different variable), today's scores are said to possess predictive validity.

In both educational and industrial settings, where there are fewer slots available than there are applicants, range restriction occurs. Because not all applicants are measured on the criterion variable (simply because they are not hired or admitted), the correlation must be calculated from

---

* Appendix B contains references for all quoted material presented in this section.

data gleaned from only a subset of those who were initially tested. This smaller group usually is more homogeneous on the variable used to make the admission or hiring decisions, thus causing the range of scores on that variable to be "restricted." This smaller group is also likely to be more homogeneous when measured on the criterion variable.

A formula exists that supposedly "corrects" the correlation for range restriction. This formula always yields a higher estimate of r than the actual value of the correlation computed from the range-restricted subgroup. Those who think that range restriction inevitably has a dampening effect on r are likely to use this formula, see that the corrected r is larger, and end up thinking that predictive validity is higher than what the original r suggests. Unfortunately, correlations that have been corrected for range restriction can be inaccurate. In some situations, range restriction can cause the r that's computed on the basis of the subgroup to be *higher* (not lower) than what r would have been had it been based on data—on both the predictor and criterion variables—from all applicants.

Undoing the Misconception

The formula that corrects r for range restriction is based on two important assumptions: linearity and homoscedasticity. The linearity assumption is met if the "path" of the data in the scatter diagram is straight rather than curved.* Homoscedasticity exists if the variability of scores on Y (the criterion variable) remains constant across different values of X (the predictor variable).† Figure 4.4.1 contains hypothetical data that conform to these two assumptions.

With data like that displayed in Figure 4.4.1, it makes intuitive sense that we can determine the value of r for the full set of data by using only a subset of the scores. For example, if we compute a range-restricted r on the basis of the nine observations that have X values of 4, 5, and 6, it makes sense that we ought to be able to guess the value of r for the full set of data (for which $N = 18$) so long as (1) we know precisely what portion of the data we used to compute our range-restricted value of r and (2) the data comply with the linearity and homoscedasticity assumptions.

---

* Stated in a more technical way, linearity exists if the set of Y means, each computed for a different value of X, are positioned in a straight line.
† Homoscedasticity is akin to the equal variance assumption that underlies certain statistical test procedures, such as the F-test in the analysis of variance.

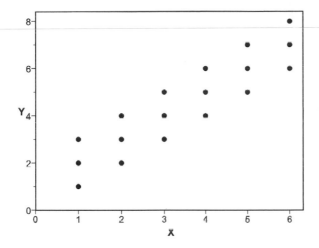

FIGURE 4.4.1 Data that are linear with equal variances for *Y*.

The formula that corrects *r* for restriction in range is not very intuitive looking, but it works. It is as follows:

$$r_N = \frac{r_n}{\sqrt{r_n^2 + \left(\dfrac{\sigma_{x(n)}^2}{\sigma_{x(N)}^2}\right)\left(1 - r_n^2\right)}}$$

where r_N = the correlation for all *N* observations, r_n = the correlation for the *n* range-restricted observations, $\sigma_{x(n)}^2$ = the variance of the *X* values of the *n* range-restricted observations, and $\sigma_{x(N)}^2$ = the variance of the *X* values of the full set of *N* observations. For the data shown in Figure 4.4.1, and presuming that we compute r_n on the basis of the nine observations where $X \geq 4$, $r_n = .707$, $\sigma_{x(n)}^2 = .667$, and $\sigma_{x(N)}^2 = 2.917$. Putting these values into the above formula produces a corrected value for r_N of .902, which is the exact value of *r* based on all 18 observations.

The formula available for correcting *r* for range restriction works fine if the conditions of linearity and homoscedasticity exist. However, the data collected in real validity studies usually do not possess the symmetry of the data displayed in Figure 4.4.1. With real data, it is possible for the original (i.e., uncorrected) range-restricted *r* to exaggerate, rather than underestimate, r_N. In that situation, correlations that are "corrected" for restriction in range move in the wrong direction!

Internet Assignment

Would you like to see "range restriction" illustrated in a scatter diagram? Would you like to be in control of how extensively range restriction is allowed to affect the data? Would you like to use an Internet-based interactive Java applet to show yourself or others that data sets can be generated for which predictive validity goes *up* in the presence of range restriction? If you would like to see and do these things, complete this Internet assignment.

If you choose to do this assignment, visit this book's companion Web site (http://http://www.psypress.com/statistical-misconceptions). Once there, open the folder for Chapter 4 and click on the link called "Range Restriction and Predictive Validity." Then, follow the detailed instructions (prepared by this book's author) on how to use the interactive Java applet. After playing with this applet, you are likely to have a deeper understanding of how range restriction can be produced and how it can affect *r*.

☐ Recommended Reading

Cohen, J. (1960). A coefficient of agreement for nominal scales. *Educational and Psychological Measurement, 20*, 37–46.

Cortina, J. M. (1993). What is coefficient alpha? An examination of theory and applications. *Journal of Applied Psychology, 78*, 98–104.

Deardorff, D. L. (2001). *Introductory physics students' treatment of measurement uncertainty.* Unpublished PhD dissertation, North Carolina State University, Raleigh.

Fleenor, J. W., Fleenor, J. B., & Grossnickle, W. F. (1996). Interrater reliability and agreement of performance ratings: A methodological comparison. *Journal of Business and Psychology, 10*(3), 367–380.

Fleiss, J. L. (1971). Measuring nominal scale agreement among many raters. *Psychological Bulletin, 76*, 378–382.

Garson, G. D. (2006). Validity. In *Statnotes: Topics in multivariate analysis.* Retrieved November 2, 2007, from http://www2.chass.ncsu.edu/garson/pa765/validity.htm.

Garson, G. D. (2007). Reliability analysis. In *Statnotes: Topics in multivariate analysis.* Retrieved November 2, 2007, from http://www2.chass.ncsu.edu/garson/pa765/reliab.htm.

Gerbing, D. W., & Anderson, J. C. (1988). An updated paradigm for scale development incorporating unidimensionality and its assessment. *Journal of Marketing Research, 25*, 186–192.

Goodwin, L. D., & Goodwin, W. L. (1999). Measurement myths and misconceptions. *School Psychology Quarterly, 14*(4), 408–427.

Green, S. (1977). Limitations of coefficient alpha as an index of test unidimensionality. *Educational and Psychological Measurement, 37*(4), 827–838.

Gross, A. L., & Fleischman, L. (1983). Restriction of range corrections when both distribution and selection assumptions are violated. *Applied Psychological Measurement, 7*(2), 227–237.

Kraemer, H. C., Periyakoil, V. S., & Noda, A. (2004). Kappa coefficients in medical research. In R. D'Agostino (Ed.), *Tutorials in Biostatistics. Vol. 1. Statistical methods in clinical studies* (pp. 85–105). West Sussex, England: John Wiley & Sons.

Müller, R., & Büttner, P. (1994, December). A critical discussion of intraclass correlation coefficients. *Statistics in medicine, 13*(23–24), 2465–2476.

Ree, M. J., Carretta, T. R., & Earles, J. A. (1998). In validation sometimes two sexes are one too many: A tutorial. *Human Performance, 12*(1), 79–88.

Schmitt, N. (1996). Uses and abuses of coefficient alpha. *Psychological Assessment, 8*(4), 350–354.

Uebersax, J. (2006). *Intraclass correlation and related methods.* Retrieved November 2, 2007, from http://ourworld.compuserve.com/homepages/jsuebersax/icc.htm.

CHAPTER

Probability

Research has shown that adults have intuitions about probability and statistics that, in many cases, are at odds with accepted theory.[*]

A number of researchers have suggested that misconceptions about basic statistical theory are relatively common [and] empirical evidence also indicates that many social scientists are misinformed about the meaning of probability values.[†]

---

* Clifford, K. (1995). *Issues in assessing conceptual understanding in probability and statistics*. Paper presented at the meeting of the American Statistical Association, San Francisco, p. 1.

† Riniolo, T. C., & Schmidt, L. A. (2000). Searching for reliable relationships with statistical packages: An empirical example of the potential problems. *Journal of Psychology, 134*, 143–151.

☐ 5.1 The Binomial Distribution and *N*

The Misconception

If a fair coin is flipped *N* times (with *N* being an even number), the potential result of "equality" (i.e., getting as many heads as tails) is more likely if *N* is large rather than small.

Evidence That This Misconception Exists*

The first of the following statements comes from an online statistics text. The second statement comes from a book on the impact of chance in our everyday lives. (Note the word and phrase *commonly-held belief* and *misconception* that appear in the first passage, as well as the first four words in the second passage.)

1. *A simple illustration of the gambler's fallacy is the commonly-held belief that a fair coin that has come up heads five times in a row is more likely than not to come up tails on the next flip. One reason for this misconception may be the notion that the number of heads and tails balances out in the long run. If there are more heads now, the balancing process will produce more tails in the future. The flaw in this reasoning is that the number of heads and tails do not balance out in the long run.*

2. *Many people mistakenly think that a number of tosses resulting in heads will be followed by a number of tosses resulting in tails, such that both heads and tails will turn up approximately the same number of times.... Indeed, the absolute difference between the numbers of heads and tails tends to become larger as the number of tosses increases. This surprising fact can be convincingly demonstrated using computer simulation.*

Why This Misconception Is Dangerous

Probability distributions are important. They are centrally connected, for example, to confidence intervals that are built around sample statistics.

---

* Appendix B contains references for all quoted material presented in this section.

Moreover, the *p*-value involved in hypothesis testing comes about by comparing a test statistic to an appropriate probability distribution. Because probability distributions are used so frequently in statistics, you are better off if you are able to visualize them and know how their shapes are influenced by various factors. One such factor is *N*, the number of observations.

The binomial distribution is probably the easiest probability distribution to understand, especially when the probability, *p*, of the outcome being focused on is equal to .50 (as is the case if we count the number of heads that turn up when a fair coin is flipped several times). However, to understand how the binomial distribution changes as a function of *N*, you need to realize that the probability of observing a result that *exactly* matches *Np* is different from the probability of observing a result that *approximates Np*. If you don't understand this difference, you are likely to be confused by illustrations or tables of the binomial distribution, prepared for various values of *N*, because the likelihood of a result turning out exactly equal to *Np* goes down (not up) as *N* increases.

Undoing the Misconception

If you flip a fair coin an even number of times, the probability of getting as many heads as tails is shown in Table 5.1.1. Note that as the number of coin flips, *N*, increases, the probability of observing "equality" decreases.*

If you flip that same fair coin an even number of times, the probability of getting a result that *approximates* the expected value (*Np*) goes up as *N* increases. This can be seen in Table 5.1.2, where the bottom row indicates the probability that the number of heads observed in *N* flips will be no more than 10% different from the expected value of 50%.

Internet Assignment

Would you like to see some convincing evidence, in the form of a picture, that the probability of getting an equal number of heads and tails decreases as the number of coin flips increases? Would you like to have that picture be interactive so you can control how many times the coin is flipped? If you would like to see and do these things, complete this Internet assignment.

---

* The probability of getting as many heads as tails when a coin is flipped an even number of times is equal to $N!$ divided by $2^N[(N/2)!]^2$. Increases in *N* cause the denominator to increase faster than the numerator.

TABLE 5.1.1. Probability of Getting as Many Heads as Tails When Flipping a Fair Coin

	Number of Times a Fair Coin is Flipped						
	2	4	6	8	10	...	100
Number of heads (N_{Heads}); number of tails (N_{Tails})	1; 1	2; 2	3; 3	4; 4	5; 5	...	50; 50
Probability of having $N_{Heads} = N_{Tails}$	.50	.375	.3125	.2734	.2461	...	.0796

TABLE 5.1.2. Probability of Having Between 40% and 60% Heads

	Number of Times a Fair Coin is Flipped						
	10	20	30	40	50	...	100
Number of heads if this outcome occurs 40%–60% of the time	4–6	8–12	12–18	16–24	20–30		40–60
Probability of getting 40%–60% heads	.6562	.7368	.7995	.8461	.8810	...	.9647

If you choose to do this assignment, visit this book's companion Web site (http://http://www.psypress.com/statistical-misconceptions). Once there, open the folder for Chapter 5 and click on the link called "The Binomial Distribution and N." Then, follow the detailed instructions (prepared by this book's author) on how to use the interactive Java applet. After playing with this applet, you are likely to have a deeper understanding of the binomial distribution.

☐ 5.2 A Random Walk With a Perfectly Fair Coin

The Misconception

If a perfectly fair coin is flipped 50 times with you betting that each flip's outcome will be heads while a friend bets against you, then your ongoing cumulative performance—based on $1 given by the loser to the winner after each flip—will cause you to be "in the black" (i.e., with positive earnings) about as often as you are "in the red" (i.e., in debt to your friend) across the series of coin flips.

Evidence That This Misconception Exists*

The first of the following statements comes from an online document dealing with statistical concepts in the field of finance. The second statement comes from an online journal dealing with communications theory and application. (In the first passage, the word *we* refers to the typical person who thinks about the coin-flipping game, and the word *expect* points to the misconception that this person has; similarly, the phase *one would expect* in the second passage indicates what the typical person will anticipate.)

1. *Imagine a game where we make a long sequence of coin tosses. Make a graph of the tosses. Each time we get heads, go up one unit on the graph. Each time we get tails, go down one unit. If the coin is fair, so the probability that we get heads or tails on any given toss is exactly 50/50 ... the graph will go up and down [and] it will wander around randomly. If the coin is fair, we "expect" that about half the time it will come up heads, and about half the time it will come up tails.*

2. *Two gamblers are engaged in a long coin tossing game (random walk). Intuitively, one would expect that each player will be on the winning side for about half of the time and that the leads will pass not infrequently from one player to the other (equivocation). The opposite is true.*

---

* Appendix B contains references for all quoted material presented in this section.

Why This Misconception Is Dangerous

If you do not thoroughly understand random processes, you are likely to mistakenly think that a person is lucky when he or she is truly skilled. Or, you may make the opposite mistake and think that a person is skilled when it's really just luck that causes him or her to be routinely on the "winning" side of the ledger. Each of these mistakes is especially likely to occur when a cumulative record is kept as to how players fare in games or contests that are repeated over time.

In some situations, the repeated game or contest is of trivial importance, and the monikers *"winner"* and *"loser"* are used in jest, or not used at all. In other situations, however, it matters greatly whether the person who accumulates victories is truly skilled or just lucky. Huge sums of money are bet on sports figures and teams that generate, over time, a winning percentage. And stockbrokers can command high fees if they can make a customer's portfolio grow rather than shrink in value.

One facet of randomness that's worth understanding is the likely "path" taken, across a series of events in time, when the binary outcome of each event is like the flip of a fair coin.

Undoing the Misconception

Figure 5.2.1 shows the actual results for a sequence of 50 flips of a perfectly fair coin, with "heads" leading to a 1-point gain and "tails" leading to a 1-point loss. In this particular sequence, there were seven occasions past the starting point when the sum of the random process turned out equal to 0. Of the 43 remaining points in the sequence, the sum was positive 42 times and negative only once!

An area of statistics dealing with *random walks* has been used to investigate what happens when a sum is calculated, over time, for a random process. Applied to our situation of two gamblers betting on coin flips, the findings are quite counterintuitive:

1. It is highly unlikely that the two gamblers will have the same amount of money (or anything close to that) after the last coin flip.

2. As the sequence of coin flips unfolds over time, the number of *equalizations*—where neither gambler is in debt to the other—is likely to be quite small relative to the number of coin flips.

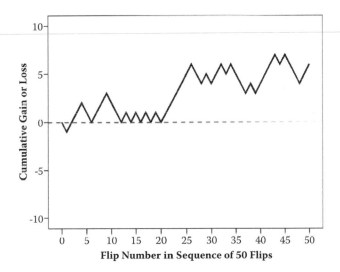

FIGURE 5.2.1 Cumulative results over time of betting on heads on each of 50 flips of a fair coin.

3. The final equalization is likely to occur early in the sequence, thus meaning that one of the gamblers is likely to be in the black for most of the sequence.

4. The three points just made are even *more* likely to be true if the number of coin flips is increased.

Internet Assignment

Would you like to take a random walk with a fair coin? Would you like to have a computer flip the coin for you and quickly display your results in a graph? Would you like to be able to control the length of your random walk, and replicate it many times within a few seconds? If you would like to see and do these things, do this Internet assignment.

If you choose to do this assignment, first go to this book's companion Web site (http://www.psypress.com/statistical-misconceptions). Once there, open the folder for Chapter 5 and click on the link called "A Random Walk With a Perfectly Fair Coin." Then, follow the detailed instructions (prepared by this book's author) on how to use the interactive Java applet. After playing with this applet, you are likely to have a better idea of what happens when a 50–50 event is repeated over and over, with a record kept as to the cumulative outcome over time.

☐ 5.3 Two Goats and a New Car

The Misconception

As a hypothetical contestant in a game show, you are shown three curtains and told that a new car is parked behind one of the curtains while a goat sits behind each of the other curtains. You then get to choose a curtain and are guaranteed that you will receive the prize behind your curtain. After making your selection, the host of the game show opens up one of two curtains you did *not* select, revealing a goat. Finally, the game show host asks you whether you want to switch from the curtain you initially selected to the other unopened curtain.*

With two unopened curtains (the one you selected and the unopened curtain you did not select), intuition suggests that the chances are equal that the car is behind either of those two curtains. Therefore, it doesn't seem to make a difference whether you stay with your original selection or switch to the other unopened curtain.

Evidence That This Misconception Exists†

The first of the following statements comes from a Web site dealing with riddles. The second comes from a book on probability. The third comes from a PhD dissertation focused on people's probabilistic reasoning. (Note the final five-word sentence in the first passage, the four-word phrase *particularly susceptible to misunderstanding* in the second passage, and the words *modal response* in the third passage.)

1. *This riddle was popularized by Marilyn vos Savant, current holder of the world's highest IQ. She introduced it in a magazine puzzle column, and was subsequently bombarded by flame mail accusing her of having the wrong solution, even though she was right. Even statistics professors were fooled!*

---

* This scenario mirrors what actually happened on a TV game show that was televised years ago. The host of the game show was Monty Hall, and the term *Monty Hall paradox* has been coined to describe the misconception that it makes no difference whether the contestant stays with his or her originally selected curtain or switches to the other unopened curtain.

† Appendix B contains references for all quoted material presented in this section.

2. *The Monty Hall problem (or three door problem) is one of the most famous examples of a "cognitive illusion," often used by psychologists, economists, and even law scientists to demonstrate people's resistant deficiency in dealing with uncertainty.*

3. *The modal response by [undergraduate] psychology subjects is to assert that each door has an equal probability of winning....*

Why This Misconception Is Dangerous

When an event has just two possible outcomes, many people think that those outcomes are equally likely to occur. In the case of a fair coin being flipped, the probability of each possible outcome—a head or a tail—*is* the same. Likewise, there's a 50–50 chance that a card randomly drawn from a regular deck of playing cards will be red. In many other situations, however, the probabilities of an event's two possible outcomes are dissimilar. Such is the case with the two remaining unopened curtains in the game show scenario described above.

The danger of having this misconception is *not* that you or someone else will end up as a contestant on a TV game show and win a goat rather than a new car. Instead, the danger is that seemingly simple situations (like the two-curtain option at the end of the game show scenario) are not considered with the care needed to figure out the probability associated with each possible outcome. In certain situations, Bayes' theorem is needed to "see through" the apparent simplicity. Because Bayes' theorem is used within a variety of disciplines—including medicine, law, psychiatry, and philosophy—the real danger of having this misconception is not having an appreciation for Bayes' theorem.*

Undoing the Misconception

The game show contestant is twice as likely to win the car if he or she switches from the originally selected curtain to the one remaining unopened curtain. This fact is surprising to many people, even some who are trained in mathematics, logic, and statistics. However, a consideration of conditional probability allows us to see that switching curtains is more likely to allow us to end up with the big prize.

---

* Bayes' theorem is named in honor of Thomas Bayes (1702–1761), who studied conditional probability, the likelihood that one thing will happen given that a different thing has already occurred.

Conditional probability permits the likelihood of a possible outcome to be "updated" (i.e., revised) on the basis of new evidence that becomes available. In the scenario of the contestant who is given the option to switch from curtain A to curtain C, the "new evidence" is the goat that is shown to be behind curtain B. With this new information now available, it makes no sense to keep thinking, as we did at the beginning, that we have a one-third chance of winning the car, regardless of which curtain we choose. Another piece of information exists as we analyze the game show story. The host, who knows where the new car is located, would never reveal it after the contestant initially selects a curtain; instead, a goat will always be revealed. As Bayes' theorem shows, it is also incorrect, after curtain B is opened, to think that there's a 50–50 chance that the car sits behind each of the unopened windows

There are many different ways to express Bayes' theorem. Here, we'll look at one that's cast in terms of our hypothetical game show. First, we must define a few things:

A, B, and C = the three curtains

A = the curtain initially selected by the contestant

B = the curtain opened by the game show host after the contestant selects A

C = the curtain that remains unopened after A is selected and B is opened

Then, we articulate some initial probabilities:

$P(A_{car}) = P(B_{car}) = P(C_{car})$ = a priori probability that the car is behind any curtain = 1/3

$P(\text{host opens } B|A_{car})$ = probability that host opens B if car is behind A – 1/2

$P(\text{host opens } B|B_{car})$ = probability that host opens B if car is behind B = 0

$P(\text{host opens } B|C_{car})$ = probability that host opens B if car is behind C = 1

$P(\text{host opens } B) = P(A_{car})*P(\text{host opens } B|A_{car}) + P(B_{car})*P(\text{host opens } B|B_{car}) + P(C_{car})*P(\text{host opens } B|C_{car}) = (1/3)(1/2) + (1/3)(0) + (1/3)(1) = 1/2$

Then, by Bayes' theorem, we can determine the probability that the car is behind the curtain initially selected by the contestant (A) or the other unopened curtain (C):

$P(A_{car}|\text{host opens B})$ = probability of winning car by *not* switching to C

$$= \frac{P(A_{car})*P(\text{host opens B}|A_{car})}{P(\text{host opens B})} = \frac{\left(\frac{1}{3}\right)\left(\frac{1}{2}\right)}{\frac{1}{2}} = \frac{1}{3}$$

$P(C_{car}|\text{host opens B})$ = probability of winning car by switching to C

$$= \frac{[P(C_{car})*P(\text{host opens B}|C_{car})]}{P(\text{host opens B})}$$

$$= \frac{\left(\frac{1}{3}\right)(1)}{\frac{1}{2}} = \frac{2}{3}$$

Internet Assignment

Would you like to pretend that you are the contestant and see what would happen under different strategies for trying to win the new car? Would you like to test out Bayes' theorem as you (the contestant) make your decision as to whether you should switch or stay after making your original selection, and then see what's behind one of the doors you don't select? If you would like to do these things, do this assignment using an Internet-based interactive Java applet.

Should you choose to do this assignment, first go to this book's companion Web site (http://www.psypress.com/statistical-misconceptions). Once there, open the folder for Chapter 5 and click on the link called "Two Goats and a New Car." Then, follow the detailed instructions (prepared by this book's author) on how to use the applet. After playing with this applet, you may end up having a bit more respect for Bayes' theorem!

☐ 5.4 Identical Birthdays

The Misconception

In a randomly selected group of 23 people, it's unlikely that two or more of the individuals have the same birthday.

Evidence That This Misconception Exists*

The first of the following statements comes from a peer-reviewed journal in mathematics. The second statement comes from a lab exercise associated with a college-level course in simulation, probability, and statistics taught at Wellesley College. The third statement comes from a textbook on statistics and computers. (In these passages, note the phrases: *erroneous reasoning made by many people, so different from the "intuitive" answer*, and *misleads us*.)

1. *The erroneous reasoning made by many people when confronted with this problem is interesting because ... people often determine the probability by considering the ratio between the number of people in the group (i.e. the number of available birthdays) and the total number of days in a year (i.e. the number of possible birthdays), so that the probability of getting a birthday match in 23 people would be 23/365 = 0.06.*

2. *The Birthday Paradox is a classic of counting and probability, because it's so darn surprising. It's a paradox not because it's logically contradictory, but because the true answer is so different from the "intuitive" answer.*

3. *[O]ur intuition about random numbers can often mislead us. Another example of this phenomenon is the famous birthday paradox.*

Why This Misconception Is Dangerous

There are times when two people in a group have the same birthday—meaning that they both were born on the same day of the same month, regardless of their birth year(s)—without knowing this piece of personal information. Most likely, there's absolutely no harm done if they fail to

---

* Appendix B contains references for all quoted material presented in this section.

say "Happy Birthday" to each other. Thus, the danger of this misconception is *not* connected to a missed opportunity for two people to realize that they blow out cake candles on the same day of the year.

The actual danger of having this misconception is twofold. First, if you expect no identical birthdays to exist in a group of 23 people, you are underestimating the influence that decimal numbers have on one another when they are multiplied. For example, if each letter of the English alphabet happens to be a decimal number, the product of $A \times B \times C \times \ldots \times Z$ turns out to be smaller than many people realize, even if each of the 26 individual decimal numbers is fairly large. The second danger of this misconception is related to the fact that solutions to probability problems such as the "birthday puzzle" require a kind of backwards thinking. In other words, it's sometimes necessary to approach a probability problem by focusing first on what you're *not* looking for, rather than focusing initially on what you *are* trying to determine.

Undoing the Misconception

Imagine a large, empty room. Also imagine hundreds of people lined up outside the door, with you being the first person in line. Finally, imagine that the people come in one at a time, with a check made—after each person enters—to see if there are any birthday matches among those who are inside the room. How many people would have to be inside the room before there would be more than a 50–50 chance of observing at least one common birthday?

To answer this question, we need to make three assumptions. First, let's assume that the people lined up outside the door are randomly selected from the general population. Second, let's assume that birthdays are spread out evenly over the 365 days of the year. Finally, let's assume that no one is born on February 29. These assumptions will make it easier to answer the question.*

Now, imagine that you walk through the door and enter the room. You are person 1. Obviously, there can't be a birthday match because there is just one person in the room. Therefore, let's imagine that another person joins you in the room. The probability that person 2 has your birthday is 1/365, or about .0027. Thus, the probability that

---

* In reality, people are *not* born with an equal likelihood on all days of the year, and people *are* born on February 29 every four years. If taken into consideration, however, these facts have only a minor impact on the probability that two or more people in a group have the same birthday.

person 2 does *not* have your birthday is 364/365, or about .9973. Clearly, we can determine the first of these probabilities by subtracting the second probability from 1. In other words, the probability of *having* a birthday match is equal to 1 minus the probability of *not having* a birthday match.

Now imagine that person 3 enters the room. The probability of having at least one birthday match among the three room inhabitants is equal to 1−[(364/365) × (363/365)] = 1 − (.9973 × .9945), or about .0082. The first fraction inside parentheses comes from the previous paragraph, and it corresponds with person 2. The second fraction inside parentheses corresponds with person 3, and its numerator is 363 because there are that many days of the year that can accommodate person 3's birthday if he or she does *not* have a match with you or person 2. We multiply those fractions together because we want to consider the case where person 2 doesn't match you *and* the case where person #3 does not create a birthday match.

As each new person enters the room, we add a new fraction inside the parentheses. The numerators of these fractions decrease by 1, while each fraction's denominator is 365. Thus, after person 6 enters the room, the probability of having you and the other five room inhabitants produce at least one birthday match is equal to

$$1-\left(\frac{364}{365}\times\frac{363}{365}\times\frac{362}{365}\times\frac{361}{365}\times\frac{360}{365}\right)$$

$$= 1 - (.9973 \times .9945 \times .9918 \times .9890 \times .9863)$$

or about .0405. With 23 people in the room, there would be 22 fractions inside the parentheses, the last of which would be 343/365, with this final fraction indicating that the probability of person 23 having a different birthday from any of the first 22 people. That probability would be about .9397.

The decimal equivalent of each of the 22 fractions would indicate, by itself, a high probability. However, the effect of multiplying those decimal numbers together produces a combined probability for the *whole* that is much lower than the probability of any of the *parts*. In fact, the product of .9973 × .9945 × ... × .9397 is equal to about .4927. This is the probability of having no birthday matches. Thus, the probability of observing at least one birthday match among 23 people is 1−.4927, or about .5073.

Clearly, the probability is extremely high (.9973) that the first two people in our imaginary room have different birthdays. When that large decimal number is multiplied by many other large decimals, however, the result turns out to be much smaller (.4927) than you might at first imagine. After we subtract that value from 1, we see that we shouldn't be surprised to discover at least one birthday match in a group of 23 people. The important point to understand is that some kind of unlikely event is likely to occur if many such events are being considered.*

The information in Table 5.4.1 shows the probability of having a birthday match for groups of different sizes. This information shows that the probability increases rapidly as *N* increases.

TABLE 5.4.1. Likelihood of Birthday Matches for Different-Sized Groups

	Group Size								
	5	10	15	20	25	30	40	50	60
Probability of at least one birthday match	.03	.12	.25	.41	.57	.71	.89	.97	.99+

Internet Assignment

Would you like to see how likely it is for there to be at least one birthday match among the members of your extended family? Would you like to know how large a group needs to be before there is a 90% chance of having at least one birthday match? If so, you can quickly determine these things with the aid of an Internet-based calculator that computes birthday-match probabilities.

If you choose to do this assignment, first go to this book's companion Web site (http://www.psypress.com/statistical-misconceptions). Once there, open the folder for Chapter 5 and click on the link called "Identical Birthdays." Then, follow the detailed instructions (prepared by this book's author) on how to use the online calculator. Finally, use the calculator to answer three birthday-match questions (again prepared by this book's author). After completing this assignment, you will be in a position to dazzle your friends with birthday-match facts that may be extremely hard for them to believe.

---

* If you flip a fair coin 10 times, you're not likely to see your coin land "heads" 10 times in a row. The probability of that happening is .00098. However, if 1,000 people each flip a fair coin 10 times, the odds are nearly 2 to 1 that at least 1 person will generate this extremely rare outcome of 10 heads in 10 flips.

☐ 5.5 The Sum of an Infinite Number of Numbers

The Misconception

The sum of an infinite number of positive numbers will be positive infinity, no matter how small the numbers are.

Evidence That This Misconception Exists*

The first of the following statements comes from a journal in mathematics. The second statement comes from a Web log dealing with Zeno's paradox. (In these passages, note the phrases *frequently considered, overcome the misconception,* and *mistaken intuition.*)

1. *[W]e must keep in mind that a sum of infinitely many addends is frequently considered by pupils as "infinitely great" (Bagni, 2000a) so first of all we must overcome the misconception "infinitely many addends, infinitely great sum."*

2. *[H]umans typically have the mistaken intuition that the sum of an infinite number of things must be infinite.*

Why This Misconception Is Dangerous

Several probability distributions extend out to infinity. For example, the curved line of a normal curve gets closer and closer to the baseline as it, the curved line, moves farther and farther away from the distribution's center. However, it never touches the baseline and instead extends out to positive infinity on one side and out to negative infinity on the other. A t distribution also extends to $\pm\infty$. Some distributions, such as χ^2 and F, start at 0 but extend to $+\infty$.

Anyone who mistakenly thinks that an infinitely long series of numbers adds up to infinity will be stumped by a thorny little paradox. First, recall that the full and complete probability connected with a Gaussian, t, χ^2, or F distribution is set equal to 1. Next, note that when such distributions are used to test null hypotheses, one or two "tails" are

---

* Appendix B contains references for all quoted material presented in this section.

established such that the proportion of the full distribution in the tail(s) is equal to α. Finally, add in the fact that there is no end to the tail(s), for it (they) extends infinitely far out from the distribution's bulky "body." How can the tail(s) have a fixed size that's small, such as .05, if it is infinitely big?

Undoing the Misconception

If the numbers being added together are all the same size, the sum is positive or negative infinity, depending on the sign of the numbers being added. This holds true no matter how small the numbers are. However, this situation does not parallel what happens with any of the probability distributions being considered (e.g., t) because the tails get smaller and smaller as they end up farther and farther away from the distribution's center.

If the numbers in the series are not the same size but rather decrease in a systematic fashion as each new number is added, the sum of the numbers is equal to a known and finite quantity. Consider, for example, this series: $4 + 2 + 1 + 1/2 + 1/4 + 1/8 + 1/16 + \ldots$ that extends out to infinity. Would the sum of these numbers be infinitely large? No. The sum is equal to 8!

For any infinite series of numbers in which (1) the beginning number is a and (2) each successive number is equal to a constant fractional multiple, r, of the preceding number, the sum of the series is a finite number. That sum is equal to $a/(1-r)$. Applied to the series in the previous paragraph, this formula produced 8 as the sum because $a = 4$, $r = .5$, and $4/(1-.5) = 8$.

To see if you've caught on to what can happen when we're dealing with a set of numbers that decrease in size by a constant fraction, here's a little puzzle for you to solve. Suppose you win a contest in which the prize is money. You are given two options for receiving your prize, and you must select one or the other of these options. Option A is a lump sum of $10,000 right now with no other money delivered to you after that. Option B is an infinite number of payments, one per day, in which the beginning payment is $100 and each successive day brings you (or your heirs) a payment that's 99% as large as the previous day's payment. Disregarding any interest you might make by investing the money you get, which option seems better?*

---

* When given these options, most people quickly choose the infinite number of payments.

Internet Assignment

Would you like to see what the sum is equal to for a series of 50 numbers, when each successive number in the series is a constant fraction of the previous number? Would you like to be able to control the beginning number in the series as well as the size of the fraction that determines the size of each successive number in the series compared to its predecessor? If you would like to see and do these things, spend a few minutes doing this assignment using an Internet-based interactive Java applet.

If you choose to do this assignment, first go to this book's companion Web site (http://www.psypress.com/statistical-misconceptions). Once there, open the folder for Chapter 5 and click on the link called "The Sum of an Infinite Number of Numbers." Then, follow the detailed instructions (prepared by this book's author) on how to use the applet. After playing with this applet, you are likely to have a better understanding of how series can be constructed and what the sum of the series is equal to, even if the series extends out to infinity!

☐ 5.6 Being Diagnosed With a Rare Disease

The Misconception

If someone is diagnosed as having a very rare and fatal disease, and if the procedure used to come up with this diagnosis is 99% accurate, then the person who's been diagnosed has a right to feel that "the end is near."

Evidence That This Misconception Exists*

The first of the following statements comes from John Allen Paulus, a leading authority on statistics and logic. The second statement comes from a chapter on probability and statistics included in a handbook on mathematics. The third statement comes from online lecture notes that accompanied a college-level course in mathematics. (In these passages, note these words and phrases: *has a way of tripping people up, misunderstanding, lead us to draw inaccurate conclusions, misconception,* and *counterintuitive.*)

1. *The psychological obstacles to rational understanding of statistics are the most familiar.... The mathematical notion of conditional probability also has a way of tripping people up.... Misunderstanding conditional probability can lead us to draw inaccurate conclusions about critical health-care issues.*

2. *Another type of misconception of conditional probabilities is the confusion between a conditional and its reverse.... If a person tests positive for AIDS, P(AIDS|+Test) does not equal P(+Test|AIDS). However, the public often sees no difference between these two conditional situations.*

3. *Doctors should be more knowledgeable about chance trees and Bayes' formula.*

---

* Appendix B contains references for all quoted material presented in this section.

Why This Misconception Is Dangerous

This misconception is dangerous because the person who's diagnosed as having the fatal disease most likely is disease-free!

Undoing the Misconception

Let's assume that the rare disease shows up in 0.05% of the population. That means only 5 people in 10,000 have the disease. Let's also assume that, on average, the diagnostic test (being 99% accurate) yields a positive result (i.e., the test indicates that the patient has the disease) for 99 out of every 100 people who really have the disease, and a negative result for 99 out of every 100 people who really are disease-free. Based on these assumptions, here's what we'd expect to happen if 200,000 people are randomly selected from the population and tested:

1. Of the 200,000 people tested, about 100 would actually have the rare disease and about 199,900 wouldn't. (The number 100 comes from multiplying .0005—that's 0.05% expressed as a decimal number—by 200,000.)

2. Of the 100 people with the disease, 99 would correctly receive a "positive" diagnosis, and 1 truly sick person would be diagnosed as being okay.

3. Of the 199,900 people without the disease, 197,901 would correctly receive a "negative" diagnosis, and 1,999 truly disease-free people would be diagnosed as being sick.

4. Altogether, we would expect 99 + 1,999 = 2,098 to be diagnosed as having the disease. However, 1,999 of these are "false positives"; in these cases, a disease-free person has been diagnosed as being sick.

5. Anyone in the group that has been diagnosed with the disease has a high probability of being one of the "false positives." To be more specific, the probability that a person is disease-free after being diagnosed as having the disease is

$$\frac{1,999}{2,098} = .9528$$

In other words, there is over a 95% chance that our hypothetical person does not have the rare disease even though the "highly accurate" diagnostic test said the opposite!

Bayes' theorem shows the same result. The probability of having the disease given a positive diagnosis is equal to

$$\frac{(.99)(.0005)}{(.99)(.0005)+(.01)(1-.0005)} = .0472$$

where .99 is the test's accuracy, .0005 is the proportion of people in the population who have the disease, and .01 is the proportion of people in the population who will end up as false positives.

Therefore, the probability of not having the disease given a positive diagnosis is equal to

$$1 - .0472 = .9528.$$

Internet Assignment

Would you like to see how likely it is for a dire diagnosis to end up being a false positive? Would you like to do this in such a way that you can control the accuracy of the diagnostic test and the prevalence of the disease? You can easily see and do these things with the aid of an Internet-based interactive Java applet.

Should you choose to do this assignment, first go to this book's companion Web site (http://www.psypress.com/statistical-misconceptions). Once there, open the folder for Chapter 5 and click on the link called "Being Diagnosed With a Rare Disease." Then, follow the detailed instructions (prepared by this book's author) on how to use the applet. After seeing the results provided by this applet, you may end up being a bit less nervous the next time a "nearly perfect" diagnostic test indicates that you have contracted a rare disease.

☐ 5.7 Risk Ratios and Odds Ratios

The Misconception

A risk ratio is the same thing as an odds ratio.*

Evidence That This Misconception Exists†

The first of the following statements comes from a peer-reviewed journal in medicine. The second statement comes from online lecture notes connected to a college-level course in medical research. The third statement comes from a textbook on medical statistics. (In these passages, note the words *misinterpretation, mistaking,* and *improperly.*)

1. *We found [in a review of articles published over two years in two peer-reviewed medical journals] that misinterpretation of an odds ratio as a risk ratio is common and can substantially affect estimates of association between a risk factor and an outcome.*

2. *Mistaking the odds ratio for a risk ratio, newspapers reported that black patients were 40% less likely to be referred for cardiac catheterization when, in fact, they were only 7% less likely to be referred.*

3. *In fact, many case-control investigators improperly used the term risk ratio or relative risk when reporting results of an odds ratio.*

Why This Misconception Is Dangerous

The statistical notions of risk and odds are two different ways of expressing the same thing. Suppose, for example, that the risk (i.e., probability) of getting a disease is 1/10 (i.e., .10). For every 10 people, 1 comes down with the disease and 9 do not. In this situation, the odds are 9 to 1 that you won't get the disease. Because the basic ideas of risk and odds are so similar, many people think that a risk ratio (RR) is the same thing as an odds ratio (OR).

---

* The term *relative risk* means the same thing as *risk ratio.*
† Appendix B contains references for all quoted material presented in this section.

It is dangerous to confuse risk ratios with odds ratios for two reasons. First, these two ratios will almost always be different when based upon the same data. For example, consider the sinking of the *Titanic*, fatality rates, and the gender of the passengers. The risk ratio indicates that the male passengers were 2.5 times more likely to die than female passengers. When the same data are used to compute an odds ratio, we find that the odds of dying were 10 times greater for males than for females.*

The second reason why it's dangerous to think that risk ratios and odds ratios are the same is the simple fact that risk ratios cannot be computed in certain kinds of studies. To be more specific, risk ratios cannot be computed in "case-control" investigations.† In such studies, odds ratios represent the only option.

Undoing the Misconception

To distinguish between an odds ratio and a risk ratio, let's consider the general case in which there are two groups, with each person in each group put into one or the other of two categories on the basis of some sort of observation or measurement. Hence, the scenario we are dealing with can be represented by Table 5.7.1.

The letters inside Table 5.7.1 represent the number of people in each group who end up being classified into each of the two available categories. When we look at some examples in a moment, there will be numbers in the chart rather than letters. For now, however, let's use the letters in order to see the different meanings of a risk ratio and an odds ratio.

TABLE 5.7.1. Group-by-Category Matrix

Groups	Category 1	Category 2
Group X	a	b
Group Y	c	d

* The details of this *Titanic* example are discussed in the next section.
† In such studies, a group of people who have some form of a disease or medical problem are compared with a group who do not possess the disease/problem; the goal is to identify characteristics (e.g., eating or exercise habits) that are more likely to be present in one group but not the other.

A risk ratio simply compares the two groups in terms of the proportion of group members that end up in one of the classification categories. For example, the proportion of people in group X that end up in category $1 = a/(a+b)$, whereas the comparable proportion in group $Y = c/(c+d)$. The risk ratio is simply the ratio of these proportions: $(a/(a+b))/(c/(c+d))$. An odds ratio compares the two groups in terms of the odds of ending up in one of the two categories. For example, the odds that people in group X end up in category $1 = a/b$, whereas the comparable odds in group $Y = c/d$. The odds ratio is simply the ratio of these odds: $(a/b)/(a/d)$.

Although a risk ratio and an odds ratio can be computed from the same data, they have certain computational similarities, and turn out equal to 1 if the same proportion of each group ends up in the designated category, these two indices are not at all identical. They differ in how they are computed, how they turn out, and what they mean. That's because one is a ratio of proportions (each indicating a risk), while the other is a ratio of odds. An example from the real world may help to make clear that $RR \neq OR$.

Table 5.7.2 contains the actual survival and gender data from the *Titanic* tragedy. Using the data in Table 5.7.2 (and rounding the results), the risk of males dying was 709/851 = .83, whereas the risk of females dying was 154/462 = .33. The male-to-female risk ratio for dying was .83/.33 = 2.50, meaning that the risk of dying was 2.5 times greater for males than females. Using the same data, the odds of a male dying were 709 to 142, whereas the odds of a female dying were 154 to 308. The odds ratio for male-to-female deaths was (709/142)/(154/308) = 9.99. Thus, the odds of a male dying were just about 10 times greater than the odds of a female dying. Note that 2.50 ≠ 9.99.*

TABLE 5.7.2. Gender by Outcome in *Titanic* Sinking

Gender	Survived	Died	Total
Males	142	709	851
Females	308	154	462
Total	450	863	1,313

---

* There is one situation where the odds ratio and the risk ratio will be nearly equal. This is the situation where a disease or other event (such as dying in a tragedy) is extremely rare. Suppose, for example, that only 5 of 1,000 males have a particular disease compared to only 2 of 1,000 females. Using these data, $RR = 2.50$, whereas $OR = 2.51$.

Internet Assignment

Would you like to see how easy it is to compute (and compare) an odds ratio with a risk ratio? Would you like to get a little practice using an Internet-based calculator that makes this possible? You can easily see and do these things with the aid of an online interactive Java applet.

If you choose to do this assignment, first go to this book's companion Web site (http://www.psypress.com/statistical-misconceptions). Once there, open the folder for Chapter 5 and click on the link called "Risk Ratios and Odds Ratios." Then, follow the detailed instructions (prepared by this book's author) on how to use the applet. After using the interactive calculator, you will likely come to understand the fundamental difference between risk ratios and odds ratios. In addition, you will come to understand how the same set of data can produce two risk ratios (or two odds ratios) that look quite different even though they tell the same story.

☐ **Recommended Reading**

Gilovich, T., Vallone, R., & Tversky, A. (1985). The hot hand in basketball: On the misperception of random sequences. *Cognitive Psychology, 17,* 295–314.

Intuitor. (n.d.). The probability of penalizing the innocent due to bad test results. In *Amazing applications of probability and statistics.* Retrieved May 1, 2007, from http://www.intuitor.com/statistics/BadTestResults.html.

Jewett, R. I., & Ross, K. A. (1988). Random walks on Z. *The College Mathematics Journal, 19*(4), 330–342.

Krauss, S. (2003). *Some issues of teaching statistical thinking.* Unpublished PhD dissertation, Fachbereich Erziehungswissenschaft und Psychologie, Freie Universität Berlin.

Liberman, A. M. (2005). How much more likely? The implication of odds ratios for probabilities. *American Journal of Evaluation, 26*(2), 253–266.

Lipkin, L. (2003). Tossing a fair coin. *The College Mathematics Journal, 34*(2), 128–133.

Monty Hall puzzle. (n.d.). Retrieved November 2, 2007, from http://staff.utia.cas.cz/vomlel/mh-puzzle.html.

Number series—A summary. (n.d.). Retrieved November 2, 2007, from http://richard bowles.tripod.com/maths/numseries/numseries.htm

Rossman, A. J., & Short, T. H. (1995). Conditional probability and education reform: Are they compatible? *Journal of Statistics Education, 3*(2). Retrieved November 2, 2007, from http://www.amstat.org/publications/jse/v3n2/rossman.html.

Sequences and series. (n.d.). Retrieved November 2, 2007, from http://www.maths.manchester.ac.uk/~gm/teaching/1P2/series.pdf.

Shoaff, W. (n.d.). *Sums, sequences, and series in the analysis of algorithms.* Retrieved November 2, 2007, from http://www.cs.fit.edu/~wds/classes/algorithms/Sums/sums/sums.html.

Sumner, D. (n.d.). *Random walk along a line.* Retrieved November 2, 2007, from http://www.math.sc.edu/~sumner/RandomWalk.html.

Weisstein, E. (2003, July 10). Random walk—1-dimensional. In *Wolfram MathWorld.* Retrieved November 2, 2007, from http://mathworld.wolfram.com/RandomWalk1-Dimensional.html.

Yudkowsky, E. (2003). *An intuitive explanation of Bayesian reasoning.* Retrieved November 2, 2007, from http://www.yudkowsky.net/bayes/bayes.html.

6

CHAPTER

Sampling

*The recurrence of regression fallacies is testimony to its subtlety, deceptive simplicity.... Galton's achievement remains one of the most attractive triumphs in the history of statistics, but it is one that each generation must learn to appreciate anew, one that seemingly never loses its power to surprise.**

Both classroom experience and research give credence to the notion that learners "do not understand that a sampling distribution is a distribution of sample statistics." (Chance et. al.) They may understand it for one fleeting instant and then lose that understanding the next.[†]

---

* Stigler, S. M. (1997). Regression towards the mean, historically considered. *Statistical Methods in Medical Research, 6,* 103–114, 113.

† Finzer, D., G Foletta, G. (2003). *Confronting some statistical inference misconceptions.* Paper presented at the Annual Meeting of ICTCM, Chicago. Retrieved January 22, 2008, from http://mtsu32.mtsu.edu:11281/presentations/CAUSEway/4technology/MisconceptionsDemoFathom.pdf.

121

☐ 6.1 The Character of Random Samples

The Misconception

If a truly random process is used to select a sample from a population, the resulting sample will turn out to be just like the population, but smaller. In other words, a random sample is like a miniature replica of the population.

Evidence That This Misconception Exists*

The first of the following statements comes from a governmental document on the statistics used in a demographic study of the country's public service agency. The second statement comes from handouts given to students in a college-level statistics course. The third statement comes from an online tutorial for students in a college-level math course. (Note the final sentence in the first passage, the word *resembles* in the second passage, and the phrase *looks just like* in the third passage.)

1. *A key point in sampling is the assumption that the sample is representative of the population from which it was drawn. That is, the sample should be a "miniature" population.*

2. *Good inference is only possible if the sample resembles the population.... Simple random sampling [means] the sample is likely to be a good representation of the population.*

3. *The sample needs to look just like the population, but smaller.*

Why This Misconception Is Dangerous

The tools of inferential statistics are used to make educated guesses regarding population parameters. Such guesses are educated for three reasons. First, statistical inferences are *empirical* (i.e., supported by data).

---

* Appendix B contains references for all quoted material presented in this section.

Second, they are based on data gathered from *random samples*. Third, they take into consideration the likelihood of *sampling error.**

If it were true that a random sample turns out to be a miniature replica of the population, characteristics of the sample could be used as error-free estimates of the population. The percentage of males in the sample would be the same as the percentage of males in the population, the sample correlation would match exactly the population correlation, and so forth. With no sampling error, inferential statistics would be quite simple. All you would need to do is summarize the sample data and then transfer that information, as a pinpoint statement of fact, to the population. There would be no need for confidence intervals, and null hypotheses would be easily rejected or retained without reliance on levels of significance, test statistics, and p-versus-α comparisons.

Those who disregard the likelihood of sampling error will make various kinds of inferential mistakes. Their thoughts about a single population most likely will be off the mark, perhaps with tragic consequences. For example, people may think that a particular pharmaceutical drug or medical procedure has a 70% likelihood of success because it was effective for 70% of people in the sample; in reality, the medical remedy might have only a 35% success rate. Or, after seeing the data from random samples drawn from two or more populations, people may erroneously conclude that one population is superior to the other(s) when in fact (1) that particular population is inferior or (2) the populations are identical. For example, in comparing three methods for training firefighters, sample data might make it seem that method A is best when in fact it's method C that produces the best-trained individuals to deal with burning buildings.

Undoing the Misconception

When a sample is extracted from a population, any numerical characteristic of the sample is likely to be different from the parallel numerical characteristic of the population. Stated differently, any sample is likely to possess sampling error. This is the case even if the sample is generated in

---

* A sampling error is not a faulty sampling process, as would be the case if people in the population are asked to volunteer to be in the sample. Rather, a sampling error is said to exist if the statistical summary of the sample is at all inaccurate in describing the population. For example, a sampling error exists if, with interest focused on the mean, the numerical value of the sample mean does not turn out to be identical to the numerical value of the population mean.

a random fashion such that every member of the population has an equal chance of being included in the sample.*

To show yourself that sampling error is to be expected, take a regular deck of playing cards, thoroughly shuffle it, put the cards face down in a pile, and then turn over the top 12 cards. Consider just the suit (spade, heart, diamond, or club) of each card, and then determine how many of your 12 cards belong to each suit. The full deck that you started with had 13 cards of each suit. Therefore, your sample of 12 cards has no sampling error—from a suit perspective—if it contains three spades, three hearts, three diamonds, and three clubs. If you actually perform this little activity, you are very unlikely to produce a sample of 12 cards that has an even suit distribution, even though your sample is a random sample.[†]

Consider now a second example, this one dealing with people and the variable of gender. Suppose we take a random sample of 40 people from a large population containing an equal number of males and females. We might, of course, end up with a sample containing 20 males and 20 females. If we did, the gender split in the sample would be identical to that in the population. But don't bet on that happening; if you do, you're likely to lose. It's far more likely that our sample will have more males than females (or vice versa).[‡]

Although the existence of sampling error is not unexpected, even with random samples, the amount of sampling error that's likely to occur follows two intuitively reasonable "laws of statistics." First, for any given sample size, sampling error is likely to be small rather than large. Thus, in our sample of 40 people taken from a large, gender-balanced population, a sample containing 55% females is more likely than one containing 80% females. Second, there is an inverse relationship between the sample size and the expected amount of sampling error. With 80 people in the sample (rather than 40), it's less likely the sample's percentage gender split would exceed 60-40 one way or the other.

---

* There are two exceptions to this general "rule." No sampling error will occur if (1) the population is totally homogeneous or (2) the sample is as large as the population. These conditions, however, rarely, if ever, exist in applied research investigations.

† The chances of your sample having three spades, three hearts, three diamonds, and three clubs are less than 1 in 10 million! (This numerical value comes from the hypergeometric distribution.)

‡ The chances are about 1 in 8 of having equal gender representation in our sample. (The exact binomial distribution was used to calculate this likelihood.)

Internet Assignment

Would you like to pull a random sample from a population and then check to see if any sampling error exists? Would you like to do this several times (within a few seconds), to see if sampling error should be looked upon as a surprising outcome of random sampling or a normal phenomenon? Would you like to do this with different sample sizes to see if n influences the magnitude of sampling error. You can do these things—and do them quickly—by using an Internet-based interactive Java applet.

If you choose to do this assignment, first go to this book's companion Web site (http://www.psypress.com/statistical-misconceptions). Once there, open the folder for Chapter 6 and click on the link called "The Character of Random Samples." Then, follow the detailed instructions (prepared by this book's author) on how to use the Java applet. By doing this little exercise, you will gather convincing evidence that you can share if someone ever asks whether random samples should be looked upon as miniature populations.

☐ 6.2 Random Replacements When Sampling

The Misconception

A sample of individuals drawn from a larger, finite group of people deserves to be called a *random* sample so long as (1) everyone in the larger group has an equal chance of receiving an invitation to participate in the study and (2) random replacements are found for any of the initial invitees who decline to be involved.

Evidence That This Misconception Exists*

The first of the following statements comes from a college textbook dealing with research methodology. The second statement comes from a peer-reviewed journal article focused on disability policy studies. The third statement comes from a university's report on individual development accounts (IDAs) for people with low incomes.

1. *Loss of subjects (also known as mortality) is perhaps the most difficult to control of all the threats to internal validity. A common misconception is that the threat is eliminated simply by [randomly] replacing the lost subjects.*

2. *Programs were stratified by region of the country, then randomly selected. Each program was solicited for participation, and random replacements were made to select another program in that region if the first refused.*

3. *Ten random "replacements" were drawn for each category, so that a randomly selected participant could be assigned to match the gender and ethnicity of any respondent who was unable to be interviewed.*

Why This Misconception Is Dangerous

Samples are typically used as the basis for making scientific guesses about populations. These guesses—referred to formally as statistical

---

* Appendix B contains references for all quoted material presented in this section.

inferences—often are made through the creation of confidence intervals and the testing of null hypotheses. To be valid, such inferences must be based on random samples.

If data are collected from nonrandom samples, numerical summaries of the gathered information most likely will be biased and lead to inferences that lack desired statistical characteristics. For example, the mean ($\bar{X}$) of a nonrandom sample cannot be said to have an expected value equal to the population mean (μ).

Undoing the Misconception

Imagine that the rectangle in Figure 6.2.1 represents a population containing 1,000 or more individuals. Also imagine that a researcher wants to make a statistical statement about this population (concerning, perhaps, the population's mean or the percentage of people in the population who support a particular political candidate). Finally, imagine that considerations of time and cost make it impossible for data to be collected from everyone in this population; accordingly, a decision is made to measure 40 individuals and then make a careful statistical inference from the sample to the population.

The small circles inside the rectangle represent the 40 individuals who have been randomly selected to be in the sample. Of these small circles, the ones that are darkened in represent 30 people who participate in the study and from whom data are gathered. The 10 small open circles, on the other hand, represent targeted sample individuals who do not fulfill their designated role. Depending on the nature of the study, these small open circles might be tied to people who forgot to complete a mailed or online survey, who declined to be interviewed, who chose not to participate in an experiment, or who for other reasons ended up not participating in the researcher's empirical investigation, even though they were randomly selected to be in the sample.

Suppose now that the researcher in our hypothetical study randomly selects 10 new individuals from the population to fill the vacant slots created by the 10 targeted sample individuals who didn't participate. Also suppose that all 10 of these individuals participate fully in the study. Thus, the researcher's data come from 30 + 10 = 40 individuals, all of whom have been randomly selected. Is this group of 40 individuals a random sample from the population? Probably not!

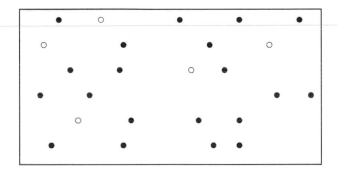

FIGURE 6.2.1 Targeted sample individuals who do (•) and don't (○) participate.

Research has shown that those individuals who choose not to participate in a study are often different, in potentially important ways, from those who accept the invitation. They generally have less free time, are unimpressed by any monetary or other kinds of incentives that accompany the invitation, and have a lower emotional connection to the topic being researched. Therefore, the population that's intended to be the target of a statistical inference actually has two parts. One part of the population contains people who, if asked to be in the study, would be willing participants. The other part is composed of individuals who will decline if invited to participate.

When invitations to participate in the study are accepted by some (but not all) of the individuals in the initial random sample, only one of the two segments of the two-part population is actually represented in the sample. The practice of securing a random replacement for each person who chooses not to be involved creates an undesirable situation of having the "random" sample come from only one of the two segments of the population. In such situations, any sample-to-population inference will be distorted to the extent that the two parts of the population differ with respect to the characteristic that's measured after the sample is drawn. Figure 6.2.2 illustrates an alternative (and better) way of conceptualizing the population that exists when random replacements are used to fill needed sample slots.

If a sample is made up of people who come from the left side of the vertical line located inside the rectangle (i.e., the population) shown in Figure 6.2.2, then any sample-based statistical inference legitimately can be directed only to the left portion of the population. This is precisely what happens when random replacements are used in a study. While the population has two parts, the sample is made up of individuals who come only from one of them.

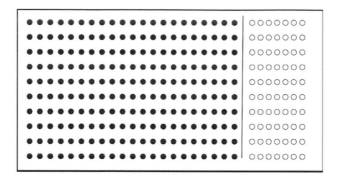

FIGURE 6.2.2 Conceptualizing a population as composed of people who will (•) and won't (○) join a study's sample.

Internet Assignment

Would you like to simulate a little study where certain people may decline your invitation to be involved as research participants? Would you like to do this quickly on the computer? If so, you can do this by using an Internet-based interactive Java applet.

If you choose to do this assignment, first go to this book's companion Web site (http://www.psypress.com/statistical-misconceptions). Once there, open the folder for Chapter 6 and click on the link called "Random Replacements When Sampling." Then, follow the detailed instructions (prepared by this book's author) on how to use the Java applet. By doing this little exercise, you will see clearly why random replacements—for those who decline to be involved or for those who drop out after a study has begun—are likely to cause a study's sample to yield biased estimates of population parameters.

☐ 6.3 Precision and the Sampling Fraction

The Misconception

Larger populations call for larger samples. In other words, the ratio of the sample size to the population size (i.e., the sampling "fraction") needs to be considered when deciding how large a sample should be.

Evidence That This Misconception Exists*

The first of the following statements comes from an online document dealing with knowledge discovery. The second comes from a government document authored by a mathematical statistician. The third comes from a statistics book for lawyers. (In these passages, note the phrases *widespread but incorrect intuition* and *common misconception*.)

1. *There is a widespread but incorrect intuition that a larger population implies the need for a significantly larger sample.*

2. *"What sample size should I take?" is one of the most frequently asked questions a statistician helps to answer.... One common misconception is thinking about an adequate sample size in terms of a proportion of the population size.*

3. *A common misconception is that a sample's precision depends on its size relative to the size of the population; in this view, samples that are a tiny fraction of the population do not provide reliable information about that population.*

Why This Misconception Is Dangerous

This misconception is dangerous to two groups of people: (1) researchers who conduct empirical investigations and (2) people who read or listen to reports that summarize research findings.

Sample data usually are costly to collect. Sometimes the cost is monetary; sometimes it involves time. Usually, the cost takes both forms.

---

* Appendix B contains references for all quoted material presented in this section.

Accordingly, researchers are not good stewards of resources if their sample sizes are unnecessarily large. If a sample size of 50 is just as good as a sample size of 500, a researcher would be wasting time and/or money, or both, if he or she decided to use the larger sample simply because the study's population is quite large and "larger populations call for larger samples."

Those who read or listen to the findings of a particular research investigation are likely to dismiss those findings if they think that the sample size was too small, given the size of the population. Operating under the misconception that the size of a sample should be proportionate to the size of the population, these individuals will find it difficult, if not impossible, to believe that a random sample of 50 individuals extracted from a population of 10,000 can provide useful insights regarding numerical characteristics of the population. Their misconception means that the study has little chance of having a beneficial impact on the way they think or act. Worse yet, such a study may cause these individuals to lose respect for those who conduct research.

Undoing the Misconception

The size of a population, N, often has little bearing on the likely accuracy, or precision, of a sample statistic. When N is large, the size of the sample, n, influences most, or totally, the precision of estimates based on sample data. The main consideration is the *absolute* size of n, not the relative size of n to N. Thus, a random sample of 50 people taken from a population where $N = 1,000$ will yield a statistic that's about as accurate in estimating the population parameter as will a random sample of 50 people drawn from a population that's 10 or 100 times that large.

By definition, the precision of a sample statistic is defined in terms of the standard error of that statistic. A standard error is like a standard deviation in that it measures dispersion. The dispersion it measures is the variability of the sample statistic, presuming that random samples of the same size are repeatedly extracted from the same population. The smaller the standard error, the greater the precision. This makes sense because a smaller standard error means that the values of the sample statistic, in the sampling distribution, will be more tightly concentrated around the population parameter.

Consider now the precision of two frequently used sample statistics, the mean and the proportion. The standard error of the sample mean is equal to

$$\frac{\sigma}{\sqrt{n}} \sqrt{\frac{N-n}{N-1}}$$

where σ is the population's standard deviation. The standard error of a sample proportion is equal to

$$\sqrt{\frac{P(1-P)}{n}\left(\frac{N-n}{N-1}\right)}$$

where P is the proportion in the population. Although each of these formulas involves consideration of both population size (N) and sample size(n), the value of the fraction, $(N - n)/(N- 1)$, approaches 1.0 as N increases for any fixed value of n. Thus, in those situations where N is large compared to n, this fraction doesn't influence the standard error very much. Stated differently, precision is determined almost totally by the absolute value of n, at least in those situations where N is large in relation to n.

Table 6.3.1 shows that the precision of the sample mean is influenced far more by the absolute size of n than by the ratio of n to N. This table assumes that $\sigma = 100$, and each entry is the standard error of the mean. Higher precision is reflected by entries that are smaller.

TABLE 6.3.1. Precision of the Sample Mean, When $\sigma = 100$, for 20 Different Combinations of n and N

	Population Size (N)				
Sample Size (n)	1,000	2,000	5,000	10,000	100,000
25	19.76	19.88	19.95	19.98	20.00
50	13.79	13.97	14.07	14.11	14.14
75	11.11	11.33	11.47	11.50	11.54
100	9.49	9.75	9.90	9.95	10.00

If you look at the entries within any row of Table 6.3.1, you will see that the sample mean's precision does not change much, even when N becomes very small relative to n. This is the case because the sampling fraction has little bearing on the standard error of the mean for any of the 20 cases considered in the table. On the other hand, the absolute value of n makes a big difference. Within any column of Table 6.3.1, precision gets better (i.e., smaller) as n increases.

It should be noted that researchers sometimes conduct studies in which the population is considered to be infinitely large. Such studies exist when there is sampling with replacement or when research participants are randomly assigned to the treatment conditions in an experiment. In these situations, precision is based exclusively on n and the variability in the population.

Internet Assignment

Would you like to see what happens to the precision of sample data when random samples of the same size are extracted from small, medium, and large populations? Would you like to do this quickly on the computer using an Internet-based interactive Java applet? If so, consider doing this Internet assignment.

If you choose to do this assignment, first go to this book's companion Web site (http://www.psypress.com/statistical-misconceptions). Once there, open the folder for Chapter 6 and click on the link called "Precision and the Sampling Fraction." Then, follow the detailed instructions (prepared by this book's author) on how to use the Java applet. Upon seeing the results of your simulation exercise, you are likely to have evidence in front of you that makes it clear that the absolute size of n affects precision far more than does the sampling fraction.

☐ 6.4 Matched Samples

The Misconception

If individuals cannot be randomly assigned to a study's treatment and control groups, the desired condition of initial equivalence between groups can be created by using existing, pretreatment data (e.g., scores on a pretest) to create matched pairs, with one member of each pair residing in the treatment group while his or her matched pair belongs to the control group.

Evidence That This Misconception Exists*

The first of the following statements comes from a book chapter on research in psychopathology. The second statement comes from an analysis of research studies dealing with efforts to improve students' math skills. The third statement comes from a peer-reviewed journal in the medical field. (In these passages, note the phrases *frequently overlooked, serious problem,* and *escaped widespread notice.*)

1. *[The] vulnerabilities of the matched-samples strategy have long been known but are frequently overlooked.*

2. *The research reviewed in this article evaluates a broad range of strategies for improving mathematics achievement.... Across most of the evaluations, lack of random assignment is a serious problem. Matched designs are used in most studies that met the inclusion criteria, and matching leaves studies open to selection bias.*

3. *The nonrandom methods of group formation in observational studies necessitate carefully assessing threats to the validity of conclusions. Regression to the mean is a source of change in clinical outcome measures that has escaped widespread notice as a potential threat to the accuracy of conclusions from observational studies and systematic reviews thereof. Failure to assess the degree to which regression confounds study results elevates the risk of making clinical decisions using biased estimates of intervention effectiveness.*

---

* Appendix B contains references for all quoted material presented in this section.

Why This Misconception Is Dangerous

The notion that matching is a good "substitute" for random assignment is dangerous for one main reason: such studies yield results that are difficult to interpret. When the comparison groups are formed by matching, any of three things can occur when the study's posttest data are analyzed: (1) a potent and beneficial treatment may end up looking like it has no impact—or worse yet, a negative impact; (2) a treatment that actually has no impact whatsoever may appear to work well; and (3) a treatment that truly hurts may seem to be inert or perhaps even helpful.

Simply stated, matched groups can cause a treatment's apparent impact to be different—and potentially *far* different—from what would have been the case if the study's participants had been randomly assigned to the treatment and control groups.

Undoing the Misconception

The phrase "matched group fallacy" refers to the belief held by many people that matching, when used as a technique for forming treatment and control groups, is just as good as random assignment. The two main "flies in the ointment" that prevent matching from achieving its goal (of creating equivalent groups) are regression toward the mean, on the one hand, and the logical limitations of any matching variable, on the other. Either one of these problems, by itself, can sabotage a study. However, it's usually the case that *both* problems exist simultaneously.

Problem 1: Regression Toward the Mean

In forming matched pairs for a study's treatment and control groups, members of the treatment group typically are selected first, either because those individuals have a special need or because the treatment must be provided to an intact group. Then, individuals for the control group are pulled from a large pool of "control group candidates." Using scores on a matching variable, a control group "twin" is identified for each person who's in the treatment group.

Suppose a study is conducted in which pretest performance functions as the matching variable. If the study's actual control group has a pretest mean that's lower than the pretest mean earned by the full pool of control group candidates, the control group probably will perform better on the posttest. This "improvement" is likely to occur even if nothing takes place between the pretest and posttest to benefit the control group's knowledge, skill, or ability. This group's upward movement, illustrated in Figure 6.4.1, is caused by regression toward the mean.

The regression that occurs will be in an upward direction (as in Figure 6.4.1) if the study's actual control group individuals, on average, come from the lower portion of the larger group of control candidates. On the other hand, regression will be in a downward direction if those in the study's control group have, on average, high scores on the pretest compared with the larger pool of control group candidates. The mean toward which regression "moves" is the posttest mean that would have been earned if all candidates for the control group had been measured on the posttest. In Figure 6.4.1, that mean is in the middle of the vertical bar on the right.

If the statistical artifact of regression causes the control group to experience "upward mobility," a truly beneficial treatment might appear to be worthless—or even harmful—when the posttest data from the treatment and control groups are compared. That's because the control group's artificial improvement could equal or even exceed the true gain made by the treatment group. On the other hand, if the control group regresses downward, a not-so-good treatment might look as if it has a positive impact.

The amount of regression toward the mean (associated with the matched control group) is influenced by two factors: (1) the degree to which the study's control group participants, on average, are located away from the mean of the larger group of individuals who were considered for inclusion in the control group, and (2) the size of the correlation between the matching variable and the posttest. Obviously, more regression is possible to the extent that the control group is atypical of the larger group from which it was drawn. Low correlations bring forth

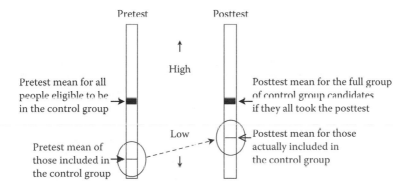

FIGURE 6.4.1 Regression toward the mean.

a lot of regression, while high correlations permit only a small amount to occur.*

Problem 2: Logical Limitations of the Matching Variable

Even if there is absolutely no regression toward the mean operating within the study, matched samples are problematic. That's because the treatment and control groups may differ in some important fashion that's not captured by data on the matching variable.

Suppose a study's treatment and control groups are formed by matching on the basis of a reliable and valid pretest that assesses knowledge. Even though matching makes the two groups equivalent on this one particular variable, the groups could be highly dissimilar in terms of other important variables, such as the motivation or opportunity to gain new knowledge. If the treatment group outperforms the control group on the posttest, there's no way to tell how much of that group's superior performance is due to the treatment it received and how much is due to other variables *not* considered when the matching process occurred.

Internet Assignment

Would you like to see a case where a group's mean changes substantially between two testing sessions (such as a pretest and a posttest) solely because of regression to the mean? Would you like to see whether the displayed amount of regression affects additional data sets that you can quickly generate using an Internet-based interactive Java applet? If so, do this Internet assignment.

If you choose to do this exercise, first go to this book's companion Web site (http://www.psypress.com/statistical-misconceptions). Once there, open the folder for Chapter 6 and click on the link called "Matched Samples." Then, follow the detailed instructions (prepared by this book's author) on how to use the Java applet. In the process of doing this assignment, you will come to realize that a study's comparison groups may be quite unequal even though they are "equated" at the beginning of the investigation.

---

* To be more specific, the complement of the correlation coefficient, when turned into a percentage, indicates how much regression will take place. For example, a study's control group mean will regress 90% of the way toward the larger group's posttest mean if the correlation is .10; in contrast, a correlation of .80 would cause the control group's mean to regress only 20%.

☐ 6.5 Finite Versus Infinite Populations

The Misconception

In an applied study involving inferential statistics, the population must have a specific and known (i.e., finite) size.

Evidence That This Misconception Exists*

The following statement comes from an online document entitled "Misconceived Relationships Among Sample, Sampling Distribution, and Population." (Note the word *misperception* in the second sentence.)

> *Problems arise when one regards the known and accessible population as the target population to which the inference is ultimately made.... Conceptually speaking, the misperception of population as finite ... has negative consequences, as it leads researchers to seek out an objective, true and final answer that does not exist.*

Why This Misconception Is Dangerous

This misconception is dangerous for two reasons. First, if the sample size, n, is smaller than the size of the larger group (N) from which the sample is drawn, the researcher may incorporate (incorrectly) the "finite population correction," $\sqrt{(N-n)/(N-1)}$ into the statistical formulas used to create confidence intervals or to test null hypotheses. Second, if data are collected from all N members of the larger group, the researcher may decide (incorrectly) that no inferential statistics are needed, because any statistical summary of the data—such as a mean or a percent—is thought (wrongly) to be a parameter rather than a statistic.

---

*Appendix B contains the reference for the quoted material presented in this section.

Undoing the Misconception

In most applied studies, the researcher's true population of interest extends, temporally, from the present into the future. The study's participants who are in the sample and provide data come from the "present" portion of this two-part population. However, the typical researcher has an equal interest in the "future" segment of the population.

Suppose a medical researcher conducts a study to see if a particular new pill can help hypertensive adults lower their dangerously high levels of blood pressure. Also suppose that 300 hypertensive adults living in the researcher's city participate in a well-controlled clinical trial to evaluate the new pill. Finally, suppose that the study yields data that strongly suggest that the pill works.

In the imaginary study, what is the researcher's intended population? In response to this question, you might inquire as to where the study's participants came from. If told that the 300 patients were randomly selected from a pool of 10,000 hypertensive adults residing in the researcher's city, would you think that the target population is comprised of those 10,000 hypertensive adults? If so, you would be wrong. That's because the researcher conducting this study would like to generalize the findings not just to the other 9,700 hypertensive adults who were living in the city when the study was conducted, but also to others who, in the future, will have high blood pressure. These "others" would include (1) adults who don't now have high blood pressure, but will; (2) children who grow up to be hypertensive adults; and (3) people who move into the city with high blood pressure already existing or soon to develop. Most likely, the researcher's intended target population would also include these kinds of people in other cities.

If you were told that the study's 300 hypertensive adults included each and every adult in the city who had high blood pressure, would you think that the researcher's intended population was that group of 300 patients? If so, that too would be an incorrect thought. Just because the researcher (in this second scenario) collected data from everyone who qualified to be in the study, this does not force the researcher into conceptualizing his or her intended target population as made up of just those research participants. Just as in the first scenario we considered (where the research participants were sampled from a larger group), the researcher here could consider the intended target population to be made up of people who, in the future and/or in other cities, are like those who served as research participants.

When a study's target population is construed to extend into the future or into geographical areas not represented by those who provide the study's data, that kind of population is hypothetical rather than real. Statistical inferences directed toward such hypothetical populations, naturally, are based on a critical assumption. We must assume that the hypothetical population is like (1) the tangible population from which the study's sample was drawn or (2) the group from which data were gathered, in the situation where no sampling was conducted. Stated differently, we assume that the study's data providers constitute a random sample that has been drawn from the hypothetical target population.

How large is the hypothetical target population? It is always viewed as being infinitely large, regardless of the size of the group that supplies the study's data. This is why the finite population correction is infrequently used when applied researchers use inferential statistics to build confidence intervals or test null hypotheses. For one thing, if we have an infinitely large population, then logic would say that we do not need a finite population correction. For another, the finite population correction would have no impact on anything even if we used it, for the ratio of $N - n$ to $N - 1$ is equal to 1 when N is infinitely large.

Some high-level authoritative justification for considering populations to be infinitely large comes from Sir Ronald A. Fisher, considered by many to be the "father of statistics." Fisher stated that the goal of inferential statistics

> ... is accomplished by constructing a hypothetical infinite population, of which the actual data are regarded as constituting a random sample.*

Fisher went on to say (p. 312) that probability—a concept of no small importance in inferential statistics—has reference to "an infinite hypothetical population," and that the normal distribution and other "curves" are based on the concept of "a hypothetical infinite population, distributed according to a mathematical law, represented by the curve."

It should be noted that the population involved in certain studies has a finite size. Such is the case when political polls are conducted. When scientific polls are taken, data are gathered from only a small portion of the population of eligible voters. The goal of the poll is to get a sense for how those in the full population would vote if the election were to be held today. There is no effort made to generalize beyond the defined population (from which the sample was drawn) or to any future point in time. Accordingly, the finite population correction is used in polling studies, and it influences decisions made regarding the needed sample size as well as the "margin of error" that's reported along with the poll's findings.

---

* Fisher, R. A. (1922). On the mathematical foundation of theoretical statistics. *Philosophical Transactions of the Royal Society of London, Series A. 222A*, (p. 311).

Internet Assignment

Would you like to see how large a sample needs to be if it is going to be drawn from a population that's small, medium sized, or enormous? Would you like to see how large a sample needs to be if it is looked upon as having been drawn from an infinitely large population? Would you like to use an Internet-based interactive Java applet to help you see these things? If so, consider doing this Internet assignment.

If you choose to do this exercise, first go to this book's companion Web site (http://www.psypress.com/statistical-misconceptions). Once there, open the folder for Chapter 6 and click on the link called "Finite Versus Infinite Populations." Then, follow the detailed instructions (prepared by this book's author) on how to use the Java applet. In the process of doing this assignment, you may be surprised by the Java applet's ability to handle the situation where the population is infinitely large.

☐ Recommended Reading

Althauser, R. P., & Rubin, D. (1971). Measurement error and regression to the mean in matched samples. *Social Forces, 50*(2), 206–214.

Austin, H. W. (1983). Sample size: How much is enough? *Quality and Quantity, 17*, 239–245.

Campbell, D. T., & Kenny, D. A. (1999). *A primer on regression artifacts.* New York: Guilford Press.

Finzer, B., & Foletta, G. (2003). *Confronting some statistical inference misconceptions.* Paper presented at the 15th Annual International Conference on Technology in Collegiate Mathematics, Chicago.

Galloway, A. (1997). *Sampling.* Retrieved November 3, 2007, from http://www.tardis.ed.ac.uk/~kate/qmcweb/scont.htm.

Garson, G. D. (2006). Sampling. In *Statnotes: Topics in multivariate analysis.* Retrieved November 3, 2007, from http://www2.chass.ncsu.edu/garson/pa765/sampling.htm.

Imai, K., King, G., & Stuart, E. A. (2006, July 26). *The balance test fallacy in matching methods for causal inference.* Retrieved April 1, 2007, from http://polmeth.wustl.edu/retrieve.php?id=632.

Jolliffe, F. R. (1988). Two sampling misconceptions. *Teaching Statistics, 10*(1), 16–19.

Regression to the mean: Three key questions. (n.d.). Retrieved October 1, 2007, from http://www.uiowa.edu/~clrc/epidemiologic/tutorials/regression.swf.

Ryan, R. S. (2006). A hands-on exercise improves understanding of the standard error of the mean. *Teaching of Psychology, 33*(3), 180–183.

Smith, M. H. (2004). A sample/population size activity: Is it the sample size of the sample as a fraction of the population that matters? *Journal of Statistics Education, 12*(2). Retrieved November 3, 2007, from http://www.amstat.org/publications/jsc/v12n2/smith.html.

Estimation

Students can be left with many misconceptions after a standard introductory discussion [of confidence intervals]. One frequent misconception is that a 99% confidence interval is narrower than a 95% confidence interval. Students also tend to misinterpret the confidence interval by considering it to be a fixed quantity, not recognizing its dependence on the particular sample observed. Another common misconception is that the interval is a statement about the distribution of the data, rather than a set of possible "guesses" for the mean of the distribution generating the dataset.*

* West, R. W., & Ogden, R. T. (1998). Interactive demonstrations for statistics education on the World Wide Web. *Journal of Statistics Education, 6*(3). Retrieved January 3, 2008, from http://www.amstat.org/publications/jse/v6n3/west.html.

☐ 7.1 Interpreting a Confidence Interval

The Misconception

If a 95% confidence interval (CI) has been created to estimate the numerical value of a population parameter, the probability of the parameter falling somewhere between the endpoints of that interval is equal to .95.

Evidence of This Misconception*

The first of the following statements comes from an online document entitled "What Are Confidence Intervals?" The second statement comes from a statistics textbook.

1. *In contrast [to tests of null hypotheses], confidence intervals provide a range about the observed effect size. This range is constructed in such a way that we know how likely it is to capture the true—but unknown—effect size. Thus the formal definition of a confidence interval is: "a range of values for a variable of interest [in our case, the measure of treatment effect] constructed so that this range has a specified probability of including the true value of the variable. The specified probability is called the confidence level, and the end points of the confidence interval are called the confidence limits."*

2. *A confidence interval is a range of values constructed to have a specific probability (the confidence) of including the population parameter. For example, suppose a random sample from a population produced an $\overline{X} = 50$. The 95% confidence interval might range from 45 to 55. That is, the probability that the interval 45–55 includes μ is .95.*

Why This Misconception Is Dangerous

Statistics is like many other academic disciplines in that it demands precision in the actions one takes and the interpretations one draws. In statistics, as in other fields, two things can look alike yet be different in

---

* Appendix B contains references for all quoted material presented in this section.

how they were created and what they mean. For example, a single set of data can have a mean equal to 14.7 as well as a standard deviation that's equal to 14.7. A knowledgeable person distinguishes between these two (identical) numbers by realizing that they were generated by different formulas and carry entirely different meanings.

It is tempting to think that the probability is .95 that the population parameter lies somewhere within a 95% CI, and many people mistakenly draw this conclusion. Those who do this, however, fail to distinguish between two quite different statistical concepts: a confidence interval, on the one hand, and a credible interval, on the other. Despite the fact that these two kinds of intervals resemble each other in both form and purpose, they are not the same in terms of the formulas used to create them or the ways in which they should be interpreted.

The danger associated with this misconception is that the person who interprets confidence intervals as if they were credible intervals will develop the habit of interpreting statistical results quickly in ways that seem to make intuitive sense (rather than interpreting such results in careful, precise ways that lead to valid thoughts and statements).

Undoing the Misconception

A 95% CI that has been built around a sample mean is a probability statement. It indicates that something has a probability of .95. But what is that something? We should not answer this question by thinking or saying that there's a .95 probability of the population mean falling somewhere between the CI's endpoints. Clearly, μ either does or does not fall in the interval that's been created. Thus, the probability of μ being inside the CI is either 1.0 or 0.0, depending on whether the CI does or does not capture μ.

To properly interpret the probability that's embedded in any CI, we must first think about two things: the sample actually drawn from the population of interest and the CI that's been created based on that sample's data. Next, we need to imagine that many random samples of that same size are drawn from that same population. We must also imagine that a 95% CI is built around each sample's mean. Next, we must imagine that somehow we could check each CI, once it was built, to see if it does or does not capture (i.e., overlap) the μ. Most of the CIs would capture μ, but some would not. If we imagine checking an infinite number of such samples and their CIs, we would find that exactly 95% of those CIs would capture μ, while 5% would not. Therefore, we can refocus our attention on the one sample that was actually drawn, consider that sample's CI that was actually created, and then say that this CI has a .95 probability of being one of the infinite number of CIs (that exist only in our imagination) that captures μ.

The probability that's properly connected to any confidence interval is said to be a classical (or frequentist) probability. This kind of probability applies to *samples* that we imagine are drawn out of a population. Repeatedly take samples of size n from a fixed and stable population, build a 95% confidence interval around each $\bar{X}$, and then we can say that 95% of those *samples* have CIs that capture μ.

A second kind of probability exists that uses a reverse kind of logic. Instead of determining the probability of getting various kinds of samples drawn from a population, this second kind of probability focuses on the likelihood that various kinds of *populations* might exist in light of the data associated with a real sample that has been drawn. This kind of probability is called a Bayesian probability.

When an interval around a sample statistic is created using Bayesian statistics, the interval is called a credible interval rather than a confidence interval. On the surface, the intervals may appear to be similar; however, they are different in how they are created and how they should be interpreted. If a 95% credible interval is built around a sample's $\bar{X}$, then we legitimately can think that the probability is .95 that μ lies somewhere between the interval's endpoints.

Because a credible interval provides a direct answer to the question most researchers would like answered, you may be wondering why confidence intervals are so popular compared to credible intervals. The answer to this question is connected to the level of difficulty associated with generating the two kinds of intervals. Confidence intervals are relatively easy to create. Credible intervals, on the other hand, are hard to develop, even though computers are readily available to crunch the numbers. This is due to the fact that the development of credible intervals requires not just sample data but prior probability statements as well. These "priors" indicate, usually in a subjective sense, how likely it is for μ to assume different values. In many applied studies, the researcher is unable to specify such priors and, as a consequence, is unable to create a credible interval.

Internet Assignment

Would you like to see 100 confidence intervals created for 100 different samples that are drawn from the same population? Would you like to have the CIs displayed graphically, with the ones that fail to overlap the population mean clearly distinguished from those that capture μ? Within the context of this simulation, would you like to be able to change the level of confidence and the values of n, μ, and σ? You can see and do these things by playing with a particular Internet-based interactive Java applet.

If you choose to do this exercise, first go to this book's companion Web site (http://www.psypress.com/statistical-misconceptions). Once there, open the folder for Chapter 7 and click on the link called "Interpreting Confidence Intervals." Then, follow the detailed instructions (prepared by this book's author) on how to use the Java applet. By doing this assignment, you will come to realize why one must be careful when interpreting a confidence interval. In addition, you will gain insight into the various factors that influence the width of a CI.

☐ 7.2 Overlapping Confidence Intervals

The Misconception

If the 95% confidence interval (CI) that's constructed for one sample partially overlaps the 95% CI that's constructed for a second sample, the two samples are not significantly different from each other at $\alpha = .05$.

Evidence That This Misconception Exists*

The first two of the following statements come from a peer-reviewed journal in medicine and a forestry document, respectively. The third statement comes from a report issued by a district's health department in New Zealand. (In these passages, note the phrases *frequently encountered misconception* and *common misconception*.)

1. *Many researchers falsely believe that for two independent group means to be statistically significantly different, the 95% confidence intervals around those means must not overlap.*

2. *We suggest that confidence intervals describing the attribute of interest be plotted.... Note however that there is a common misconception that overlapping confidence intervals indicate a statistically non-significant difference between two populations.*

3. *A common misconception is that overlapping CIs imply that there is "no difference" between two means, which is not necessarily true.*

Why This Misconception Is Dangerous

Many studies involve two groups. In experiments, for example, the people or animals in one group might be given some form of treatment, while members of a different but equivalent group are given a placebo (or nothing). Many nonexperimental studies also involve two groups, as when data come from groups distinguished from each other on the

* Appendix B contains references for all quoted material presented in this section.

basis of a demographic characteristic (e.g., gender) or a variable reflecting people's behavior or preference (e.g., smoker versus nonsmoker).

Realizing that the groups in such studies are samples, researchers often construct a confidence interval (CI) around the sample statistic of interest (e.g., a mean or a proportion). Once the two CIs have been created, it is tempting to compare them to see if the two groups are significantly different with respect to the measured variable. The decision rule that's used to make this decision seems, on the surface, to be simple: If the CIs don't overlap, the groups *are* significantly different; however, if the two CIs overlap, the groups *are not* significantly different.

Comparing CIs like this is dangerous because it can lead to the wrong inference about the two groups. To be more specific, it is possible for two groups that truly are significantly different from each other to be declared not significantly different when the two CIs are compared.

Undoing the Misconception

Comparing two separate but overlapping CIs is not proper because each of these CIs is created using data from a single sample, with the data from the other sample totally disregarded. Yet, the comparison of interest involves both samples. If data from the two samples are examined simultaneously, an inference based on a single CI created for the difference between the samples' means has more precision than does an inference based on separate CIs created for the two samples. This added precision makes it possible, in certain circumstances, for the single CI based on data from both samples to detect a significant difference that is overlooked when separate CIs are compared.

The added precision that's associated with a CI created for the difference between two means is brought about, for the most part, by an interesting little number: $\sqrt{2}$. This number's involvement can be seen most easily if we assume that the two samples are the same size and have come from populations with equal standard deviations. Under those conditions, let's contrast two approaches in terms of what it would take for the two sample means to show up as significantly different from each other.

If separate CIs are placed around the two sample means, a significant difference between the means would be declared if there is no overlap between the two CIs. For this to occur, the difference between the sample means would need to exceed the width of either of the CIs. For example, if each CI has a width equal to 20, there would be no overlap between the two CIs only if the difference between the two means equals or exceeds 20.

If a single CI is placed around the *difference* between the two sample means, a significant difference between the means will be declared if this single CI does not overlap zero. For this to happen, the CI's half-width needs to be smaller than the difference between the two means. As it turns out, this CI's half-width is smaller than the full width of the CIs created separately for the two samples. In fact, the half-width of the single CI that's built for the mean difference turns out to be about 1.414 times as large as the full length of the separate CIs constructed for each sample.

The number $\sqrt{2}$ comes from a comparison of the estimated standard error used in the two approaches just considered. If the data from a single sample are used to create a CI around that sample's mean, the estimated standard error is equal to $s/\sqrt{n}$, where s is the sample estimate of the population standard deviation. If we have two samples and place a confidence interval around the difference between the two sample means, the estimated standard error of the difference is equal to $\sqrt{2s^2/n}$, assuming that the samples are equally large and come from populations with a common variance. This can be rewritten as $\sqrt{2} \times (s/\sqrt{n})$. Note that this standard error is *smaller than* twice the size of $s/\sqrt{n}$.

Internet Assignment

Would you like to see a graphical display of two 95% confidence intervals that overlap, with these CIs tied to the data of two different samples? Moreover, would you like these CIs to represent the situation where a statistically significant difference exists between the two sample means? Finally, would you like the graph of the CIs to come from an Internet-based Java applet that allows you to control the mean and n of each sample? If so, do this Internet assignment.

If you choose to do this exercise, first go to this book's companion Web site (http://www.psypress.com/statistical-misconceptions). Once there, open the folder for Chapter 7 and click on the link called "Overlapping Confidence Intervals." Then, follow the detailed instructions (prepared by this book's author) on how to use the Java applet. By doing this assignment, you will deepen your understanding of why it is wrong to conclude that two means must be significantly different from each other if the CI built around one of those means overlaps the CI built around the other mean.

☐ 7.3 The Mean ± the Standard Error

The Misconception

If $\bar{X}$ and SE represent the sample mean and the estimated standard error of the mean, respectively, data presented in the form $\bar{X} \pm SE$ is simply a 68% confidence interval. If you double SE and compute $\bar{X} \pm 2SE$, you'll have a 95% CI.

Evidence That This Misconception Exists*

The following statement comes from a professional journal in the biomedical and life sciences. (Note that each of the means referred to in this passage came from a sample of two observations.)

> *Mean GUS activity values are shown [in one of the research report's figures], ±2 standard errors of the mean (the 95% confidence interval). It should be noted that if the means were plotted ±1 standard error bar, the endpoints of these 1 standard error bars would correspond exactly to the two data values used to obtain each of the respective mean values shown.*

Why This Misconception Is Dangerous

Written summaries of research investigations often include a numerical value for the sample mean. As a point estimate of μ, $\bar{X}$ is likely to be "off the mark" to some degree because sample statistics rarely match perfectly the population parameters they estimate. Knowing this, researchers typically build intervals around their sample means. Such intervals sometimes appear in the text of the report or its tables, and sometimes they take the form of error bars in histograms, bar graphs, and other kinds of charts. Whatever their form, these intervals convey useful information regarding the precision that X has in estimating the mean of the population. Narrow intervals imply high precision; wide intervals don't.

When an interval around a sample mean is presented, it will usually be a standard error interval or a 95% confidence interval (CI). Although it is tempting to think that $\bar{X} \pm SE$ can be interpreted as a 68% CI, this

---

* Appendix B contains the reference for the quoted material presented in this section.

interpretation will overestimate the precision of the mean. In other words, what appears to be a 68% CI actually will be an interval for which there is *lower* confidence. Of course, this same overestimation of precision occurs if an interval is formed by doubling the value of *SE* and then adding this amount to and subtracting it from $\bar{X}$. Doing this leads to an interval for which the actual confidence level is lower than 95%.

Undoing the Misconception

A CI around $\bar{X}$ is formed via the formula $\bar{X} \pm (_{1-\alpha}t_{\upsilon})$ *SE*, where $_{1-\alpha}t_{\upsilon}$ represents the value from the *t* distribution with $1 - \alpha$ confidence and $df = n - 1$. In this formula, *SE* is computed as $s/\sqrt{n}$, where *s* is the sample-based estimate of the population standard deviation.

Suppose we have these scores from a small sample: 11, 7, 13, 10, and 9.* Based on these data:

$$95\% \text{ CI} = 10 \pm 2.78$$

$$\bar{X} \pm SE = 10 \pm 1.00$$

Clearly, these two intervals are not the same. One extends from 7.22 to 12.78, whereas the other extends from 9.00 to 11.00. Such intervals will never turn out equal to each other, except in the unrealistic situation where there is no variability whatsoever in the sample data (i.e., where $s = 0$).

Even if we double *SE* in the process of forming a standard error interval, the result will not be exactly the same as a 95% CI. If *n* is small, the difference between these two kinds of intervals can be sizable. For example, when created on the basis of the sample data presented in the preceding paragraph, the interval created as $\bar{X} \pm 2SE$ is only about 72% as wide as a true 95% CI. For larger *n*'s, there is a smaller difference between the two intervals. If $n = 10$, an interval formed as $\bar{X} \pm 2SE$ is about 90% as wide as a 95% CI.

Table 7.3.1 shows the level of confidence associated with standard error intervals built around the means of samples of different sizes.[†]

---

* In some disciplines (e.g., exercise physiology applied to elite athletes), very small samples are used because the pool of potential participants is limited and because the cost and time required for data collection are enormous.

[†] If this table were to be extended for larger *n*'s, the level of confidence in the middle column would exceed 68% when $n > 94$. Similarly, the values in the right-hand column would exceed 95 when $n > 63$.

TABLE 7.3.1. Levels of Confidence for Two Kinds of Standard Error Intervals

n	$\bar{X} \pm SE$	$\bar{X} \pm 2SE$
2	50.00%	70.00%
3	58.00%	82.00%
4	60.00%	86.00%
5	63.00%	89.00%
10	66.00%	92.00%
15	66.60%	93.00%
20	67.02%	94.00%
30	67.44%	94.50%

Internet Assignment

Would you like to see some evidence that convincingly shows why intervals formed as $\bar{X} \pm 2SE$ should not be interpreted to be 95% confidence intervals? Would you like to be the one who creates this evidence via an Internet-based interactive Java applet? Would you like to see the evidence displayed graphically (as well as summarized by a single numerical value)? If you would like to see and do these things, do this Internet assignment.

If you choose to do this exercise, first go to this book's companion Web site (http://www.psypress.com/statistical-misconceptions). Once there, open the folder for Chapter 7 and click on the link called "The Mean ± the Standard Error." Then, follow the detailed instructions (prepared by this book's author) on how to use the Java applet. By doing this assignment, you will demonstrate that the notion of 95% confidence should not be attached to intervals created by computing $\bar{X} \pm 2SE$, at least in those situations where n is small.

☐ 7.4 Confidence Intervals and Replication

The Misconception

If a 95% CI is constructed around a sample mean, one legitimate way to interpret the CI is to think that the chances are 95 out of 100 that the mean of a new sample of the same size drawn randomly from the same population will fall somewhere between the endpoints of the first sample's CI.

Evidence That This Misconception Exists*

The first of the following statements comes from a journal article entitled "Confidence Intervals and Replication: Where Will the Next Mean Fall?" The second statement comes from a reference manual of scientific evidence. (Note the phrases *majority of researchers, erroneous belief,* and *misconception.*)

1. *Confidence intervals (CIs) give information about replication, but many researchers have misconceptions about this information.... Cumming et al. (2004) investigated researchers' beliefs about the chance that a replication mean would fall within an original CI. They found that a majority of researchers in the three disciplines [psychology, behavioral neuroscience, and medicine] hold the confidence-level misconception (CLM), which is the erroneous belief that about C% of future replication means will fall within an original C% CI, where C is the confidence level of a CI. A holder of the CLM believes that, on average, a 95% CI will include about 95% of future means.*

2. *Another misconception is that the confidence level gives the chance that repeated estimates fall into the confidence interval.*

Why This Misconception Is Dangerous

There are two dangers associated with this misconception. One concerns what we might call sloppy thinking and the possibility that a person might be publicly embarrassed if he or she says or writes things about

---

* Appendix B contains references for all quoted material presented in this section.

confidence intervals that are not true. The other danger is associated with actual replications of applied studies. Here, the misconception could cause one to have unjustifiably high confidence that an initial study's findings will be replicated.

Undoing the Misconception

When interpreting statistically based inferential statements, it's important to be clear about what two entities are at the opposite ends of the inferential bridge. Confusion regarding this basic (yet highly important) aspect of inferential statistics can lead to trouble.

When a CI is constructed around $\bar{X}$, this figurative inferential bridge connects the study's sample and its population. At the sample end of this bridge, data are analyzed to determine the sample's mean and standard deviation. Then, these pieces of statistical information are used inferentially to estimate two items at the bridge's other end, the population's mean and standard deviation. Those two estimates—along with knowledge of n, N (if the population has a finite size), and an appropriate value from the Gaussian or t distribution—become needed ingredients in the formula that's used to create the CI. Because of the way the CI is created and then interpreted, its double focus is sample and population.

If one sample is used to make statements about the likely result of a second sample, the inferential bridge is not connecting sample to population. Instead, the first sample (for which data are available) is being conceptually linked to a second, replicated sample that truly or hypothetically will come into existence after the first sample has been created. Both of these samples, of course, are considered to be randomly drawn (with n held constant) from the same population; therefore, the notion of a population most certainly is involved in this scenario. Nevertheless, the primary inferential concern is sample-to-sample in nature.

If a 95% CI is created around the mean of one sample, the probability is less than .95 that the mean of a second, yet-to-be-created sample will lie somewhere between the endpoints of the first sample's CI. This probability is not .95 because the CI that's created for the first sample is dealing, inferentially, with one pair of entities (sample and population), whereas the question about the replicated sample's mean involves a different pair of entities (samples 1 and 2). Although both inferential bridges are identical in terms of what's at one end (i.e., the sample that provides data to create the CI), what they connect at the other end is different.

An illustration may help to explain why a 95% CI overestimates the precision of replicated samples. In Figure 7.4.1, the heavy vertical line represents the mean, μ, of a population. The 10 horizontal lines represent the 95% CIs for 10 separate samples that we'll imagine have been or could be drawn from the population. (There could be many more horizontal lines in Figure 7.4.1, but only 10 or so are required to illustrate the point being made.)

Each of the CIs displayed in Figure 7.4.1 has the sample's mean positioned midway between the CI's endpoints. These sample means, along with the means for other samples we could imagine being drawn from the population, are distributed around the vertical line, with more of the sample means located near to rather than far away from the value of μ. If *n* is large, this sampling distribution of the means would be approximately normal in shape.*

In Figure 7.4.1, look at the fifth CI from the top. Half of this CI is located to the right of μ and the other is half located to the left of μ. This is the case because this sample's $\bar{X}$ turned out to be equal to μ. If the one sample you have in an applied study has this feature (i.e., if $\bar{X} = \mu$), then a 95% CI created from that sample *would* have a 95% chance of capturing the mean of a second, replicated sample. However, it's highly unlikely that the initial sample's $\bar{X}$ will equal μ. If that sample's CI is like any of

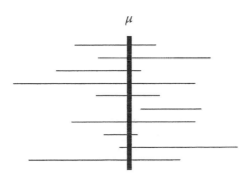

FIGURE 7.4.1 The 95% CI around $\bar{X}$ for 10 different samples.

---

* The central limit theorem says that the distribution of sample means approaches normality as *n* increases.

the other nine CIs displayed in Figure 7.4.1, then the curved shape of the implied sampling distribution of $\bar{X}$ causes the probability to be only .834 that a replicated sample's mean will lie between the endpoints of the initial sample's CI.*

Internet Assignment

Would you like to conduct a fast little simulation study to investigate whether an initial confidence interval ought to be interpreted as a replication interval? Would you like to do this using an Internet-based interactive Java applet that shows graphically how many of the means computed from future samples fall between the endpoints of the CI created on the basis of data from the initial sample? If so, spend a few minutes doing this Internet assignment.

If you choose to do this exercise, first go to this book's companion Web site (http://www.psypress.com/statistical-misconceptions). Once there, open the folder for Chapter 7 and click on the link called "Confidence Intervals and Replication." Then, follow the detailed instructions (prepared by this book's author) on how to use the Java applet. By doing this assignment, you will come to realize why it is wrong for confidence intervals to be used in a predictive fashion to forecast what will happen if one or more additional samples are drawn from the same population.

---

* This probability is derived in the appendix of Cumming, G., Williams, J., & Fidler, F. (2004). Replication and researchers' understanding of confidence intervals and standard error bars. *Understanding Statistics*, 3(4), 299–311.

☐ Recommended Reading

Barrowman, N. J. (2002). Missing the point (estimate)? Confidence intervals for the number needed to treat. *Canadian Medical Association Journal, 166*(3), 1676–1677.

Belia, S., Fidler, F., Williams, J., & Cumming, G. (2005). Researchers misunderstand confidence intervals and standard error bars. *Psychological Methods, 10*(4), 389–396.

Bower, K. M. (n.d.). *Some misconceptions about confidence intervals.* Retrieved March 23, 2007, from http://www.minitab.com/resources/articles/Some MisconceptionsAboutConfidenceIntervals.pdf.

Cumming, G., & Maillardet, R. (2006). Confidence intervals and replication: Where will the next mean fall? *Psychological Methods, 11*(3), 217–227.

Cumming, G., Williams, J., & Fidler, F. (2004). Replication and researchers' understanding of confidence intervals and standard error bars. *Understanding Statistics, 3*(4), 299–311.

Juslin, P., Winman, A., & Hansson, P. (2007). The naïve intuitive statistician: A naïve sampling model of intuitive confidence intervals. *Psychological Review, 114*(3), 678–703.

Larson, S. G. (2003). Misunderstanding margin of error. *Harvard International Journal of Press/Politics, 8*(1), 66–80.

Payton, M. E., Greenstone, M. H., & Schenker, N. (2003). Overlapping confidence intervals or standard error intervals: What do they mean in terms of statistical significance? *Journal of Insect Science, 3*(34), 1–6.

Schenker, N., & Gentleman, J. F. (2001). On judging the significance of differences by examining the overlap between confidence intervals. *The American Statistician, 55,* 182–186.

Teigen, K. H., & Jøgensen, M. (2005). When 90% confidence intervals are 50% certain: On the credibility of credible intervals. *Applied Cognitive Psychology, 19*(4), 455–475.

Hypothesis Testing

A common misconception among beginning researchers is the notion that if you reject a null hypothesis you have "proven" your research hypothesis. [*]

Unfortunately, many researchers have the misconception that alpha and beta are inversely related, and believe that if they set alpha at a low level, beta would automatically become high. [†]

---

[*] Ouyang, R. (n.d.). *Basic concepts of quantitative research: Inferential statistics*. Retrieved March 23, 2007, from http://ksumail.kennesaw.edu/~rouyang/ED-research/i-statis.htm.

[†] Asraf, R. M., & Brewer, J. K. (2004). Conducting tests of hypotheses: The need for an adequate sample size. *Australian Educational Researcher, 31*(1), 79–94.

☐ 8.1 Alpha and Type I Error Risk

The Misconception

Alpha, the level of significance, defines the probability of a Type I error. For example, if α is set equal to .05, there will then necessarily be a 5% chance that a true null hypothesis will be rejected.

Evidence That This Misconception Exists*

The first and second of these statements come from online documents called *Testing Hypotheses* and *Statistics Glossary,* respectively. The third statement comes from a college textbook dealing with business statistics. (Note the word *always* in the first and third passages.)

1. *The probability of type I error is always equal to the level of significance that is used as the standard for rejecting the null hypothesis; it is designated by α, and thus α also designates the level of significance.*

2. *This probability of a type I error can be precisely computed as P(type I error) = significance level = α.*

3. *The maximum probability of Type I error is designated by the Greek α (alpha). It is always equal to the levels of significance used in testing the null hypothesis.*

Why This Misconception Is Dangerous

In most scientific fields, researchers are taught to conduct their empirical studies in such a way that Type I errors have a low probability of occurrence.† They are also taught that the way to exert control over this kind of inferential error is to select a rigorous level of significance (α). In many fields of study, this means that the alpha level should be no higher than. 05.

---

* Appendix B contains references for all quoted material presented in this section.
† A Type I error is made if a true null hypothesis is rejected.

Clearly, it would be unfortunate (and perhaps dangerous to the evolving progress of scientific knowledge) if conclusions were drawn on the basis of studies in which Type I error risk is different from what researchers think and claim it is. If the actual probability of a Type I error is lower than α, a false null hypothesis has a greater than α chance of being retained. Worse yet, true null hypotheses will be rejected at too high a rate in studies wherein α understates Type I error risk.

Undoing the Misconception

Unfortunately, the probability of a Type I error may or may not be equal to the level of significance that's selected. If the true Type I error risk matches the selected α, then this aspect of the hypothesis testing procedure is operating as it should. On the other hand, if the selected alpha level either exaggerates or understates the actual likelihood of a Type I error, then such an α clearly is not doing its job.

In recognition of the fact that α can fail to specify Type I error risk, a special term has been coined to describe poor-performing alpha levels. Such an alpha level is referred to as a nominal level of significance. In this context, the word *nominal* means "in name only." The longer definition that fits here is "of, being, or relating to a designated or theoretical size that may vary from the actual."*

There are two main reasons why the selected level of significance can be misleading as to the chance of a Type I error. One of these concerns underlying assumptions. The other deals with the number of tests being conducted.

If one or more of the assumptions underlying a statistical test are violated, the actual probability of a Type I error can be substantially higher or lower than the nominal level of significance. For example, if a t-test comparing the means from two unequally sized samples is conducted with $\alpha = .05$, and if the assumption of equal population variances does not hold true, the actual probability of a Type I error can be greater than .35. That's seven times higher than the nominal level of significance! The Type I error rate can also be far smaller than .05.†

---

* This definition comes from the *Merriam-Webster Online Dictionary*. Retrieved March 25, 2007, from http://www.m-w.com/cgi-bin/dictionary?book=Dictionary&va= nominal.

† A computer simulation I conducted with $\mu_1 = \mu_2$, $\sigma_2^2 = 16\sigma_1^2$, $n_1 = 25$, and $n_2 = 5$ revealed that Type I errors occurred 35.4% of the time over the 100,000 replications of the simulation. When I did the simulation a second time, reversing the sizes of the two samples, the empirical Type I error rate was .00037.

A statistical test is said to be robust if it functions as it should, even if its underlying assumptions are violated. However, certain statistical tests are robust only in specific situations (e.g., when sample sizes are large and equal), while other statistical tests are never robust if their assumptions are violated.*

Even if a statistical test's underlying assumptions are valid, it still is possible for the level of significance to understate Type I error risk. This will happen if the test is applied more than once. Within the full *set* of tests being conducted, the probability of a Type I error occurring in one or more of the tests will exceed α, even if each test is conducted with a level of significance set equal to α.

The phrase "inflated Type I error rate" describes this situation. A coin-flipping analogy may help to illustrate why the chances of a Type I error get elevated over α in the situation where multiple tests are conducted. Let's consider flipping a fair coin, and let's further consider that it's bad to end up with the coin landing on its tails side. If we flip the coin just once, the probability of a bad result is .50. But what if we flip the coin twice? Now, the probability of getting tails (on the first flip, on the second flip, or on both flips) is .75. If the first coin is flipped 10 times, the probability of getting at least 1 tail increases to .999.

With the level of significance set at a low level in each of 10 tests, the probability of making one or more Type I errors is not as high as getting one or more tails in our coin-flipping example. However, the Type I error risk would be substantially higher than the nominal level of significance. If α is set equal to .05 in each of the tests, that risk is equal to about .40. With 20 tests, there would be almost a 65% chance of rejecting a true null hypothesis at least once. With 50 tests, the Type I error risk would be .92.†

Internet Assignment

Would you like to see some evidence that Type I error rate can be higher (and, in some situations, *much* higher) than the level of significance? Would you like to have this information come from an Internet-based

---

* No inferential test is robust to the assumption that data come from *random* samples, and a repeated measures ANOVA is not robust to violations of the sphericity assumption.

† With k independent tests being conducted, each using the same level of significance, the probability of having one or more Type I errors occur in the full set of tests is equal to $1 - (1 - \alpha)^k$.

interactive Java applet? If you have responded affirmatively to these two questions, take a few minutes to do this Internet assignment.

Your first task is to go to this book's companion Web site (http://www.psypress.com/statistical-misconceptions). Once there, open the folder for Chapter 8 and click on the link called "Alpha and Type I Error Risk." Then, follow the detailed instructions (prepared by this book's author) on how to use the Java applet. By doing this assignment, you will come to understand that a stated level of significance, under certain circumstances, can grossly misrepresent the actual probability of rejecting a true null hypothesis.

☐ 8.2 The Null Hypothesis

The Misconception

The null hypothesis is always a statement of "no difference."

Evidence That This Misconception Exists*

The first of the following statements comes from a college textbook in statistics. The second statement comes from a book designed to help students prepare for the GRE in psychology. The third statement comes from an online document on practical inference. (Note the word *always* in the first and third passages.)

1. *The null hypothesis ... is always a statement of no difference.*

2. *Null hypothesis means "no difference."*

3. *The null is always a statement of no difference; the alternate is that a difference exists.*

Why This Misconception Is Dangerous

There are two bad consequences of thinking that null hypotheses must be statements of "no difference." First, doing this disregards an important kind of flexibility that's built into certain statistical tests designed to compare two samples. Thinking that the H_o of such a test *must* articulate equality can lead to a situation where a "no difference" null hypothesis becomes the focus of a study when it would make far more sense to test a null hypothesis that specifies a particular nonzero difference. Second, when a statistical test involves a single sample, the "no difference" thought usually leads one into a logical quagmire in which the only escape is to think, incorrectly, that H_o should be defined as no difference between the sample statistic and the population parameter.

---

* Appendix B contains references for all quoted material presented in this section.

Undoing the Misconception

When comparing two sample means with a t-test, researchers usually test a null hypothesis that says H_o: $\mu_1 = \mu_2$. Likewise, when researchers statistically compare two sample proportions, the null hypothesis under investigation typically states that the two populations have the same proportion (i.e., H_o: $P_1 = P_2$). Each of these null hypotheses, of course, is a statement of no difference between the two populations. However, there is no law that says only "no difference" null hypotheses are legal when comparing two samples.

The first null hypothesis we considered (H_o: $\mu_1 = \mu_2$) comes into existence whenever a researcher sets D, the difference between the two population means, equal to 0 in the t-test's actual (and more flexible) null hypothesis: H_o: $\mu_1 - \mu_2 = D$. Other values of D can be used, however, and a t-test's null hypothesis can easily state that $\mu_1 - \mu_2$ is equal to 2, 10, −.8, or any other numerical value. That's also the case when two sample proportions are compared. In that situation, the null hypothesis can be set up to say that $P_1 - P_2$ is equal to 0 or to any other value that's selected for D in the expression, H_o: $P_1 - P_2 = D$.

Clearly, if H_o can be set up to specify a nonzero difference between the parameter values of two populations, it is wrong to think that a null hypothesis must be a statement of no difference. There is, however, a second reason for avoiding the "no difference" notion of null hypotheses. Let's now consider the case where a single sample has been drawn from a single population.

In a one-sample t-test focused on the mean, H_o deals with μ. With only one population mean being focused upon, there can be no notion of a difference—large, small, or nonexistent—embodied in the null hypothesis. In this situation, H_o: $\mu = X$, where X is any numerical value of the researcher's choosing. In one-sample tests focused on a correlation coefficient, a proportion, a variance, or any other statistical summary, there logically cannot be the notion of no difference (or any other kind of difference) because the null hypothesis specifies a numerical value of the single population involved in the study.

It should be noted that the evidence gathered from a study's sample(s) is used to *evaluate* the null hypothesis; however, the sample data never are employed to *define* H_o. The null hypothesis is always a statement about a study's population(s), and H_o never makes reference to data. Thus, it's wrong to think that the null hypothesis is a statement of no difference between the sample statistic(s) and the population parameter(s). Based on this same reasoning, it is not correct to think or say that a null hypothesis means that no significant difference will be found once the data are analyzed.

Internet Assignment

Would you like to see some proof that a null hypothesis can be something other than a statement of no difference? Would you like this proof to come from an Internet-based interactive Java applet? If so, take a few minutes to do this Internet assignment.

Your first task is to go to this book's companion Web site (http://www.psypress.com/statistical-misconceptions). Once there, open the folder for Chapter 8 and click on the link called "The Null Hypothesis." Then, follow the detailed instructions (prepared by this book's author) on how to use the Java applet. By doing this assignment, you will come to realize that it is easy to set up a null hypothesis that articulates a nonzero difference between two population means or between two proportions.

☐ 8.3 Disproving H_o

The Misconception

Although the null hypothesis cannot be proven true, it *can* be proven false. This is because science and hypothesis testing are based on the logic of falsification. If someone claims that all swans are white, confirmatory evidence (in the form of lots of white swans) cannot prove the assertion to be true. However, contradictory evidence (in the form of a single black swan) makes it clear that the claim is invalid.

Evidence That This Misconception Exists*

The first of the following statements comes from an online document entitled "Converting Research Questions into Statistical Hypotheses." The second statement comes from an article authored by a medical statistician at the University of Cambridge. The third statement comes from a university's online study-skills document. (Note the phrases *can disprove* and *to be disproved* that appear in the second and third passages.)

1. *Remember we can never prove the null hypothesis. All we can prove is that there is a relationship or effect (H_1) between two or more variables.*

2. *The point is that we can disprove statements, but we can not prove them. This is the principle of disconfirmation, and it forms the basis for scientific inquiry.... Now, knowing that we can't prove a hypothesis but can disprove it, we take the tact of attempting to disprove the null hypothesis. If we are successful then we have, in an admittedly backwards and somewhat convoluted manner, supported our real hypothesis, the alternative hypothesis. While you can't prove that a statement or hypothesis is true, you can disprove that its opposite is true, thereby obtaining the desired result, provided that there are no possibilities other than your hypothesis and its opposite. It is really a rather ingenious system.*

3. *A null hypothesis is a working hypothesis that is to be disproved by a statistical test in favour of the alternative hypothesis.*

---

* Appendix B contains references for all quoted material presented in this section.

Why This Misconception Is Dangerous

The danger in thinking that null hypotheses are proven wrong if rejected is twofold. Both of these dangers are related to the word *prove*. Although this word has different meanings in different contexts (e.g., mathematics, printing, and cooking), most dictionaries indicate that we prove something when we establish its genuineness or authenticity. Proof, therefore, leaves no room for error. If you prove something, you and others can be 100% confident that your claim is true.

Those who think that null hypotheses can be proven false have mixed together, inappropriately, the logic of falsification and the statistical procedure of hypothesis testing. As will be indicated in the next section, nothing is truly falsified when a null hypothesis is rejected. The observation of one black swan is sufficient to falsify the claim that all swans are white. That single black swan proves that the claim is wrong. It is dangerous to accept or promote the belief that a rejected H_o has been proven wrong because sample data never constitute a black swan.

There is a second danger associated with the belief that null hypotheses can be proven wrong. This concerns the important scientific practice of replication. If a study's null hypothesis were to be rejected, and if this rejection constituted proof that H_o is wrong, no replication would be necessary. Why bother to replicate a statistically significant finding if the tested null hypothesis has been *proven* to be wrong?

Undoing the Misconception

If you test a null hypothesis, reject it, and then think that you have *proven* H_o to be false, you have deceived yourself. To think that a "$p < \alpha$" result disproves the null hypothesis is to forget completely that a Type I error can occur whenever the hypothesis testing procedure yields information that causes H_o to be rejected.

The only way a particular H_o can be proven false (or true) is to know the precise numerical value of the population parameter(s) specified in the null hypothesis. However, sample data do not provide that kind of information. Instead, summaries of sample data (e.g., $\bar{X}$) are nothing more than estimates of population parameters (e.g., μ), and the two are likely to be different due to sampling error. Therefore, to think that sample-based information can prove H_o wrong is to disregard the inferential guesswork that's involved in hypothesis testing.

If you flip a fair (i.e., unbiased) coin 10 times, the chances are about 2 in 3 that you'll end up with somewhere between 4 and 6 heads. However, it's clear that you might end up with a result that's more lopsided than this. In fact, there's about a 2% chance that your 10 flips will produce a 9-to-1 or 10-to-0 split between heads and tails. If you actually got one of these more extreme splits (for which $p < .05$), would it prove that the fair coin that you've been flipping was not fair? Of course not!*

Researchers are encouraged to replicate their studies, and this concern for replication does not vanish simply because a researcher's initial study leads to a rejection of the null hypothesis. The objective of replication is to see if the conclusions reached in the first investigation show up again in the second, replicated study. Clearly, the call for replication is based on the awareness that conclusions drawn from the first study might be erroneous. If the initial study had the ability to prove things, no replication would be needed.

Internet Assignment

Would you like to see some proof that H_o is not proven wrong if it is rejected? Would you like this proof to be both easy to understand and totally convincing? Would you like to generate the convincing evidence by means of an Internet-based interactive Java applet? If you would like to see and do these things, do this Internet assignment.

To begin this assignment, go to this book's companion Web site (http://www.psypress.com/statistical-misconceptions). Once there, open the folder for Chapter 8 and click on the link called "Disproving H_o." Then, follow the detailed instructions (prepared by this book's author) on how to use the Java applet. By doing this simple assignment that involves a computer-based coin-flipping activity, you will come to realize that sample data, by themselves, never can prove a null hypothesis to be false.

---

* The binomial distribution was used to determine the "chances" and p referred to in this paragraph.

☐ 8.4 The Meaning of *p*

The Misconception

In testing a null hypothesis, the *p*-value based on the sample data indicates the probability that H_o is true.

Evidence That This Misconception Exists*

The first of the following statements comes from a textbook in nursing. The second statement comes from a peer-reviewed article in a medical journal. The third statement comes from an online document that contained a section entitled "Some Common Misconceptions Students Should NOT Have."

1. *One common misconception is to equate the P value with the probability that the null hypothesis is true.*

2. *A common misconception is to interpret the p-value, in this example, p < .0001, as "the probability the null hypothesis is true is less than .0001."*

3. *A p-value is the probability that the null hypothesis is true.*

Why This Misconception Is Dangerous

One important area of statistics is probability, and one important kind of probability is a *conditional* probability. This is the kind of probability that says, for example, "Given that you've pulled a face card from a well-shuffled deck of cards, what's the probability that your card is a King?" In our everyday lives, we frequently—though informally—compute conditional probabilities in our minds. For instance, if we must decide whether to take an umbrella with us when we leave home, we typically ask ourselves the question, "Given the weather forecast for today, what's the likelihood that it will rain?"

---

* Appendix B contains references for all quoted material presented in this section.

In making everyday decisions, in dealing with questions concerning a deck of cards, or in using data to evaluate a null hypothesis, it's important to realize that the probability of "X given Y" is often different from the probability of "Y given X." It can matter greatly whether it is X or Y that's assumed to be true. (The probability of having a King given that you've drawn a face card is .33; however, the probability of having a face card given that you've drawn a King is much higher!) Because the p-value plays such an important role whenever a null hypothesis is evaluated, it's important for you to understand that p is a conditional probability and to be aware of what's "given."

Undoing the Misconception

The data-based p that computers spit out whenever a null hypothesis is tested provides an answer to this specific question:

> If the null hypothesis concerning the study's population(s) were true, what is the probability of getting sample data like those actually observed or other sets of sample data that are even more at odds with H_o.

In this explanation of what p means, note the order of the two main thoughts. First, we assume H_o to be true. Next, we compute (perhaps with the help of a friendly computer) the p-value. Thus, we have a conditional probability: Given a true H_o, what's the probability of the sample?*

Conditional probability is not "bidirectional" like a bivariate correlation. If we collect data on variables X and Y and then compute Pearson's r, the result can be referred to as the correlation between X and Y, or as the correlation between Y and X. The order of X and Y is immaterial. That's not the case with conditional probabilities because it's often the case that the probability of Y given X is different from the probability of X given Y. Sometimes, it's possible to determine the probability of X given Y, but fully impossible to do the reverse.

The best way to show that conditional probability is not bidirectional is with a picture called a Venn diagram.† There are many kinds of Venn diagrams, and they can be drawn with different shapes and with varying numbers of components. The one we'll consider here has just

---

* To be technically correct, this sentence should contain, at the end, these additional words: "or other possible samples that would conflict with H_o even more than does the sample that was actually observed."
† John Venn, a British mathematician and philosopher, invented this kind of picture in 1881.

two parts, a rectangle that represents X and a different rectangle that represents Y. As illustrated in Figure 8.4.1, the two rectangles in such a Venn diagram usually overlap and can be of different sizes.

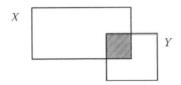

FIGURE 8.4.1 Venn diagram with two full rectangles.

In this kind of Venn diagram, the notion of conditional probability is represented as the ratio of two areas. The numerator is the area defined by the place where the two rectangles overlap (i.e., the shaded area). The denominator is the total area of one or the other of the two rectangles. Note that it makes a big difference which rectangle determines the denominator. The probability of being in X given that you're already in Y looks to be about one fourth, or .25. In contrast, the probability of being in Y given that you're already in X seems to be about one seventh, or approximately .14.

Now consider Figure 8.4.2. Here, only a portion of rectangle Y is visible. Because we can see only the upper-left-hand corner of the Y, we don't know how large this rectangle is.

FIGURE 8.4.2 Venn diagram with one full and one partial rectangle.

In Figure 8.4.2, it's possible to determine the probability of being in Y given that you're already in X. (That probability is about .14, just as it was in Figure 8.4.1.) For that particular kind of conditional probability, the unknown size of the Y rectangle is not problematic. However, note that there is no way to figure out the probability of being in X given that you're already in Y. If the Y rectangle is gigantic, this particular conditional probability would be tiny. On the other hand, if the Y area is only slightly larger than the darkened overlap area, this probability would be huge.

The p-value that's produced whenever data are analyzed to test a null hypothesis is analogous to the overlap area of Figure 8.4.2, with X representing the null hypothesis and Y representing the data. If we assume H_o to be true, we can determine the probability of getting sample data that deviate as much as, or more than, the actual data gathered in the study. In other words, we *can* compute $P(Y|X)$, the probability of the data given the null hypothesis. However, it's impossible to compute the reverse, $P(X|Y)$, the probability that H_o is true given the data.

Internet Assignment

Would you like to see a convincing "visual" explanation as to why p does not indicate the probability that the null hypothesis is true? Would you like to gain insights into this explanation by using an Internet-based interactive Java applet? If you would like to see and do these things, do this Internet assignment.

To do this assignment, first go to this book's companion Web site (http://www.psypress.com/statistical-misconceptions). Once there, open the folder for Chapter 8 and click on the link called "The Meaning of p." Then, follow the detailed instructions (prepared by this book's author) on how to use the Java applet. By gaining a deeper understanding of conditional probability, you will realize why a data-based p does not indicate the probable truth of the null hypothesis.

☐ 8.5 Directionality and Tails

The Misconception

A nondirectional alternative hypothesis always leads to a two-tailed test, whereas a directional H_a always brings about a one-tailed test.*

Evidence That This Misconception Exists[†]

The first of the following statements comes from a recently published dictionary of research for students and researchers in nursing. The second statement comes from a technical report dealing with the human–computer interaction within factory settings. The third statement comes from a book on quantitative research methods. (In these passages, note how the number of tails is said to be determined by the nature of the alternative hypothesis.)

1. *If the alternative hypothesis is "directional" or "one-sided" (e.g., there is an inverse relationship between X and Y), a "one-tailed test" is called for. If the alternative hypothesis is nondirectional (e.g., there is a relationship between X and Y), a "two-tailed test" is called for. Those names derive from the area of the sampling distribution in which the "rejection region" (alpha region) for the test is located.*

2. *If the alternative hypothesis is non-directional, a two-tailed test is employed. However, if the hypothesis is directional, a one tailed test is used.*

3. *It is also important to point out at this point that if the alternative hypothesis has the form "not equal to," then the test is said to be a two-tailed test and if the alternative hypothesis is an inequality (< or >), the test is one-tailed.*

Why This Misconception Is Dangerous

Any applied researcher ought to have a conceptual understanding of how a p-value has been computed when this data-based index is used to tag

---

* Some authors and teachers prefer to represent the alternative hypothesis as H_1 rather than H_a.
[†] Appendix B contains references for all quoted material presented in this section.

results as being (or not being) statistically significant. It is not necessary that the researcher be able to *compute* the *p*-value, because that can be done easily by computers. However, he or she should be able to *visualize* the sampling distribution of the test statistic and then be able to explain, with reference to that visualized picture, why it is that a given study's *p* turned out as it did.

If a person thinks that a nondirectional H_a always leads to a split critical region (whereas only directional H_a's are "one-sided"), he or she will not be able to interpret properly the data-based *p*-value associated with several popular statistical tests. For example, the *p*-value from an ANOVA *F*-test will be problematic because this test (as usually applied) is one-tailed even though the null hypothesis specifies no difference among the population means.

Undoing the Misconception

With certain statistical tests, the nature of the alternative hypothesis determines whether the test is one-tailed or two-tailed in nature. The way such tests work is straightforward. If H_a is set up to be nondirectional, the critical region will be located in both tails of the test statistic's distribution. On the other hand, if H_a is directional, the entirety of the critical region is positioned in a single tail.

Consider, for example, Figure 8.5.1. Here we see the null distribution for a binomial test in which $N = 10$, $P = .50$, and $\alpha = .05$. The critical region here is positioned in both tails, as indicated by the darkened bars over the baseline values of 0 and 1 (on the left) and 9 and 10 (on the right). This binomial test is two-tailed because H_a is nondirectional in nature: H_a: $P \neq .50$.

With the binomial test, the *t*-test, tests that utilize the normal distribution for evaluating null hypotheses, and certain other test procedures, a directional alternative hypothesis leads to a one-tailed test. This situation is illustrated in Figure 8.5.2, where we see the entirety of the 5% critical region located in the right tail of a normal distribution. This one-tailed distribution would be used, for example, in a *z*-test employed to evaluate H_o: $\mu = 100$ and H_a: $\mu > 100$.

Certain tests operate differently than those considered in the preceding paragraphs and pictures. In other words, certain test procedures have a critical region that's located entirely in one tail of the null distribution even though the test's alternative hypothesis is nondirectional. Two such tests are the one-way ANOVA *F*-test and the chi-square test of proportions.

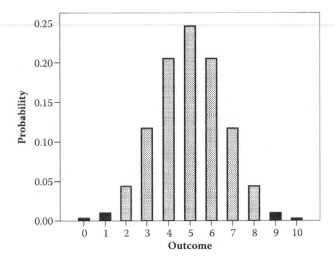

FIGURE 8.5.1 The critical region in a binomial test with a nondirectional H_a.

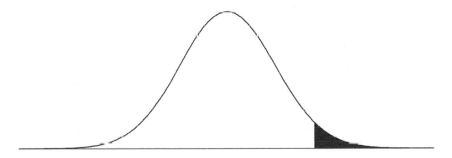

FIGURE 8.5.2 The normal distribution's critical region if H_a is directional.

Suppose a one-way analysis of variance is used to compare two sample means, with the alternative hypothesis being nondirectional (i.e., $H_a: \mu_1 \neq \mu_2$). This ANOVA's calculated value is referred to an F distribution, in which the full critical region is positioned in the distribution's upper tail.* The null distribution is set up to be one-tailed (even though H_a is nondirectional) because the calculated F (1) cannot assume negative values, (2) is expected to be greater than 1 to the extent that the sample means differ, and (3) pays no attention to which mean is larger.

---

* The fact that F is one-tailed when testing $H_o: \mu_1 = \mu_2$ against $H_a: \mu_1 \neq \mu_2$ ought to seem reasonable to anyone who knows that $t^2 = F$. If all values in a t distribution are squared, those t-values that are smaller than 0 have their sign changed from negative to positive. In a very real sense, therefore, the left tail of a two-tailed t-test gets merged together with the right tail when t is converted to F.

A chi-square test is often used to compare two samples in terms of frequency-based proportions. Suppose, for example, that a 2 × 2 chi-square test is used to compare men and women in terms of the proportion, P, of people in each group who have received at least one speeding ticket over the past five years. Suppose further that the null hypothesis asserts that there is no difference between the two population proportions, while the alternative hypothesis is set up to be nondirectional (i.e., $H_a: P_{men} \neq P_{women}$). Even with this H_a, this test's critical region in the χ^2 distribution is located in just the upper tail.*

It should be noted that both F and χ^2 distributions are not inherently one-tailed. Each is simply a theoretical distribution that's based on a mathematical formula. These distributions are tail-less in their raw form. Tails are created when a researcher comes along and stipulates that a certain proportion of the distribution will function as the critical region (i.e., region of rejection). Sometimes (but not often), researchers use these distributions in a two-tailed fashion. For example, the variance of a single sample (s^2) can be compared against a predetermined "standard" (σ_o^2) via a χ^2 test. In conducting this test, a nondirectional alternative hypothesis would demand that the critical region be located in both the upper and lower tails of the F distribution. Thus, an F-test or a chi-square test *can* be two-tailed. That's not the case, however, when two sample means are compared with an ANOVA F-test or two sample proportions are compared by a chi-square test.

Internet Assignment

Would you like to see some convincing evidence that a nondirectional alternative hypothesis sometimes leads to a one-tailed test? Would you like that evidence to come from two Internet-based interactive Java applets? And would you like one of those applets to provide a picture showing how the value of the data-based p-value is based on what occurs in just one of the distribution's two tails? If you would like to see these things, do this Internet assignment.

Your first task in doing this assignment involves going to this book's companion Web site (http://www.psypress.com/statistical-misconceptions).

---

* The fact that there's just one tail in this chi-square test ought to make sense to anyone who knows how to compute the χ^2 test statistic for an $R \times C$ contingency table. Because this formula involves summing the quantity $(O - E)^2/E$ across all cells, the value of the test statistic becomes larger and larger (in only a positive direction) as the data conflict more and more with H_o.

Once there, open the folder for Chapter 8 and click on the link called "Directionality and Tails." Then, follow the detailed instructions (prepared by this book's author) on how to use the Java applet. By doing this assignment, you will come to realize why it is wrong to think or state that non-directional alternative hypotheses are always evaluated with two-tailed tests. Also, you are also likely to gain a better understanding of how the t and F distributions are related to each other.

☐ 8.6 The Relationship Between Alpha and Beta Errors

The Misconception

There is a simple inverse relationship between the probability of a Type I error (i.e., "alpha" error) and the probability of a Type II error (i.e., "beta" error), and the level of significance should be selected to balance the risks of these two opposing kinds of inferential error.

Evidence That This Misconception Exists*

The first of the following statements comes from a recently published statistics guide for students in geography. The second statement comes from an online document entitled "Hypothesis Testing." The third statement comes from an online document used in conjunction with a college-level course in biostatistics.

1. *As Type I error decreases, Type II increases and vice versa.*

2. *Type I and II Errors have an inverse relationship. If you reduce the probability of one error, the other one increases so that everything else is unchanged.*

3. *If you choose to lessen the type I error rate by using a small α, it comes at the expense of increasing the probability of making a type II error.*

Why This Misconception Is Dangerous

In one particular situation, it *is* true that an inverse relationship exists between the probabilities associated with Type I and Type II errors. If everything else about a study is held constant, making the level of significance more rigorous (say by changing α from .05 to .01) will reduce Type I error risk but increase Type II error risk. Or, changing the level of

---

* Appendix B contains references for all quoted material presented in this section.

significance to make it more "lenient" (say by changing α from .05 to .15) will cause the probability of a Type II error to decrease but the probability of a Type I error to increase.

If you think that Type I and Type II error risks are inversely related, then you have not yet come to realize that it's possible to "have your cake and eat it too." In other words, this misconception, if you have it, is preventing you from seeing that both kinds of error risks can be lowered at the same time. Those who fail to realize this are likely to (1) conduct poorly designed studies and (2) render less than adequate evaluations of others' investigations. Moreover, those individuals are likely to be perplexed when well-trained researchers talk about performing an a priori power analysis, specifying effect size, or computing the needed sample size for their studies.

Undoing the Misconception

If a single null hypothesis is tested and if no important assumptions of the statistical test are violated, α determines the probability of a Type I error. Thus, there is a clear and simple connection between the level of significance and the likelihood of an "error of the first kind." If alpha is set equal to .05, there is a 5% chance that a Type I error will be made. If that level of risk for falsely rejecting H_o is thought to be too high, then alpha can be made more rigorous. For example, changing α from .05 to .01 lowers the chance of a Type I error to 1 out of 100.

By definition, the power of a test is equal to $1 - \beta$, where β is the probability of a Type II error. Thus, if β is equal to .15, power is equal to .85. In a very real sense, therefore, power and Type II error risk are like two sides of the same coin. Just as you know that a coin's down side is "tails" if you see that the up side is "heads," you know what risk exists for a Type II error if you know the power level of a statistical test. Therefore, any discussion of power is a discussion of Type II error risk (and vice versa).

Power (or its complement, Type II error risk) is influenced by several factors. These include (1) α, (2) sample size, (3) the degree to which H_o is false, (4) the directional-versus-nondirectional nature of H_a, (5) the amount of variability in the study's population(s), and (6) the statistical test used to evaluate the null hypothesis. If one or more of these factors other than α is changed, power will be impacted even though the probability of a Type I error remains stable.

Of the various things that affect power without altering the likelihood of a Type I error, sample size is often the easiest thing to change. There is a direct relationship between sample size and power, so increases in n cause power to increase. Because power and Type II error risk are

TABLE 8.6.1. Beta Error Probability of a One-Tailed z-Test in Evaluating H_o: $\mu \geq 75$ (If $\mu = 80$ and $\sigma = 10$) for Three Different Alpha Levels and Eight Different Sample Sizes

		Sample size (n)							
		10	20	30	40	50	60	70	80
Alpha level	.05	.53	.28	.14	.06	.03	.01	.01	.01
(α)	.01	.77	.54	.34	.20	.11	.06	.03	.02
	.001	.93	.80	.64	.47	.33	.22	.14	.08

opposite sides of the same coin, there's an inverse relationship between sample size and the chance that a false null hypothesis will be retained. Increase n and the probability of a Type II error decreases.

Table 8.6.1 shows the relationships among sample size and the two kinds of error probabilities for a situation in which (1) a single population exists with $\mu = 80$ and $\sigma = 10$, (2) a single-sample z-test is used to test H_o: $\mu = 75$ in a one-tailed fashion, (3) α is set equal to .05, .01, or .001, and (4) the sample size ranges from 10 to 80. Look carefully, and you'll see that it's possible to decrease Type I *and* Type II risks at the same time. When n = 20 and α = .05, there is a 28% chance of a Type II error. Reduce α to .01 (but double n), and the probability of not rejecting the false null hypothesis *decreases* to .20. Further reduce alpha to .001 and Type II error risk decreases even further (to .08) if n is doubled once again.*

Internet Assignment

Would you like to see a picture of some sampling distributions that show how Type I and Type II error risk can be decreased simultaneously? Would you like such a picture to be part of an Internet-based interactive Java applet that gives you the opportunity to change certain things about the study (such as its sample size), and then see the effect of such changes on other features of the study (such as the probability of a beta error)? If you would like to see and interactively control such a picture, do this Internet assignment.

---

* The entries in Table 8.6.1 were determined by using Rollin Brant's online power and sample size calculator (http://stat.ubc.ca/~rollin/stats/ssize/n1.html).

To begin this assignment, go to this book's companion Web site (http://www.psypress.com/statistical-misconceptions). Once there, open the folder for Chapter 8 and click on the link called "The Relationship Between Alpha and Beta Errors." Then, follow the detailed instructions (prepared by this book's author) on how to use the Java applet. By doing this assignment, you will demonstrate in a convincing fashion that the risks of Type I and Type II errors can be decreased at the same time. This assignment's Java applet will also help you understand that Type II error risk is determined by several features of a study beyond the selected level of significance.

☐ Recommended Reading

Ancker, J. S. (2006). The language of conditional probability. *Journal of Statistics Education, 14*(2). Retrieved April 1, 2007, from www.amstat.org/publica tions/jse/v14n2/ancker.html.

Balluerka, N., Gómez, J., & Hidalgo, D. (2005). The controversy over null hypothesis significance testing revisited. *Methodology: European Journal of Research Methods for the Behavioral and Social Sciences, 1*(2), 55–70.

Cohen, J. (1994). The earth is round (p < .05). *American Psychologist, 49,* 997–1003.

Finch, S., Cumming, G., & Thomason, N. (2001). Colloquium on effect size: The role of editors, textbook authors, and the publication manual: Reporting on statistical inference in the *Journal of Applied Psychology*: Little evidence of reform. *Educational and Psychological Measurement, 61,* 181–210.

Fraley, R. C., & Marks, M. J. (n.d.). *The null hypothesis significance testing debate and its implications for personality research.* Retrieved October 13, 2007, from http://psych.nmsu.edu/faculty/marks/pubs/FraleyMarksNHST.pdf.

Haller, H., & Krauss, S. (2002). Misinterpretations of significance: A problem students share with their teachers? *Methods of Psychological Research, 7*(1). Retrieved November 3, 2007, from www.mpr-online.de/issue16/art1/haller.pdf.

Hoenig, J. M., & Heisey, D. M. (2001). The abuse of power: The pervasive fallacy of power calculations in data analysis. *The American Statistician, 55,* 19–24.

Hubbard, R., & Armstrong, J. S. (2006). Why we don't really know what "statistical significance" means: Implications for educators. *Journal of Marketing Education, 28*(2), 114–120.

Intuitor. (n.d.). Type I and type II errors—Making mistakes in the justice system. In *Amazing applications of probability and statistics.* Retrieved April 16, 2007, from http://www.intuitor.com/statistics/T1T2Errors.html.

Koehnle, T. (2005). The proof is not in the P value. *American Journal of Physiology— Regulatory, Integrative, and Comparative Physiology, 288,* 777–778.

Lenth, R. V. (n.d.). *Two sample-size practices that I don't recommend.* Retrieved March 29, 2007, from http://www.stat.uiowa.edu/~rlenth/Power.

Sawyer, A. G., & Peter, J. P. (1983, May). The significance of statistical significance tests in marketing research. *Journal of Marketing Research, 20*(2), 122–133.

Sotos, A. E. C., Vanhoof, S., Noortgate, W. V., & Onghena, P. (2007). Students' misconceptions of statistical inference: A review of the empirical evidence from research on statistical education. Retrieved July 21, 2008, from https://lirias.kuleuven.be/bitstream/123456789/136347/1/CastroSotos.pdf.

t-Tests Involving One or Two Means

Research has shown that students typically hold statistical misconceptions that are persistent and resistant to change....*

---

* Scanlon, E., Blake, C., Joiner, R., & O'Shea, T. (2005). Technologically mediated complex problem-solving on a statistics task. *Learning, Media and Technology, 30,* 165–183.

☐ 9.1 Correlated *t*-Tests

The Misconception

A correlated *t*-test focuses on the measured relationship (i.e., correlation) between two variables, with the null hypothesis being H_o: $\rho = 0$.

Evidence That This Misconception Exists*

The following two statements were posted on an electronic discussion board connected to a college-level research methods course.

> *[Question] If my study adopts a within-subjects design, in which repeated measures are taken on a single sample, why is this not a correlation study?*

> *[Response] Technically it is, and in fact the usual statistical test for the typical two-trial repeated measures study, is sometimes known as the correlated t-test. However, the determining factor here is the intent of the researcher— within-subjects designs are adopted to examine [mean] differences in measures, as a result of some intervention or treatment....*

Why This Misconception Is Dangerous

Those who mistakenly think that a correlated *t*-test deals with correlation are likely to end up analyzing data incorrectly (if they are conducting their own studies) or misinterpreting others' findings (if they are reading or listening to summaries of other people's research projects). Either of these mistakes can have grave consequences.

By thinking that a correlated *t*-test deals with the correlation between two sets of data, a person will wrongly interpret a statistically significant *t*-value from a pretest–posttest comparison to mean that the pretest scores are significantly correlated with the posttest scores, when it's fully possible that the actual correlation (both in the sample data and in the population) is equal to 0. Or, our misinformed person will mistakenly think that a nonsignificant *t*-test result means that there's little

---

* Appendix B contains the reference for the quoted material presented in this section.

or no correlation between the pretest and posttest scores, when it's fully possible that the actual correlation is moderate, high, or even perfect!

Undoing the Misconception

A correlated t-test focuses on means, not correlations. To be more specific, this kind of t-test compares the means of two sample sets of data, with the null hypothesis dealing with the means of the populations corresponding to the two samples. In its typical application, the null hypothesis for this t-test is H_o: $\mu_1 = \mu_2$.

As shown here, the formula for a correlated t-test contains r, the observed correlation between the two sets of sample data:

$$t = \frac{\left(\overline{X}_1 - \overline{X}_2\right) - \left(\mu_1 - \mu_2\right)}{\sqrt{\dfrac{1}{n}\left(s_1^2 + s_2^2\right) - 2rs_1 s_2}}$$

Despite the fact that r is contained in this formula's denominator, it is the numerator that establishes the primary focus of this t-test. That focus is on means. The two μ's in the numerator come from the null hypothesis, and if they are identical (as is usually the case), the numerator reduces to the observed difference between the sample means.

To prove to yourself that a correlated t-test is focused on means rather than a correlation, take a close look at the "inner workings" of the t-test formula. The calculated t-value that pops out of this formula will be large even if $r = 0$, so long as there is a big difference between the two sample means relative to variability within the two sets of sample data. On the other hand, the calculated t will turn out to be 0 if r is large (or even perfect), so long as the two sample means are identical.

Perhaps the term *correlated-samples t-test* would be less confusing than the term *correlated t-test*, as the former term implies that this t-test uses data from correlated samples. However, the best way to avoid creating the misconception that correlation is the focus is to refer to this kind of t-test by any of its other three names: (1) a paired t-test, (2) a matched t-test, or (3) a dependent t-test.

Internet Assignment

Would you like to see some evidence that a correlated *t*-test focuses on means rather than a correlation coefficient? Would you like to have this evidence come from a correlated *t*-test applied to data that you supply. And would you like the analysis to be done on an Internet-based interactive Java applet? If you would like to see and do these things, this Internet assignment will be worth doing.

To begin this assignment, go to this book's companion Web site (http://www.psypress.com/statistical-misconceptions). Once there, open the folder for Chapter 9 and click on the link called "Correlated *t*-Tests." Then, follow the detailed instructions (prepared by this book's author) on how to use the Java applet. By doing this short assignment, you will see that (1) correlated *t*-tests are sometimes referred to as paired *t*-tests, (2) correlated *t*-tests always involve two equally large sets of scores, and (3) the word *correlation* never appears in the output of some computer programs that perform this kind of *t*-test.

9.2 The Difference Between Two Means If $p < .0001$

The Misconception

If it turns out that $p < .0001$ when a *t*-test is used to evaluate H_o: $\mu_1 = \mu_2$, one is safe in thinking that the two sample means are radically different from each other.

Evidence That This Misconception Exists*

The following statements come from peer-reviewed journals in the fields of education, psychology, and information technology. (In these passages, note the words *misinterpretation* and *confusion*.)

1. *Outcomes with lower p values are sometimes interpreted by students as having stronger treatment effects than those with higher p values; for example, an outcome of p < .01 is interpreted as having a stronger treatment effect than an outcome of p < .05.... How prevalent is this misinterpretation? ... Oakes found that researchers in psychology grossly overestimate the size of the effect based on a significance level change from .05 to .01.*

2. *It is difficult to know how common this belief is [that a small value of p means a treatment effect of large magnitude] ..., however, researchers often use language that lends itself to this type of misinterpretation.*

3. *So why the confusion and what is the difference between statistical significance testing and effect sizes? The confusion stems from misconceptions of what statistical significance testing tells us. First, as Nickerson (2000) explains, there is a belief that a small value of p means a treatment effect of large magnitude, and that statistical significance means theoretical or practical significance.*

Why This Misconception Is Dangerous

Whenever an independent-samples *t*-test is used to evaluate a null hypothesis concerning two population means (e.g., H_o: $\mu_1 = \mu_2$), both

---

* Appendix B contains references for all quoted material presented in this section.

the researcher and those who read the research report ought to have an appreciation for the various factors that influence the *t*-test's result. In many people's minds (especially those who like to reject null hypotheses), the *t*-test's primary result is the data-based *p*-value. It follows, then, that these individuals ought to know what statistical forces are at work when a *t*-test compares two sample means.

One of the factors that influence the size of the *p* produced by a *t*-test is the magnitude of the difference between the two sample means. Clearly, if H_o says that the two population means are the same (and if all other factors are held constant), then *p* will be small to the extent that $\bar{X}_1$ differs from $\bar{X}_2$. Unfortunately, many people forget that other factors also impinge upon the *p*-value that is produced by the *t*-test. When this happens, erroneous conclusions can be drawn about the difference between the sample means. A very small *p* may mislead someone into thinking that $\bar{X}_1$ and $\bar{X}_2$ were far apart. The reverse can occur as well, with a large *p* misleading one into thinking that the sample means were nearly identical.

A *t*-test's *p* can provide useful information. But it must be interpreted properly.

Undoing the Misconception

The *p*-value produced by a *t*-test comparison of the means of two independent samples is influenced by three factors in addition to the difference between $\bar{X}_1$ and $\bar{X}_2$. These include (1) the directional versus nondirectional nature of H_a, (2) the sample size (i.e., n_1 and n_2), and (3) the variability within each sample (i.e., SD_1 and SD_2).* Because most researchers conduct their *t*-tests in a two-tailed fashion, our focus here will be on the two other factors: sample size and within-group variability.

A *t*-test's *p* is influenced in opposite ways by sample size and within-group variability. The impact of *n* and *SD* on *p* (presuming all other things are held constant) is as follows:

- *n* is inversely related to *p*. (In other words, big *n*'s make *p* small, whereas small *n*'s make *p* big.)

---

* Violations of underlying assumptions can also affect a *t*-test's *p*. Because the purpose of the current discussion is to show the way sample size and within-group variability impact *p*, here we consider all assumptions to be valid.

- Within-group variability is directly related to p. (In other words, big SD's make p big, whereas small SD's make p small.)

The impact that sample sizes and within-group variability have on the *t*-test's calculated value shows up clearly in the formula used to compute *t* from sample data. This formula (for the case where independent samples are used to test H_0: $\mu_1 = \mu_2$ against H_0: $\mu_1 \neq \mu_2$ with a pooled estimate of population variability) is

$$t = \frac{X_1 - X_2}{\sqrt{\dfrac{(SS_1 + SS_2)}{n_1 + n_2 - 2}\left(\dfrac{1}{n_1} + \dfrac{1}{n_2}\right)}}$$

where SS_1 and SS_2 are the within-group sums of squares.* Note that large within-group variability (as indicated by SS) functions to make *t* small. In contrast, large *n*'s function to make *t* large. Because large values of *t*—disregarding *t*'s algebraic sign—lead to small values of p, small within-group variability and large sample sizes each function to make p small.†

Consider now these two facts: (1) p is determined by the calculated value of *t* (along with its *df* value), and (2) the calculated value of *t* is determined by three things: the observed difference between the two sample means, sample size, and within-group variability. Because of these connections, a *t*-test's *p*-value is determined as much by sample size or within-group variability as it is by the difference between the two sample means. Stated differently, an unusually small p could have come about for any one (or a combination) of three reasons: a large difference between $\bar{X}_1$ and $\bar{X}_2$, a large sample size, or small within-group variability.

If a *t*-test comparing two sample means produces an unusually small p, it is improper to think that the values for $\bar{X}_1$ and $\bar{X}_2$ must have been quite different in order to generate such an impressive p. It may be the case that the sample means were close together but the sample sizes were enormous. Or, it may have been the case that the sample means were close together but the within-group variability was tiny. Because of

---

* Within each group, SS measures dispersion from the mean. It is equal to the sum of the squared deviation scores.

† Large *n*'s function to make p small for two reasons. Increases in *n* cause the calculated value for *t* to get larger. In addition, larger *n*'s cause the *t*-test's *df* to increase. With *df* being larger, the calculated value is referred to a *t* distribution with tails that begin closer to the distribution's center.

these possibilities, a t-test's p should never be thought of as a good ruler that measures the degree to which $\bar{X}_1$ differs from $\bar{X}_2$.

Internet Assignment

Would you like to see some convincing evidence that the p-value from an independent-samples t-test is influenced by several factors in addition to the degree to which the sample means differ? Would you like to generate this evidence yourself via an Internet-based interactive Java applet? If you would like to see and do these things, spend a few minutes completing this Internet assignment.

To start, go to this book's companion Web site (http://www.psy press.com/statistical-misconceptions). Once there, open the folder for Chapter 9 and click on the link called "The Difference Between Two Means If $p < .0001$." Then, follow the detailed instructions (prepared by this book's author) on how to use the Java applet. By doing this short assignment, you will prove that a statistical comparison of two sample means can yield a result that is "highly significant," even if the means being compared are almost identical to each other. You will also come to realize why this is possible.

☐ 9.3 The Robustness of a *t*-Test When $n_1 = n_2$

The Misconception

An independent-samples *t*-test is robust to violations of assumptions if the two sample sizes are equal. In other words, the *t*-test will function properly, even if the normality assumption or the equal variance assumption is violated (or even if both of these assumptions are violated), so long as $n_1 = n_2$.

Evidence That This Misconception Exists*

The first of the following statements comes from a peer-reviewed journal in second-language acquisition. The second comes from a textbook in biostatistics. The third comes from a message posted to an online discussion group focused on applied statistics.

1. *In the case of t-tests ... Brown (2001) stated that "if the sample sizes are the same for the two groups involved, the t-test is robust to violations of the assumption of equal variances."*

2. *What is the solution when the standard deviations are not equal? Fortunately, this assumption can be ignored when the sample sizes are equal.... This is one of several reasons many researchers try to have fairly equal numbers in each group. (Statisticians say the t-test is robust with equal sample sizes.)*

3. *What are you worried about? With equal Ns, the t-test is VERY robust.*

Why This Misconception Is Dangerous

When a *t*-test is used to evaluate a null hypothesis concerning two population means (e.g., $H_o, \mu_1 = \mu_2$), the level of significance is supposed to define the probability that a Type I error will be made. If the chance of mistakenly rejecting a true null hypothesis fails to match (or closely

---

* Appendix B contains references for all quoted material presented in this section.

approximate) the selected α level, the t-test is not functioning as it is supposed to.

In many scientific disciplines, there is an unofficial (yet widely accepted) "rule" stipulating that Type I error risk must not exceed 5% unless the researcher can justify the selection of some higher risk level for this kind of error. Because of this, those in the scientific community look askance at studies wherein α is set equal to .10 (or higher) without explanation. Evidence of this bias against lenient alpha levels can be found in the articles published in statistically based journals.

The t-test is widely thought to be robust to violations of the normality and equal variance assumptions, so long as $n_1 = n_2$. However, when the two equal sample sizes are small, the probability of a Type I error can be as much as four times as large as the selected level of significance. As indicated in the previous paragraph, α is considered to specify Type I error risk. If alpha fails to do its job, then the entire hypothesis testing procedure does not function properly.

Undoing the Misconception

Table 9.3.1 contains the results of 18 computer simulations conducted to investigate the alleged robustness of the t-test under the condition of equal sample sizes. The common sample size in these simulations was set equal to 25, 10, or 5. There were 100,000 replications of the t-test in each simulation, with results presented here for both the .05 and .01 levels of significance. The two populations being compared were set up

TABLE 9.3.1. Type I Error Rates for t-Tests Conducted With Equal Sample Sizes and Assumptions Violated

		Assumption(s) Violated		
Sample Size	α	Normality	Equal Variance	Both
$n_1 = n_2 = 25$	.050	.051	.056	.054
	.010	.011	.012	.013
$n_1 = n_2 = 10$	.050	.054	.063	.064
	.010	.013	.017	.017
$n_1 = n_2 = 5$	.050	.055	.076	.107
	.010	.014	.023	.045

in three ways: (1) only the normality assumption was violated, (2) only the equal variance assumption was violated, and (3) both assumptions were violated.

The results in Table 9.3.1 show that the *t*-test's Type I error risk approximated the level of significance when each *n* was 25. This was the case for both the .05 and .01 levels of significance when the normality and/or equal variance assumptions, or both, were violated. However, the occurrence of Type I errors was elevated when *n* was 5 and when the equal variance assumption was violated either alone or in conjunction with a violation of the normality assumption.

Most researchers who use an independent-samples *t*-test have sample sizes that are substantially larger than 5. In certain scientific disciplines (e.g., exercise physiology), however, it is not unusual to see published studies in which *t*-tests are used with very small samples. In such studies, the normality and equal variance assumptions should be tested on a routine basis, even if $n_1 = n_2$. As the bottom two rows of Table 9.3.1 clearly show, the *t*-test is not robust when the sample sizes are equal, but small.

Internet Assignment

Would you like to see the results of a computer simulation designed to investigate the *t*-test's ability to be robust? Would you like to be the person who conducts this simulation study (with the entire investigation completed in a matter of minutes)? Finally, would you be more inclined to do the simulation study if it could be done via an Internet-based interactive Java applet? If you responded affirmatively to each of these questions, do this Internet assignment.

To start, go to this book's companion Web site (http://www.psypress.com/statistical-misconceptions). Once there, open the folder for Chapter 9 and click on the link called "The Robustness of a *t*-Test When $n_1 = n_2$." Then, follow the detailed instructions (prepared by this book's author) on how to use the Java applet. By doing this assignment, you will demonstrate that the condition of equal sample sizes does not guarantee that a *t*-test's nominal level of significance will be equal to the probability of a Type I error. Seeing this to be the case, you are more likely to view the *t*-test as a delicate instrument that will not function properly if used indiscriminately.

☐ Recommended Reading

Boneau, C. A. (1960). The effects of violations of assumptions underlying the t test. *Psychological Bulletin, 57*(1), 49–64.

David, H. A., & Gunnink, J. L. (1997). The paired *t* test under artificial pairing. *American Statistician, 51*(1), 9–12.

DeCarlo, L. T. (1997). On the meaning and use of kurtosis. *Psychological Methods, 2*(3), 292–307.

Keselman, H. J., Othman, A. R., Wilcox, R. R., & Fradette, K. (2004). The new and improved two-sample *t* test. *Psychological Science, 15*(1), 47–51.

Livingston, E. H., & Cassidy, L. (2005). Statistical power and estimation of the number of required subjects for a study based on the t-test: A surgeon's primer. *Journal of Surgical Research, 126*(2), 149–159.

Rock, A. J. (2007). Is the logic of the t-test for two independent samples fallacious? An analysis of the ontological status of the treated population. *North American Journal of Psychology, 9*(1), 163–172.

Tarasińska, J. (2005). Confidence intervals for the power of student's t-test. *Statistics & Probability Letters, 73*(2), 125–130.

Wuench, K. A. (2005). *Skewness, kurtosis, and the normal curve.* Retrieved March 29, 2007, from http://core.ecu.edu/psyc/wuenschk/docs30/Skew-Kurt.doc.

Zimmerman, D. W. (2004). Inflated statistical significance of student's t test associated with small intersubject correlation. *Journal of Statistical Computation & Simulation, 74*(9), 691–696.

ANOVA and ANCOVA

There is an abundance of research on incorrect statistical reasoning, indicating that statistical ideas are often misunderstood and misused by students and professionals alike.... This body of research indicates that inappropriate reasoning about statistical ideas is widespread and persistent, similar at all age levels (even among some experienced researchers), and quite difficult to change.*

* Garfield, J. (2002). The challenge of developing statistical reasoning. *Journal of Statistics Education, 10*(3). Retrieved September 2, 2007, from www.amstat.org/publications/jse/v10n3/garfield.html.

☐ 10.1 Pairwise Comparisons

The Misconception

If a study involves three (or more) comparison groups, one independent variable, one dependent variable, and a concern for possible differences between pairs of means, the researcher must first obtain a statistically significant F from a one-way analysis of variance (ANOVA) before having the right to make pairwise comparisons with a procedure such as Tukey's HSD (Honestly Significant Difference) test.

Evidence That This Misconception Exists*

The first of the following statements comes from a governmental document summarizing social development research focused on work, the family, and parenting. The second statement comes from a statistics book for health-care workers. The third statement comes from an online book dealing with psychological statistics. (In these passages, note the phrases *only if* and *only when*.)

1. *Step 4: Pairwise Multiple Comparisons. Multiple comparison methods are used to investigate differences between pairs of group means. They are conducted only when ANOVA is significant (at the 95% confidence level), in other words, only when there is evidence of overall difference will individual pairwise comparisons be made.*

2. *You need to do this test [Tukey] only if the result of your ANOVA is significant.*

3. *When three or more groups are being analyzed in the ANOVA, there frequently arises the need to carry out more specific two-group comparisons in order to determine where the major treatment effect is occurring. These two-group comparisons are commonly referred to as "individual" comparisons, "follow-up" tests, or "post-hoc" tests. ... There are a number of guidelines that one needs to know in order to properly carry out these two-group comparisons. For example, most researchers agree that it is appropriate to perform individual comparisons only if the result of the overall ANOVA is significant.*

---

* Appendix B contains references for all quoted material presented in this section.

Why This Misconception Is Dangerous

Applied researchers who suffer from this misconception conceivably will encounter one or both of two problems in their research investigations. One is a perplexing situation that they will easily recognize, if they stumble across it. The other is like a missed opportunity that they won't even know they had.

Those who believe that a one-way ANOVA F must be significant before pairwise comparisons are tested can end up in an apparent logical bind. If the ANOVA F is significant in the first of this two-stage approach to the data analysis, this result is often interpreted to mean that at least one pairwise comparison will show up as significant in the second, post hoc stage of the analysis. However, there is no guarantee that this will happen. All pairwise comparisons can turn out nonsignificant even though the omnibus null hypothesis (H_o: $\mu_1 = \mu_2 = \ldots = \mu_k$, where k represents the last of the comparison groups) is rejected. This perplexing situation can occur even though (1) the same α is used in both stages of the analysis, (2) the various sample sizes are identical, and (3) a liberal test procedure is used in the post hoc investigation.

The missed opportunity can occur if the ANOVA F turns out to be nonsignificant. In this situation, most researchers will not bother to test any pairwise comparisons. Their logic is simple. They view the ANOVA F like a traffic signal. A nonsignificant F is considered to be analogous to a red light that says, in essence, "Don't conduct any post hoc tests because nothing will show up as significant." Unfortunately, a decision not to conduct pairwise comparisons can cause the researcher to miss detecting one or more pairs of sample means that are significantly different.

Undoing the Misconception

The two problems that an applied researcher may encounter—a significant ANOVA F followed by nothing significant in a post hoc investigation, or significant pairwise differences that remain undetected because a nonsignificant ANOVA F prevents a post hoc investigation from taking place—both occur because the ANOVA's F-test and the tests typically conducted to make pairwise comparisons are doing different things. This difference comes to light if we consider what the level of significance protects against in each kind of analysis.

Suppose a researcher uses the Tukey HSD procedure to make all possible pairwise comparisons among means *without* an ANOVA being performed first. Also suppose that the same level of significance is used in making each of the pairwise comparisons. Here, the selected α indicates the probability that one or more of these comparisons will yield a significant result when in fact each pairwise H_o is true. With five groups in the study, there would be 10 pairwise comparisons. If α is set equal to .05 when making these tests, there would be a 5% chance of at least one Type I error somewhere among the 10 tests.

When a level of significance is used with a one-way ANOVA, the selected α protects against Type I errors being made in a much larger set of comparisons. That's because the ANOVA F considers all possible comparisons that conceivably could be set up and tested. This set includes both pairwise and nonpairwise comparisons * Because more comparisons are taken into consideration by the ANOVA F-test, this analysis turns out to be more conservative than a set of Tukey tests applied only to pairwise comparisons.† This added protection is built into the internal working of the F-test, thus making it possible for the ANOVA to yield a nonsignificant result, whereas a set of Tukey comparisons, applied to the same data, might reveal a significant difference.

Because an ANOVA F-test considers both pairwise and nonpairwise comparisons, it is possible for it to yield a significant result due to a nonpairwise comparison. For example, in a study involving five groups, suppose the ANOVA yields a significant result because, unbeknownst to the researcher, the mean of the two highest scoring groups combined together is quite different from the mean of the two lowest scoring groups that are pooled together. If the researcher performs just pairwise comparisons (in an effort to determine why the ANOVA's omnibus H_o was rejected), this kind of post hoc investigation conceivably might not reveal *anything* to be significant.

A leading expert on the correct (and incorrect) ways to make comparisons among means is Jason C. Hsu. His thoughts about how best to perform pairwise comparisons are both clear and concise:

An unfortunate common practice is to pursue multiple comparisons only when the null hypothesis of homogeneity H_o: $\mu_1 = \mu_2 = \ldots = \mu_k$ (typically based on the F-test) is rejected, due to the mistaken beliefs that:

---

* Nonpairwise comparisons involve more than two groups. For example, in a study with three groups, a comparison of the first group's mean against the mean of the second and third groups pooled together would be nonpairwise in nature.

† A test procedure is said to be conservative if the probability of rejecting the null hypothesis is smaller than the level of significance.

1. Magical "protection" is endowed by first performing a test of homogeneity.

2. No useful result will be found if the test of homogeneity accepts.*

After defending his position by means of statistical theory as well as geometric illustrations of rejection regions, Hsu reiterated his main point: "In short, to consider multiple comparisons as to be performed only if the F-test rejects is a mistake" (p. 178).

It should be noted that planned (i.e., a priori) comparisons, by their very nature, can be conducted without an ANOVA F being computed. Therefore, if a researcher has a priori interest in pairwise comparisons, such comparisons can be investigated directly because they are planned. It should also be noted that there is no theoretical or statistical justification for considering the Tukey HSD procedure to be post hoc in nature. It is simply a technique for making pairwise comparisons among means. Therefore, the Tukey procedure for making pairwise comparisons can be used directly without any needed "green light" coming from a significant ANOVA F-test.

Internet Assignment

Would you like to see some proof that a pairwise comparison can be significant in the presence of a nonsignificant omnibus F-test from a one-way ANOVA? Would you like this proof to come from an Internet-based Java applet that allows you to enter the data? Finally, would you like (or at least be willing) to have the pairwise comparisons evaluated by means of Tukey's HSD test? If so, do this Internet assignment.

To start, go to this book's companion Web site (http://www.psy press.com/statistical-misconceptions). Once there, open the folder for Chapter 10 and click on the link called "Pairwise Comparisons." Then, follow the detailed instructions (prepared by this book's author) on how to use the Java applet. By doing this assignment, you will see a case where the ANOVA's omnibus F-ratio yields a "$p > .05$" finding, whereas Tukey's HSD procedure yields a "$p < .05$" result. By seeing and thinking about his seemingly paradoxical set of results, you will deepen your understanding of what an ANOVA F-test is really testing (and why it might fail to detect a significance difference between a pair of means).

---

* Hsu, J. C. (1996). *Multiple comparisons: Theory and methods* (p. 177). London: Chapman & Hall.

☐ 10.2 The Cause of a Significant Interaction

The Misconception

If all but one of the cell means are similar in a two-way ANOVA that produces a significant interaction, the single cell $\bar{X}$ that's different from the others can legitimately be thought of as the reason why the interaction null hypothesis was rejected.

Evidence That This Misconception Exists*

The first of the following statement comes from a peer-reviewed article dealing with research in *otolaryngology*. The second statement comes from an agricultural report issued by a U.S. university. (In each passage, note that a single subgroup is identified as the source of the interaction in each study's two-way ANOVA.)

1. *The source of the interaction [F(1,90) = 6.85, p = 0.01] is the poorer performance of the high-JND RD subgroup compared with the other [three] subgroups.*

2. *In this study, we had 2 grass species [Bermuda and Paspalum], and 3 levels of chemical treatment (none, 500 and 1000 ppm).... Based on the 15 daily individual ET measurement events, a significant statistical interaction occurred on only 2 of 15 days. In these cases, it was the non-treated paspalum turf (Pasp C) which caused the interaction, because of its high water use.*

Why This Misconception Is Dangerous

This misconception is dangerous for two reasons. On the one hand, applied researchers may feel a sense of embarrassment by saying or writing things that indicate they don't understand either the meaning of a significant two-way interaction H_o or the formula used to compute the interaction MS. On the other hand, those who listen to or read research reports may place less confidence in a study's findings and recommendations if the

---

* Appendix B contains references for all quoted material presented in this section.

recipients of the research report are distracted by incorrect comments made about the two-way ANOVA's significant interaction.

Undoing the Misconception

In a two-way ANOVA, any interaction that is present in the sample data is created by *all* of the cell means. No one cell is ever responsible, by itself, for interaction that shows up in the ANOVA summary table. Every cell mean matters.

The fact that interaction is tied to all cell means can be seen most easily if we examine the "inner workings" of a 2 × 2 ANOVA in which three of the four cells have identical sample means. Consider, for example, the data in Table 10.2.1.

If each of the four cells has an n of 10, and if the within-groups MS is equal to 20, there is a significant A × B interaction, $F(1, 36) = 8.0$, $p < .05$. It is tempting to think that this interaction is attributable to the "outlier" cell mean (of 4). On first glance, it seems plausible to think that way because there would have been no interaction if the mean in the bottom-right-hand cell had turned out like the other three, equal to 12. However, the same result—of no interaction—would have been created if the upper-right-hand cell's mean had turned out to be equal to 4. Or if the bottom-left-hand cell had turned out to be equal to 4. Or if the upper-left-hand cell had turned out to be equal to 20. Thus, if any of the four cells can be changed to eliminate the interaction that's present, then it follows logically that no single cell is the "culprit" behind any interaction that's in the data to begin with.

TABLE 10.2.1. Hypothetical Sample Means for a 2 × 2 ANOVA

Factor A	Factor B	
	b_1	b_2
a_1	$\bar{X} = 12$	$\bar{X} = 12$
a_2	$\bar{X} = 12$	$\bar{X} = 4$

Looking at interaction in a more formal and more generalizable manner, the linear score model for a two-way ANOVA takes the form

$$Y_{ijk} = \mu + \alpha_j + \beta_k + \gamma_{jk} + \varepsilon_{ijk}$$

where Y_{ijk} = the ith score in the jth row and the kth column, α_j = the effect associated with the jth row, β_k = the effect associated with the kth column, γ_{jk} = the interaction effect in the cell found at the intersection of the jth row and the kth column, and ε_{ijk} = the random error associated with score Y_{ijk}. The interaction sum of squares in the ANOVA summary table is based on the estimated values of the cell interaction effects. These estimated effects, symbolized as $\hat{\gamma}_{jk}$, are computed from the data as follows:

$$\hat{\gamma}_{jk} = \overline{X}_{jk} - \overline{X}_j - \overline{X}_k + \overline{\overline{X}}$$

where $\overline{X}_{jk}$ = the cell mean in the jth row and the kth column, $\overline{X}_j$ = the mean of all data in the jth row, $\overline{X}_k$ = the mean of all data in the kth column, and $\overline{\overline{X}}$ = the mean of all data in all cells.

Table 10.2.2 contains the estimated interaction effects for each of the cells shown in Table 10.2.1.

To compute the interaction sum of squares for the ANOVA summary table, each cell's $\hat{\gamma}_{jk}$ is squared and then multiplied by the cell n. Then these products are summed. Thus, for the data in our hypothetical 2×2 ANOVA,

TABLE 10.2.2. Estimated Interaction Effects Based on Data in Table 10.2.1.

Factor A	Factor B	
	b_1	b_2
a_1	$\hat{\gamma}_{11} = -2$	$\hat{\gamma}_{12} = +2$
a_2	$\hat{\gamma}_{21} = +2$	$\hat{\gamma}_{22} = -2$

$$SS_{A \times B} = 10(\hat{\gamma}_{11})^2 + 10(\hat{\gamma}_{12})^2 + 10(\hat{\gamma}_{21})^2 + 10(\hat{\gamma}_{22})^2$$

$$= 10(-2)^2 + 10(+2)^2 + 10(+2)^2 + 10(-2)^2$$

$$= 160$$

In this calculation, notice that each cell contributes the same amount to $SS_{A \times B}$, the interaction SS. That is the case in any 2 × 2 ANOVA (having equal n's across the four cells), regardless of how similar or diverse the cell means might be.

If a two-way ANOVA has more than two levels in either or both of its factors, it is also the case that the amount of measured interaction is influenced by all of the cell means. In such ANOVAs, the various values of $\hat{\gamma}_{jk}$ are likely to vary (and some of the estimated interaction effects in certain cells may turn out to be equal to 0), and thus the degree to which different cells contribute to $SS_{A \times B}$ will likely vary. Nevertheless, it will never be the case that one cell is fully responsible for the interaction turning out as it does. Regardless of the pattern of cell means in a two-way ANOVA, it is impossible for there to be only one nonzero $\hat{\gamma}_{jk}$.

Internet Assignment

Would you like to use an Internet-based interactive Java applet to demonstrate why one cell in a two-way ANOVA should not, by itself, be thought of as the cause of interaction? Would you like this demonstration to involve a 2 × 3 ANOVA? Finally, would you like the applet to display a graph of the interaction that's created by your data? If you responded affirmatively to these questions, you will find this Internet assignment to be both instructive and interesting.

To start, go to this book's companion Web site (http://www.psypress. com/statistical-misconceptions). Once there, open the folder for Chapter 10 and click on the link called "The Cause of a Significant Interaction." Then, follow the detailed instructions (prepared by this book's author) on how to use the Java applet. In the process of doing this assignment, you will see an interaction graph created by six cell means, all of which will be identical except one. The last portion of the assignment will help you gain a better understanding of why the interaction sum of squares turns out as it does in any two-way ANOVA.

□ 10.3 Equal Covariate Means in ANCOVA

The Misconception

If the comparison groups in a study have identical or highly similar means on a covariate variable (e.g., a pretest), there's no reason to use an analysis of covariance (ANCOVA) to analyze the data. In this situation, data on the covariate variable should be discarded and the scores on the study's dependent variable should be subjected to a *t*-test or ANOVA.

Evidence That This Misconception Exists*

The following statement comes from a recent PhD dissertation dealing with intercultural sensitivity.

> *It should be noted that independent samples t-tests were performed ... instead of ANCOVA [because] there were no significant differences between the groups on the pre-test thus making pre-test scores an inappropriate covariate.*

Why This Misconception Is Dangerous

When used properly, the analysis of covariance reduces within group variability. As a result, ANCOVA increases statistical power. ANCOVA can achieve this objective even if comparison groups have similar, or even identical, means on the covariate variable.[†]

To discard data on a good covariate variable unnecessarily increases the probability of a Type II error when group means on the study's dependent variable are compared. If the power is high regardless of whether the covariate data are or aren't used, then the increase in the risk of a Type II error will be negligible. However, it's often the case that (1) power is below desirable levels and (2) other features of the study that

---

* Appendix B contains the reference for the quoted material presented in this section.

† The discussion here is limited to the case where data exist on a single covariate variable. However, ANCOVA can accommodate two or more covariate variables.

affect Type II error rate—such as the sample size or the level of significance—cannot be altered so as to increase power. In these situations where surplus power does not exist, it is simply a waste of available and useful information not to use ANCOVA.*

Undoing the Misconception

If the means of independent samples are compared by any fixed-effects analysis of variance, the within-groups mean square, MS_{wg}, serves as the denominator in the ANOVA's F-ratio(s).† Thus, an inverse relationship exists between the size of MS_{wg} and the size of the computed F. Because a false ANOVA H_o is more likely to be rejected when an F-value is large (presuming that α and df values remain constant), a decrease in MS_{wg} will bring about an increase in power.

The primary purpose of an ANCOVA is to reduce within-group variability. This goal is accomplished by using data on one or more covariate variables to "account for" a portion of the individual differences that exist inside comparison groups. This accounted for portion of the within-group variability is taken out of MS_{wg}, and what remains is referred to as the "adjusted" MS_{wg}.

The degree to which ANCOVA helps to reduce MS_{wg} depends mainly on the correlation between the covariate and dependent variables. If this correlation is large (in either a positive or negative direction), there will be a sizable reduction in MS_{wg}; conversely, if this correlation is small, so too will the reduction be small. The approximate relationship between MS_{wg}, the correlation, and the adjusted within-group mean square is as follows:

$$\text{Adjusted } MS_{wg} \approx (1 - r^2)\, MS_{wg}$$

where r is the pooled within-group correlation between scores on the covariate and dependent variables. This correlation is said to be "pooled"

---

* The assumption here, of course, is that ANCOVA's assumptions are met so that its use is appropriate.
† This is the case regardless of how many factors are involved, regardless of how many levels make up each factor, regardless of how large the samples are, and regardless of whether the ANOVA model is additive or nonadditive.

because sums of squares and sums of cross-products are first computed separately within each group and then aggregated across groups.*

The use of covariate data accomplishes a second, desirable goal. In addition to reducing within-group variability, ANCOVA equates the comparison groups on the covariate variable. Utilizing the techniques of linear regression, ANCOVA adjusts each group's mean on the dependent variable to compensate for that particular group having a higher or lower mean on the covariate variable. The logic behind this adjustment is both simple and straightforward. A group with a below-average covariate mean has its mean on the dependent variable adjusted upwards, whereas a group with an above-average mean on the covariate has its mean on the dependent variable adjusted downward.† The resulting adjusted means on the dependent variable provide the best guess as to how the comparison groups would have scored on the dependent variable if they had had identical means of the covariate variable.

If a study's comparison groups have identical means of the covariate variable, each group's adjusted mean on the dependent variable turns out identical to that group's unadjusted mean. This should make sense, as the purpose of the adjustment is to remove any visible "inequalities" associated with the covariate variable. If no such inequalities exist, no adjustment is required.

Even if the means on the dependent variable require little or no adjustment (because comparison groups have highly similar or identical covariate means), ANCOVA can still be useful because of its ability to reduce within-group variability. This is the case because ANCOVA's internal formulas that function to increase power do not involve any consideration whatsoever of group means on the covariate variable. If scores on the covariate variable have a high within-group correlation with scores on the dependent variable, power will increase regardless of whether the comparison groups' means on the covariate variable are close together or far apart.

---

* To better approximate adjusted MS_{wg}, the term $(1 - r^2)MS_{wg}$ should be multiplied by $[1 + 1/(df_{wg} - 2)]$, where df_{wg} is the degrees of freedom for the within-groups error term that would be used if the study's data were to be analyzed by an ANOVA. Except for studies involving tiny n's, this added term takes the form of a very small fraction.

† The direction of the adjustments in this example assume that a positive correlation exists between the covariate and dependent variables.

Internet Assignment

Would you like to see some convincing evidence that data on a covariate variable can be useful even if comparison groups have identical means on this variable? Would you like to use an Internet-based Java applet to create this evidence? If so, do this Internet assignment.

To start, go to this book's companion Web site (http://www.psypress.com/statistical-misconceptions). Once there, open the folder for Chapter 10 and click on the link called "Equal Covariate Means in ANCOVA." Then, follow the detailed instructions (prepared by this book's author) on how to use the Java applet. In the process of doing this assignment, you will have the applet analyze a small set of data in two ways. First, you will perform a one-way ANCOVA. Next, you will conduct a one-way ANOVA. You may be surprised when you compare the results yielded by these two analyses!

☐ Recommended Reading

Colliver, J. A., & Markwell, S. J. (2006). ANCOVA, selection bias, statistical equating, and effect size: Recommendations for publication. *Teaching & Learning in Medicine*, *18*(4), 284–286.

Dimitrov, D. M., & Rumrill, P. D. (2003). Pretest-posttest designs and measurement of change. *Work*, *20*, 159–165.

Hsu, J. C. (1996). *Multiple comparisons: Theory and methods*. London: Chapman & Hall.

Jaccard, J. (1998). *Interaction effects in factorial analysis of variance*. Thousand Oaks, CA: Sage.

Jaccard, J., & Guilamo-Ramos, V. (2002). Analysis of variance frameworks in clinical child and adolescent psychology: Advanced issues and recommendations. *Journal of Clinical Child Psychology*, *31*(2), 278–294.

Miller, G. A., & Chapman, J. P. (2001). Misunderstanding analysis of covariance. *Journal of Abnormal Psychology*, *110*(1), 40–48.

Ottenbacher, K. J. (1991). Interpretation of interaction in factorial analysis of variance design. *Statistics in Medicine*, *10*(10), 1565–1571.

Pairwise comparisons. (n.d.). Retrieved November 11, 2007, from http://core.ecu.edu/psyc/wuenschk/StatHelp/Pairwise.htm.

Rogan, J. C., & Keselman, H. J. (1977). Is the ANOVA F-test robust to variance heterogeneity when sample sizes are equal? An investigation via a coefficient of variation. *American Educational Research Journal*, *14*(4), 493–498.

Tomarken, A. J., & Serlin, R. C. (1986). Comparison of ANOVA alternatives under variance heterogeneity and specific noncentrality structures. *Psychological Bulletin*, *99*(1), 90–99.

Wright, D. B. (2006). Comparing groups in a before–after design: When t test and ANCOVA produce different results. *British Journal of Educational Psychology*, *76*(3), 663–675.

Practical Significance, Power, and Effect Size

There is clear evidence that many people, including some researchers, have serious and persisting misconceptions about fundamental aspects of probability and statistics. Even successful completion of statistics courses does not guarantee that misconceptions will be overcome.*

* Cumming, G., & Thomason, N. (1996). Educational strategy and cognitive change: From Prolog to Stat Play. *Educational Computing, 11*, 22–25, 23.

☐ 11.1 Statistical Significance Versus Practical Significance

The Misconception

Statistically significant results signify strong relationships between variables or big differences between comparison groups.

Evidence That This Misconception Exists*

The first of the following statements comes from a peer-reviewed journal article in the behavioral sciences. The second statement comes from a book designed to help people become better able to understand research in applied linguistics. The third statement comes from a book dealing with a subfield of statistics called *forecasting*. (In these passages, note the words *common, misconception, often,* and *confuse*.)

1. *A common misuse of NHST [null hypothesis significance testing] is the implication that statistical significance means theoretical or practical significance. This misconception involves interpreting a statistically significant difference as a difference that has practical or clinical implications.*

2. *Two other misconceptions are common regarding statistical significance. One is to think that because something is statistically significant, there is a strong relationship between variables or a big difference between groups.... The other common misconception about statistical significance is to confuse it with practical significance.*

3. *[R]esearchers often misinterpret statistical significance.... One problem is that researchers (and editors and reviewers) often confuse statistical significance with practical significance.*

Why This Misconception Is Dangerous

There are two kinds of significance—statistical significance and practical significance—and they refer to entirely different concepts. To think

---

* Appendix B contains references for all quoted material presented in this section.

that one implies the other is tantamount to thinking that a bridal shower and a bathroom shower are the same thing, or that the King of Hearts is equivalent to the King of England. Whereas few people would ever confuse these two kinds of showers or these two kinds of kings, it unfortunately is the case that statistical significance is often interpreted—even by some researchers—to mean significance in a practical manner.

If you think that statistical significance implies practical significance, you are likely to disappoint others or be disappointed yourself. If you are a researcher and talk about your statistically significant findings in a way that makes others think that you've discovered something big, important, and noteworthy, the recipients of your results may be disappointed (or even angry) when they discover, after taking action on your study's findings, that what they expected to be large or strong in reality is small or weak. If you are the one who spends time, energy, or money on something and expect your actions to make a big difference (because you think statistical significance = practical significance), it may be you who gets disappointed.

If you or others fail to distinguish between these two kinds of significance, what appears to you or them to be a mountain may actually be only a molehill!

Undoing the Misconception

Statistical significance involves, among other things, null and alternative hypotheses, a level of significance (α), sample data, and a data-based probability (p). The numerical value of p documents the degree to which the sample data differ from what would be expected if the null hypothesis were true. If p is small enough (i.e., if p turns out equal to or smaller than (α), the empirical evidence is viewed as being in conflict with H_o. Accordingly, the null hypothesis is rejected and a statistically significant finding is said to exist.

Practical significance, in contrast to statistical significance, is focused on a study's possible impact on the work of practitioners or other researchers. Here, the question being asked is: "Will people who read or hear about a study's findings consider altering what they do or think because of the investigation's 'discoveries'?" If this question is answered "yes," practical significance is said to exist. Thus, the determination of practical significance necessarily involves anticipating people's subjective reaction to a study's findings.

Statistical significance can (and often does) exist in the absence of any practical significance. One of the main reasons why this can happen

TABLE 11.1.1. Smallest r That Rejects H_o: $\rho = 0$ in Favor of H_1: $\rho \neq 0$ at $\alpha = .05$

| | \multicolumn{10}{c}{Sample Size} |
	10	20	30	40	50	100	200	500	1,000	5,000
Pearson's r	±.55	±.38	±.31	±.27	±.24	±.17	±.12	±.08	±.06	±.03

is sample size (n). Because p and n are inversely related, a large n can cause results to be statistically significant (with $p < \alpha$) even though the measured relationship or effect is small, tiny, or practically nonexistent! For example, Table 11.1.1 shows a variety of sample correlation coefficients, each of which is statistically significant (two-tailed with $\alpha = .05$) if based upon the sample size shown above each value of r.

Table 11.1.1 indicates that a correlation of .03 (or –.03) will turn out to be statistically significant in the situation where a two-tailed test is conducted with $\alpha = .05$ and $n = 5,000$. In light of this fact, four questions are worth asking: (1) Do researchers ever use sample sizes this large? (2) In such studies, do r's ever turn out as small as ±.03? (3) Are such r's ever reported to be statistically significant? (4) Can r's this small signal practical significance? The answer to each of the first three questions is "yes." The answer to the fourth question is "probably not."*

It should be noted that both statistical significance and practical significance are inherently subjective. The subjectivity involved in claims of practical significance sits on the surface for all to see. For example, whether a correlation of .50 has practical significance is purely a matter of judgment. One researcher might claim that such an r is important, while a different researcher (in the same discipline) might claim that it does not. What's viewed as being important in a practical way, in a very real sense, "is in the eye of the beholder."

The subjectivity involved in claims of statistical significance is not as visible, at least to many people who conduct studies or come into contact with research findings. In the process of designing a study

---

* If $r = .03$, the coefficient of determination is equal to .0009. This means that only nine one-hundreds of 1% of the variability in X is associated with (i.e., explained by) variability in Y. It is hard to imagine that a researcher could persuasively argue that this amount of explained variability has utility in any practical or theoretical manner.

and analyzing its data, a researcher makes several decisions that influence whether or not the result is statistically significant. For example, the researcher must decide what population(s) to use, how to sample the population(s), what statistical test(s) to employ, how large n will be, whether H_1 will be directional or nondirectional, and what level of Type I error risk should be tolerated. In many studies, a statistically significant result would vanish (or suddenly appear) if the researcher were to go back in time and alter one or more of these decisions.

Internet Assignment

Would you like to look at a set of results from a one-way ANOVA that are statistically significant even though they lack any practical significance? Would you like these results to come from an Internet-based Java applet that allows you to enter the data that produce the statistically significant result? Finally, would you like the applet to accommodate input information that takes the form of sample means, standard deviations, and n's (rather than raw scores)? If so, do this Internet assignment.

To start, go to this book's companion Web site (http://www.psypress. com/statistical-misconceptions). Once there, open the folder for Chapter 11 and click on the link called "Statistical Significance Versus Practical Significance." Then, follow the detailed instructions (prepared by this book's author) on how to use the Java applet. By doing this assignment, you will gain an appreciation for the fact that significance can be, at the same time, both present in and absent from a study's results.

☐ 11.2 A Priori and Post Hoc Power

The Misconception

A study's statistical power has the same meaning regardless of whether it is estimated prior to or after the data have been gathered and analyzed.

Evidence That This Misconception Exists*

The first of the following statements comes from a recent article that appeared in a peer-reviewed journal in statistics. The second statement comes from a peer-reviewed journal in ergonomics. The third statement comes from a research biostatistician's Web log. (In these passages, note the phrases *most widely reported misapplication, fundamentally flawed,* and *a referee was insisting.*)

1. *The most widely reported misapplication of statistical power is in retrospective or post hoc power calculations [that] determine the power of a study after data has been collected and analyzed*

2. *It is well known that statistical power calculations can be valuable in planning an experiment. There is also a large literature advocating that power calculations be made whenever one performs a statistical test of a hypothesis and one obtains a statistically nonsignificant result. Advocates of such post-experiment power calculations claim the calculations should be used to aid in the interpretation of the experimental results. This approach, which appears in various forms, is fundamentally flawed.*

3. *Someone wrote in and was upset that a referee was insisting on post hoc power for all the outcome measures.... If a referee asks you to include a post hoc power calculation, just say no.*

Why This Misconception Is Dangerous

For obvious reasons, an applied researcher cannot create confidence intervals or test null hypotheses until data are gathered. Simply stated,

---

* Appendix B contains references for all quoted material presented in this section.

data collection must precede data analysis. Despite this fact, well-trained researchers think carefully, in the design phases of their studies, about the statistical procedures that will be applied once data gathering is complete. Such thinking typically takes the form of an a priori power analysis that indicates either (1) how large samples should be (in the situation where n is flexible) so as to have adequate power, or (2) whether the power for a fixed n is high enough to justify proceeding with the investigation.*

A power analysis can also be conducted in a post hoc sense, after a study's data have been gathered. The erroneous belief that this kind of power analysis is as good as one done in an a priori manner can lull one into thinking, incorrectly, that it's OK to forego considering power at the beginning of a study so long as one is willing to compute power at the end of the investigation. Such a thought is dangerous because the statistical notion of power is not the same within these two kinds of power analyses. Because of that, it's possible for a study to have high a priori power but low post hoc power.† Or, just the opposite is also possible!

Undoing the Misconception

In the planning stages of a study, researchers often ask, "How large should my study's sample(s) be?" A power analysis provides an answer to this query. First, the researcher must specify these five features about the planned statistical treatment of the yet-to-be-collected data:

- The specific statistical test that will be used to analyze the study's data

- The one-tailed or two-tailed option for testing the null hypothesis

- The selected level of significance

- The desired level of statistical power

- The effect size

These five items constitute the ingredients that go into the power analysis "recipe." What pops out is a clear and specific answer to the

---

* Statistical power is the probability of correctly rejecting a null hypothesis. Thus, power = $1 - \beta$, where β represents the probability of committing a Type II error.
† The terms *post hoc power, observed power,* and *retrospective power* mean the same thing.

sample size question.* Suppose, for example, that I am planning to conduct a two-tailed test of Pearson's r (in which H_o: $\rho = 0$) with α and power set equal to .05 and .90, respectively. Also, suppose I set the effect size set equal to ±.40. Given these items of input information, a power analysis would indicate that n needs to equal 58.

Sometimes a slightly different question is asked during the planning phase of the investigation. If the size of the researcher's sample(s) is predetermined due to the constraints of cost, time, access, or other considerations, the relevant question becomes: "What level of statistical power will there be if the study is conducted with the available sample size(s)?" In this situation, sample size and power switch sides in the power analysis equation, with sample size becoming one of the five pieces of input information and power being what's determined. In the example involving Pearson's r, suppose my sample size is fixed at 35. In this case, my study's power would be only .71. Knowing this, I would have three choices: (1) move forward with the study as planned, (2) modify the study in some fashion in order to increase power, or (3) put the investigation on the back burner.

In either form of these a priori power analyses, the effect size (ES) takes the form of a numerical value that divides possible nonnull situations into those that are considered trivial versus those that are noteworthy. The placement of this dividing line is purely a matter of opinion, and what one researcher chooses for ES may not be the same as what a different researcher might choose. In other words, the researcher doing the investigation is able to set ES however he or she sees fit.

In the example of the test on Pearson's r, I set ES equal to ±.40. This means that if the correlation in the population is not as strong as +.40, then it's my opinion that the correlation is too weak to be important. (With such a correlation, no more than 16% of the variability in one of the variables would be associated with variability in the other variable.) On the other hand, if ρ happens to have an absolute value of .40 or higher, then my ES decision indicates that any such correlation is important to me in some practical or theoretical fashion.

A post hoc power analysis is different from an a priori power analysis because the ES is different. In a power analysis that's conducted *prior* to the execution of the study, the ES takes the form of a judgment, or opinion, as to the dividing line between trivial and noteworthy deviations from the null hypothesis. In a power analysis conducted *after* the study's data have been gathered, the ES is a data-based index of the degree to which the data were found to deviate from H_o.

---

* For certain tests, such as a t-test involving one or two means, another needed ingredient for the power analysis is the variability that exists in the population(s).

Consider again the hypothetical study focused on Pearson's correlation wherein $n = 58$. Suppose that the data, once gathered, indicate that $r = .12$. With a correlation this size, the null hypothesis (H_o: $\rho = 0$) cannot be rejected because $t(56) = 0.905$, $p = .37$. If a post hoc power analysis is conducted to examine the correlation that was in the sample data, the power estimate turns out to be equal to approximately .15. This indicates that my t-test has about a 15% chance of rejecting the null hypothesis if ES = .12, that is, if the correlation in the population is equal to .12.

As this little example shows, a given study's power can be radically different depending on whether power is computed in an a priori or post hoc manner. Power means different things because ES is defined differently in the two kinds of power analysis. In one situation, ES represents a judgment call as to what kinds of statistical results possess practical significance. In the other situation, ES is an empirical measure of how extensively the gathered data deviate from the null hypothesis.

It should be noted that the purpose of an a priori power analysis is quite different from the purpose of a post hoc power analysis. In an a priori power analysis, the goal is to determine how to set up a study—with concern for n—so it has adequate sensitivity to detect meaningful deviations from H_o. In a post hoc power analysis, on the other hand, researchers try to determine whether power-related features of the study—such as sample size—were inadequate for bringing about a statistically significant finding. (The answer to this post hoc question is *always* affirmative, because the study would not have turned out as it did unless one or more aspects of the study were inadequate!)

Aware that an a priori power analysis is conceptually and computationally different from a post hoc power analysis, many statistical authorities recommend that applied researchers do the former but not the latter. Perhaps the main reason for this admonition can be illuminated by asking a simple question: If the features of a study need to be changed so as to cause the study to have adequate power, isn't it more logical to determine this before the study is conducted?

Internet Assignment

Would you like to test your understanding of how an a priori power analysis differs from a post hoc power analysis? Would you like to do this using an Internet-based Java applet that performs these two kinds of power analyses? Finally, would you like the applet to accommodate input information that takes the form of sample means, standard deviations, and n's (rather than raw scores)? If so, do this Internet assignment.

To start, go to this book's companion Web site (http://www.psy-press.com/statistical-misconceptions). Once there, open the folder for Chapter 11 and click on the link called "A Priori and Post Hoc Power." Then, follow the detailed instructions (prepared by this book's author) on how to use the Java applet. By doing this assignment, you will see clearly how a study's statistical power can be quite different depending on whether the power analysis is conducted before or after the study has been conducted. This assignment will also illuminate the fact that a study's effect size, like its power, can be conceptualized (and quantified) in either an a priori or post hoc manner.

☐ 11.3 Eta Squared and Partial Eta Squared

The Misconception

In a two-way or higher-order ANOVA, both eta squared and partial eta squared provide equally good estimates of effect size.

Evidence That This Misconception Exists*

The first of the following statements comes from a PowerPoint slide presentation given in a university course called Statistical Measures 2. The second statement comes from a peer-reviewed journal article in business. The third statement comes from an online discussion forum at Queen's University in Canada.

1. *Practically any effect size measure is better than none particularly when there is a non-significant result.*

2. *An experimental design highlights another complicating factor in deriving an effect size. Consider a study in which a researcher examined the effects of task variety (high vs. low) and performance feedback (specific vs. general) on job satisfaction. It is common for a researcher to report an effect size for each of the independent variables. In the study described, reporting an effect size such as d or η^2 could be misleading.*

3. *What SPSS reports as eta squared is really partial eta squared. Hence, researchers obtaining estimates of eta squared from SPSS are at risk of reporting incorrect values.*

Why This Misconception Is Dangerous

Because it is possible for a main or interaction effect to lack practical significance even though it turns out to be statistically significant, researchers in several disciplines now regularly compute estimates of effect size to accompany their ANOVA's F-tests. Many researchers are forced to do this. That's because many professional journals have a rule that says research reports will be considered for possible publication only if estimates of effect size have been computed.

---

* Appendix B contains references for all quoted material presented in this section.

Various procedures can be used to estimate effect size. Two of them—eta squared and partial eta squared—have similar sounding names, use the same "variance explained" notion of effect size, and have symbols (η^2 and η_p^2) that resemble each other. Moreover, the conventions for labeling an effect size as small, medium, or large are the same for both η^2 and η_p^2. (According to these conventions, values of .01, .06, and .14 are considered to be small, medium, and large effects, respectively.)

Despite their many similarities, η^2 and η_p^2 have different meanings and can lead to vastly different numerical values when computed from the same data. Therefore, those who mistakenly think that η^2 and η_p^2 are interchangeable will make an undisciplined choice as to which one to use. Or, they might use whichever one is included as output (perhaps never realizing that a choice existed). Either way, an effect might end up being tagged as "large" when it's really "small" (or vice versa).

Undoing the Misconception

For any main or interaction effect, eta squared is defined as the ratio of the sum of squares for that effect to the ANOVA's total sum of squares. Thus, $\eta^2 = SS_{effect} / SS_{total}$. Partial eta squared, for that same main or interaction effect, is defined as the ratio of the sum of squares for that effect to an adjusted total sum of squares that's composed of just two parts: (1) the sum of squares for the effect in question and (2) the sum of squares for error. Thus, $\eta_p^2 = SS_{effect} / (SS_{effect} + SS_{error})$.

In a one-way ANOVA, there will be no difference between η^2 and η_p^2 because the two denominators will be identical. In a two-way ANOVA, it is possible for η^2 and η_p^2 to be identical; however, this is unlikely to happen in any applied study. In order for these two measures of effect size to be the same, the sums of squares would need to equal 0 for both main effects and the interaction, or for one of the main effects and the interaction. Data yielding such results are found only in textbooks!

In the typical two-way ANOVA, the sums of squares for each main effect and for the interaction effect all turn out greater than 0. In this situation, η_p^2 will be larger than η^2. The degree to which these two indices of effect size are similar or different depends on two considerations: (1) the size of SS_{error} compared to SS_{total} and (2) the relative sizes of SS_A, SS_B, and $SS_{A \times B}$. The way these two forces impinge on η^2 and η_p^2 is illustrated in Table 11.3.1, which contains summary information from a hypothetical two-way ANOVA. Focus on the main effect of factor B, and

TABLE 11.3.1. Comparison of η^2 and η_p^2 in a Two-Way ANOVA

Source of Variation	df	SS Case 1	Case 2	Case 3	Case 4
A	4	0	12	54	39
B	1	4	4	4	2
A × B	4	0	8	26	43
Error	90	96	76	16	16
Total	99	100	100	100	100
Effect size for the B source	η^2	.04	.04	.04	.02
	η_p^2	.04	.05	.20	.11

note the values of η^2 and η_p^2 for the four cases. Case 1 illustrates the unlikely situation where η^2 and η_p^2 are identical. Cases 2 to 4 make it clear that η^2 and η_p^2 define "proportion of explained variability" differently. For η^2, it's the proportion of *all* variability explained by B. For η_p^2, on the other hand, it's the proportion of variability explained by B after discounting any variability associated with other effects.

Two features of eta squared and partial eta squared are worth noting. First, if η^2 is computed in a two-way ANOVA for each main effect, for the interaction, and for error, these four values necessarily sum 1.00. Thus, any one of the values of η^2 indicates how much of the total variability is associated with that particular source of variation. This is not the case with η_p^2. Using the data from case 3 in Table 11.3.1, the three values for η_p^2 are equal to .77, .04, and .62 for the two main effects and the interaction, respectively.

The second thing to note about η^2 and η_p^2 is that each of these measures is descriptive rather than inferential. In other words, eta squared and partial eta squared describe the proportion of data-based variability that's accounted for by each main effect and the interaction. If used in an inferential manner to estimate the proportion of explained variability in the populations represented by a study's samples, both η^2 and η_p^2 are positively biased. In other words, each of these measures will exaggerate the strength of effect that actually exists in the population. The amount of the bias, however, will be small so long as the sample sizes are large or the true effect size is large.

Internet Assignment

Would you like to see some convincing evidence that eta squared can be quite different from partial eta squared? Would you like this evidence to come from an Internet-based Java applet that performs a two-way analysis of variance? Finally, would you like the applet to accommodate raw data that you submit? If so, do this Internet assignment.

To start, go to this book's companion Web site (http://www.psy press.com/statistical-misconceptions). Once there, open the folder for Chapter 11 and click on the link called "Eta Squared and Partial Eta Squared." Then, follow the detailed instructions (prepared by this book's author) on how to use the Java applet. By doing this assignment, you will deepen your understanding of two popular variance-accounted-for measures of effect size that are used in conjunction with factorial ANOVAs. Moreover, you will acquire a small data set (for a 2 × 2 ANOVA) that you can provide to anyone who makes the claim that eta squared and partial eta squared are equivalent measures of effect size.

☐ Recommended Reading

Algina, J., Keselman, H. J., & Penfield, R. D. (2006). Confidence interval coverage for Cohen's effect size statistic. *Educational & Psychological Measurement, 66*(6), 945–960.

Feinberg, W. E. (1971). Teaching the type I and type II errors: The judicial process. *American Statistician, 25*(3), 30–32.

Hoenig, J. M., & Heisey, D. M. (2001). The abuse of power: The pervasive fallacy of power calculations in data analysis. *The American Statistician, 55*, 19–24.

Huberty, C. J. (2002). A history of effect size indices. *Educational & Psychological Measurement, 62*(2), 227–240.

Kraemer, H. C., Morgan, G. A., Leech, N. L., Gliner, J. A., Vaske, J. J., & Harmon, R. J. (2003). Measures of clinical significance. *Journal of the American Academy of Child and Adolescent Psychiatry, 42*(12), 1524–1529.

Lenth, R. V. (2001). Some practical guidelines for effective sample size determination. *The American Statistician, 55*(3), 187–193.

Lenth, R. V. (2007). *Post hoc power: Tables and commentary*. Technical report No. 378,. Department of Statistical and Actuarial Science, University of Iowa. Retrieved November 16, 2007, from http://www.stat.uiowa.edu/techrep/tr378.pdf.

Lochner, H. V., Bhandari, M., & Tornetta, P., III. (2001). Type-II error rates (beta errors) of randomized trials in orthopaedic trauma. *Journal of Bone & Joint Surgery, 83*(11), 1650–1655.

Nakagawa, S., & Cuthill, I. C. (2007). Effect size, confidence interval and statistical significance: A practical guide for biologists. *Biological Reviews, 82*(4), 591–605.

Nugent, W. R. (2006). The comparability of the standardized mean difference effect size across different measures of the same construct: Measurement considerations. *Educational & Psychological Measurement, 66*(4), 612–623.

Onwuegbuzie, A. J., Levin, J. R., & Leech, N. L. (2003). Do effect-size measures measure up? A brief assessment. *Learning Disabilities, 1*(1), 37–40.

Schmitz, C. C. (2007). *The ubiquitous p < .05: Practical versus statistical significance revisited*. Retrieved June 30, 2007, from http://www.facs.org/education/rap/schmitz0207.html.

Sohlberg, S., & Andersson, G. (2005). Extracting a maximum of useful information from statistical research data. *Scandinavian Journal of Psychology, 46*, 69–77.

Wilcox, R. R. (2006). Graphical methods for assessing effect size: Some alternatives to Cohen's d. *Journal of Experimental Education, 74*(4), 353–367.

Zumbo, B. D., & Hubley, A. M. (1998). A note on misconceptions concerning prospective and retrospective power. *Journal of the Royal Statistical Society, 47*(2), 385–388.

Regression

*One could further argue that multivariate modeling has increased the prevalence of statistical fallacies in biological inference. An example is the naive belief that product terms in a model correspond to or reflect biological interactions, such as synergy or antagonism.**

* Greenland, S. (1989). Modeling and variable selection in epidemiologic analysis. *American Journal of Public Health, 79,* 340–349.

☐ 12.1 Comparing Two *r*'s; Comparing Two *b*'s

The Misconception

If two independent samples have been measured on the same two variables, a test to see if the two correlation coefficients are significantly different from each other is equivalent to a test to see if the two regression coefficients are significantly different.

Evidence That This Misconception Exists*

The first of the following statements comes from a statistician's contribution to an online discussion group. The second statement comes from a PowerPoint presentation focused on regression.

1. *[A] whole lot of people do ask to compare two correlations when they ought to be asking to compare two regression coefficients or regression lines.*

2. *Comparing two regression equations can be accomplished with the correlation difference test. This is a statistical test to determine whether two correlation coefficients differ.*

Why This Misconception Is Dangerous

When data come from a single sample, a test to see if *r* is significantly different from zero is both logically and mathematically identical to a test to see if the regression coefficient, *b*, is significantly different from zero. Because of this equivalence, there is a temptation to expect the results of a comparison of the *r*'s from two independent samples to match the results of a comparison of the *b*'s from those same two samples. Though this "extrapolation" may seem reasonable, it is simply wrong and can lead to a misinterpretation of data.

There are times when a researcher ought to be concerned about both correlation coefficients and regression coefficients. For example, in the analysis of covariance, both *r* and *b* should be considered. Each group's *r*

---

* Appendix B contains references for all quoted material presented in this section.

is important, because the covariate's ability to reduce within-group variability is directly related to the within-group correlation between the covariate and dependent variable.* Just as the within-group r's should be homogenous, so too should the b's be similar. That's because one of ANCOVA's important assumptions is equality of regression coefficients across the populations that correspond to the study's comparison groups. In ANCOVA and other situations, this misconception might well encourage one to perform a formal test to compare r's but not b's, or to compare b's but not r's. As a consequence, further comparisons of the two groups may be made improperly.

Undoing the Misconception

As is well known, the value of r, when computed for a single set of data, is insensitive to the variability of the data on either the X or Y variable. In contrast, the value of b is influenced by the comparative variability in the two variables. Therefore, two independent samples can have identical r's but different b's, or the two samples can have identical b's but different r's. Logically, therefore, a statistical test that compares two r's is doing something different from a statistical test of the two b's.

If the preceding logic is not fully persuasive, then perhaps a look inside the two statistical procedures will do the trick. If the test for comparing r's were equivalent to the test for comparing b's, the procedures for computing the tests' calculated value ought to be similar. However, this is *not* the case.

To compare the r's from two independent samples, each r must first be transformed into a z-score using Fisher's r-to-z transformation. Then, the difference between these two z's is divided by the standard error of the difference, given by

$$\sqrt{\frac{1}{n_1 - 3} + \frac{1}{n_2 - 3}}$$

with the result compared against critical values from the normal distribution.

---

* Studies have shown that the population value of the within-group correlation should be equal to or larger than |.20|; otherwise, the covariate should be discarded with the data subjected to an ANOVA instead of to an ANCOVA.

To compare the b's from two independent samples, the raw differ-ence between the two b's is divided by the standard error of the differ-ence, given by

$$\sqrt{\left[\frac{1}{(n_1-1)s_{x1}^2}+\frac{1}{(n_2-1)s_{x2}^2}\right]\times\left[\frac{(n_1-2)s_{y1}^2(1-r_1^2)+(n_2-2)s_{y2}^2(1-r_2^2)}{n_1+n_2-4}\right]}$$

with the result compared against a critical value from a t distribution with n_1+n_2-4 degrees of freedom.*

Internet Assignment

Would you like to see some convincing evidence that a test comparing two beta coefficients is not equivalent to a test comparing two correlation coefficients? Would you like this evidence to be connected to a small set of data? Finally, would you like to see an Internet-based interactive Java applet that compares two r's (with the applet needing only information on the two r's and the two sample sizes)? If so, do this Internet assignment.

To start, go to this book's companion Web site (http://www.psy press.com/statistical-misconceptions). Once there, open the folder for Chapter 12 and click on the link called "Comparing Two r's; Comparing Two b's." Then, follow the detailed instructions (prepared by this book's author) on how to use the Java applet. By doing this assignment, you will see an example wherein the b's computed for two groups are signifi-cantly different from each other, whereas the two r's (computed from the same data) are almost identical. This assignment has a secondary benefit: It makes clear the fact that a statistical comparison of two r's involves a null hypothesis stating that the correlations in the two populations are equal (i.e., $H_o: \rho_1 = \rho_2$), and not a null hypothesis stating that each popula-tion correlation is equal to 0 (i.e., $H_o: \rho_1 = 0$ and $\rho_2 = 0$).

---

* This formula comes from Howell, D. C. (2007). *Statistical methods for psychology.* Belmont, CA: Thomson Wadsworth, p. 259.

☐ 12.2 R^2

The Misconception

If R^2 is high, this indicates that the regression model is good in explaining variance in the dependent variable.

Evidence That This Misconception Exists*

The first of the following statements comes from a message that a statistician posted to an online discussion group. The second statement comes from a peer-reviewed journal in medicine. The third statement comes from a textbook on advanced statistics. (In these passages, note the phrases *as it is commonly used, many who use these techniques,* and *far too many researchers.*)

1. *R^2 as it is commonly used is inflated due to overfitting.*

2. *Statistical models, such as linear or logistic regression or survival analysis, are frequently used as a means to answer scientific questions in psychosomatic research. Many who use these techniques, however, apparently fail to appreciate fully the problem of overfitting, i.e., capitalizing on the idiosyncrasies of the sample at hand.*

3. *Far too many investigators have abused multiple regression by "by throwing everything into the hopper," often merely because the variables are available.*

Why This Misconception Is Dangerous

In bivariate regression, the coefficient of determination, r^2, is frequently used as a measure of the strength of the association between the single independent variable (X) and the single dependent variable (Y). When converted from a decimal to a percentage, the result indicates the percentage of variability in the dependent variable that is explained by variability in the independent variable. Even if the correlation between the X and Y variables is tested and found to be statistically significant (with

---

* Appendix B contains references for all quoted material presented in this section.

$p < .05$), r^2 provides a better measure of predictability than does p, as the latter (but not the former) is affected by sample size.

In multiple regression, it is tempting to think of R^2 as the "purest" measure of how well the set of X variables predicts Y. Because R^2 will increase as additional X variables are entered into the model (so long as no pair of X variables is perfectly correlated), it might seem as though the best model should include as many predictor variables as possible. Doing this *will* maximize R^2. However, it creates simply the illusion of predictability. R^2 will be high when computed from the data used to build the regression model, but lower when computed from a different random sample drawn from the same population, especially when N is not much larger than the number of X's.

Undoing the Misconception

Multiple regression is a delicate statistical tool that can produce inaccurate results if not used with care. For example, data gathered with unreliable measuring instruments will make R^2 lower than it ought to be, and multicollinearity (caused by highly correlated independent variables) can cause regression weights to be untrustworthy. Another possible problem is created if an excess of X variables is used.

The problem of having too many X variables is referred to as *overfitting*. The notion here of "too many" is determined by comparing the number of X variables to N, the number of individuals from whom data are collected. As the number of X variables approaches N, the problem of overfitting rears its ugly head.

In Table 12.2.1, we see data for a group of people or objects measured on 10 independent variables and 1 dependent variable. These scores did not come from a real study. Instead, the data in each column were drawn randomly from a normally distributed population with mean = 0 and $SD = 1$.*

A hierarchical approach was used to analyze these data, with four X variables randomly selected to be control variables in step 1, followed by three randomly selected pairs of X's entered in steps 2 to 4.† With no restrictions on the X's as they entered the model, R^2 turned out equal .32 in step 1, .88 in step 2, .93 in step 3, and 1.00 in step 4.

Despite the fact that the data in Table 12.2.1 are random numbers (meaning that the population correlation between any two variables is 0.00), the multiple regression produced high values for R^2 in the second,

---

* These data were generated in Excel using the formula $f_x = $ SQRT(-2*LN(1-RAND()))*COS(RAND()*2*PI()).

† Predictor variables 6, 5, 3, and 4 were entered in step 1, followed by variables 1 and 2, 8 and 7, and 10 and 9 in steps 2, 3, and 4, respectively.

TABLE 12.2.1. Random Data on 10 X and 1 Y Variables

Person or Object	X_1	X_2	X_3	X_4	X_5	X_6	X_7	X_8	X_9	X_{10}	Y
A	.99	-.85	.51	-.09	-.20	-1.13	1.48	-1.21	-1.82	-.42	1.80
B	1.47	1.37	.54	-1.05	-1.47	-.96	.07	-1.65	-.49	.34	2.74
C	.38	.31	-.15	1.48	.95	-.11	.56	1.27	.47	-1.76	.44
D	-.34	-1.49	1.15	.70	-.07	-1.08	-1.57	.55	.14	-.18	-.47
E	-1.03	-.57	-1.67	.40	-.44	-.62	-1.56	1.43	-.96	-.63	-2.48
F	1.77	.49	-.43	-2.53	.70	-.05	-1.65	-1.47	.94	1.15	-1.20
G	1.23	-1.84	-.59	.42	.66	1.33	.89	1.41	.31	-.61	-.15
H	1.31	1.30	.53	.63	.92	-1.45	.64	2.08	.42	.45	.60
I	-.27	-1.44	1.07	-1.14	-.87	.52	-.39	-.89	1.11	-.47	.46
J	1.39	-.60	1.77	-1.13	.36	.85	-1.40	-1.76	-.12	-1.25	.58

third, and fourth steps of the hierarchical multiple regression. In step 4, R^2 turned out to be equal to 1.00. Thus, the full set of independent variables in this example explained 100% of the variance in the dependent variable. The reason behind this silly result is overfitting. The number of X variables was equal to N. Whenever this is the case, R^2 will turn out equal to 1.00.

The way to avoid overfitting, of course, is to make sure that N exceeds the number of independent variables. However, it's not good enough to have N be just slightly larger than the number of X variables. Instead, recommended rules-of-thumb say there should be a given number of cases for every X variable considered for inclusion in the regression model. Many statisticians assert that this ratio should be at least 20 to 1.

Is the problem of overfitting real? In other words, do applied researchers use multiple regression with N's that are too small relative to the number of independent variables? One pair of answers to these two questions comes from Michael Babyak—an authority on overfitting in regression analyses—who laments the fact that

> . . . [W]e have been overfitting models for years, in some cases, very badly. In some cases, this may be of little consequence. However, it is not hard to imagine that millions of research dollars and uncountable hours of work are spent each year chasing findings or ideas that arose from the failure to appreciate this concept more fully.*

Internet Assignment

Would you like to use an Internet-based interactive Java applet to compute R^2 for a small amount of data? Would you like to be the one who supplies the data that get analyzed? Finally, would you like to see what happens to the computed value of R^2 when you quickly enter data that are generated in your brain in a semirandom fashion? If so, do this assignment.

To start, go to this book's companion Web site (http://www.psypress. com/statistical-misconceptions). Once there, open the folder for Chapter 12 and click on the link called "R^2." Then, follow the detailed instructions (prepared by this book's author) on how to use the Java applet. By doing this assignment, you will understand why R^2 can sometimes be a misleading summary statistic in a multiple regression study. This assignment will also allow you to see a perfect example of overfitting.

---

* Babyak, M. (2004). What you see may not be what you get: A brief, nontechnical introduction to overfitting in regression-type models. *Psychosomatic Medicine, 66*, 411–421.

□ 12.3 Predictor Variables That Are Uncorrelated With *Y*

The Misconception

In multiple regression, an independent variable that is uncorrelated with the dependent variable ought to be left out of the model because its inclusion won't help to make R^2 larger.

Evidence That This Misconception Exists*

The first of the following statements comes from a peer-reviewed journal in higher education. The second comes from a paper presented at a professional conference. The third comes from a peer-reviewed journal dealing with advanced statistics. (In these passages, note the phrases *often overlooked*, *many researchers*, and *on a regular basis*.)

1. *Often, suppressor variables [i.e., predictor variables that have a low correlation with the criterion] are viewed as unfavorable attributes of regression models ... [and] are often overlooked in favor of reporting only positive, best predictors.... Yet, suppressor variables can tell us a lot ... and have the ability to alter research results dramatically.*

2. *Understanding suppressor variables, and how they operate in multiple regression analyses is crucial in reporting accurate research results. However, many researchers are unfamiliar with the influences and importance of these variables.*

3. *Researchers may overlook suppressor effects on a regular basis because of the algorithm typically employed for selecting variables in standard regression programs.*

Why This Misconception Is Dangerous

Multiple regression can address a variety of different research questions. In one of its uses, the goal is to identify the best set of independent (i.e.,

---

* Appendix B contains references for all quoted material presented in this section.

predictor) variables that collectively can explain variability in a dependent (i.e., criterion) variable. When used for this purpose, the multiple correlation coefficient, R, is first computed, for this summary of the data is conceptually and statistically equal to the bivariate correlation between the criterion variable and a linear composite of the predictor variables. Then, the multiple correlation coefficient is squared, with R^2 indicating the proportion of variability in the dependent variable that's been explained by the set of independent variables.

An important task for a researcher using multiple regression is setting up the "model." In doing this, decisions must be made as to which potential independent variables will and won't be included as predictors. If such decisions are made by looking only at the bivariate correlation between each independent variable and the dependent variable, the end result might be a model that falls short of its potential. That's because it's possible for a predictor variable that doesn't look very useful on its own—because it has a low (or even a zero) correlation with the dependent variable—to actually increase R^2 if other predictors are included in the model.

Undoing the Misconception

The term *suppressor variable* denotes an independent variable that helps to increase R^2 even though it has a low correlation with the dependent variable. Such a variable makes a contribution because it suppresses (i.e., reduces) the error variance that's "in" the other independent variable(s), thus permitting the full set of independent variables to work better than would be the case if the suppressor variable is kept out of the model.

A Venn diagram may be helpful in illustrating the way a suppressor variable works. In Figure 12.3.1, there are three circles, two for independent variables (X_1 and X_2) and one for the dependent variable (Y). In such diagrams, the area within each circle corresponds to the variability among the scores on that circle's variable, and the overlap between two circles corresponds to $r^2 \times 100$, the percentage of variability in one of the two circles that's associated with variability in the other circle.

In Figure 12.3.1, the circles for X_1 and Y overlap, indicating that X_1 explains a portion of the variability in the dependent variable. It looks like approximately 25% of Y's variability is explained by the first independent variable. In contrast, the second independent variable is not correlated at all with Y. However, X_1 and X_2 are related. Within the

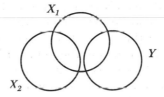

FIGURE 12.3.1 Illustration of a suppressor variable.

context of multiple regression, X_2 is not a worthless independent variable. That's because it helps to explain (i.e., account for) error variance in X_1. By "eliminating" extraneous variability in X_1, X_2 functions to increase R^2 above the level attainable by using just the first independent variable.*

It should be noted that different kinds of suppression can occur in multiple regression, depending on the sign and size of the bivariate correlations and the standardized regression coefficients. The kind illustrated in Figure 12.3.1 is called *classical suppression* because the second independent variable and the dependent variable are fully independent (i.e., completely uncorrelated). Other situations involve independent variables that create *net suppression* and *cooperative suppression*.[†]

Internet Assignment

Would you like to see some convincing evidence that a predictor variable can help in the prediction effort even though it (i.e., the predictor variable) is uncorrelated with the criterion variable? Would you like this evidence to come from an Internet-based interactive Java applet? Finally, would you like to have a simple regression model (and easy-to-follow results) so you can easily determine if the prediction is improved because a seemingly worthless predictor is included in the model? If so, do this assignment.

---

* A description of a suppressor variable functioning within the context of a "real-world" situation is presented in: Meyers, L. S., Gamst, G., & Guarino, A. J. (2005). *Applied multivariate research: Design and interpretation* (pp. 182–184). Thousand Oaks, CA: Sage.

† These two kinds of suppression occur when an independent variable has a non-zero correlation with the dependent variable. With net suppression, the sign of the bivariate r differs from the sign of the independent variable's beta weight; with cooperative suppression, the sign of r matches the sign of the beta weight.

To start, go to this book's companion Web site (http://www.psy press.com/statistical-misconceptions). Once there, open the folder for Chapter 12 and click on the link called "Predictor Variables That Are Uncorrelated With Y." Then, follow the detailed instructions (prepared by this book's author) on how to use the Java applet. By doing this assignment, you will deepen your understanding of the "inner workings" of multiple regression. You will also see a suppressor variable in action.

☐ 12.4 Beta Weights

The Misconception

When multiple regression is used to predict scores on a criterion variable, the worth of a particular predictor variable is indicated by that variable's estimated beta weight (i.e., its standardized regression coefficient).

Evidence That This Misconception Exists*

The first of the following statements comes from a book published by the Harvard University Press. The second comes from a master's thesis. (Note the final sentence in the first passage. In the second passage, note how the final sentence differs from the others in that it is neither past tense in nature nor tied to the model that produced the standardized regression coefficient of .44.)

1. *The result of a multiple regression analysis can be expressed as a linear equation in which the value of the target [dependent] variable is predicted from a weighted sum of the predictor variables. Regression techniques select a set of beta weights for each variable that permit the best prediction. Roughly speaking, the greater the beta weight associated with each independent (predictor) variable, the greater its predictive value.*

2. *After controlling for the demographic variables, the model accounted for 27% of the variance in perceived racism (F(4,86) = 8.29, p < .001). Thus, both the Assimilation (β = .49, p < .05) and the Asian Sociopolitical Awareness (β = .44, p < .001) proved to be good predictors of perceived racism (see Table 8 [not included here]). More specifically, the more assimilated the individuals were to U.S. society the more racism they perceived and the more they were aware of Asian specific injustices in the society [the] more likely they were to perceive racism . . . Clearly, Asian specific Sociopolitical Awareness is a good predictor of perceived racism.*

---

* Appendix B contains references for all quoted material presented in this section.

Why This Misconception Is Dangerous

Multiple regression is often used to shed light on the relationship between predictor (i.e., independent) variables, on the one hand, and a criterion (i.e., outcome) variable, on the other. In studies wherein multiple regression is used for this purpose, researchers often focus their attention on the individual predictor variables, with two questions often being of primary interest: (1) Which predictor variable(s) should be left in the model? (2) Within the final model that's created, which predictor variable is the best predictor in the sense that it contributes most to explaining variability in the outcome variable?

A predictor variable's standardized regression coefficient $\hat{\beta}$ is often looked upon as the main indicator of an independent variable's predictive worth. However, an estimated β can be misleading as to the true value of a given predictor variable. What appear to be the best and worst predictors may be just the reverse! Or, perhaps the best predictor does not show up at all!

Undoing the Misconception

Beta weights can be interpreted properly only if we restrict our thoughts to (1) the type of individuals from whom data were gathered, (2) the measuring instruments used to generate the data, and (3) the specific variables that were included in the model that produced the beta weights being examined. Change any of these three things, and the beta weight might also change. Although the populations sampled and instrument quality are highly important issues in their own right, we will focus here only on the issue of beta weights and models.

In a very real sense, the strength (i.e., worth) of a beta weight is like the strength of an ingredient that's included in a recipe for chili. Onions will play a prominent role in affecting how the end product tastes if the other ingredients—especially the beans and spices—are mild. However, add in a double dose of chili powder or use extra hot beans, and the impact of the onions is dramatically reduced. It's the same situation with multiple regression. Add a new predictor variable to the mix, and what seemed strong or weak to begin with can take on a new level of importance within the expanded model.

Let's shift our focus from analogies to formulas. If a multiple regression is conducted using a single predictor variable, that predictor's estimated beta weight is equal to the correlation between X and Y. In other words, $\hat{\beta} = r$. If we change the model by adding in a second predictor variable, the beta weight for that first predictor variable is likely to change. That's because

$$\hat{\beta}_1 = \frac{r_{Y1} - (r_{Y2})(r_{12})}{1 - (r_{12}^2)}$$

where the subscripts 1, 2, and Y represent the first predictor variable, second predictor variable, and dependent variable, respectively. Clearly, the first predictor's $\hat{\beta}$ will be different from r_{Y1}—its value when no other predictor variables are used—unless the second predictor variable is uncorrelated with the first predictor variable.

The term *bouncing betas* is sometimes used to describe the fact that a predictor variable's estimated beta weight is highly likely to change as other predictor variables are added to or deleted from the regression model. Because of this instability of estimated beta weights across different models, it is important that any $\hat{\beta}$ be interpreted relative to the specific model that produced it. Thus, an estimated beta weight is like a conditional probability in the sense that there's an important "given" element that affects the result. With estimated beta weights, the interpretation should always be $\hat{\beta}$|model. This point has been made nicely by L. S. Meyers:

> Another concern regarding using beta coefficients to evaluate predictors is that beta weight values are partly a function of the correlations between the predictors themselves. That is, a certain independent variable may predict the dependent variable to a great extent in isolation, and one would therefore expect to see a relatively high beta coefficient associated with that predictor. Now place another predictor that is highly correlated with the first predictor into the analysis and all of a sudden the beta coefficients of both predictors can plummet. The first predictor's relationship with the dependent variable has not changed in this scenario, but the presence of the second correlated predictor could seriously affect the magnitude of the beta weight of the first. This "sensitivity" of the beta weights to the correlations between the predictors, reflected in the beta values, places additional limitations on the generality of the betas and thus their use in evaluating or comparing predictive effectiveness of the independent variables.*

* Meyers, L. S., Gamst, G., & Guarino, A. J. (2005). *Applied multivariate research: Design and interpretation* (pp. 168–169). Thousand Oaks, CA: Sage.

Internet Assignment

Would you like to see some proof that a predictor variable's beta weight is "context dependent" in the sense that its value depends on the other predictor variables included in the model? Would you like this proof to come in the form of the results that come from analyzing data? Finally, would you like the analysis to be conducted by means of an Internet-based interactive Java applet? If so, do this assignment.

To start, go to this book's companion Web site (http://www.psy press.com/statistical-misconceptions). Once there, open the folder for Chapter 12 and click on the link called "Beta Weights." Then, follow the detailed instructions (prepared by this book's author) on how to use the Java applet. By doing this assignment, you will be able to watch what happens to the beta weight for a particular predictor variable when other predictor variables are added to the model. You may be surprised by the degree to which changes occur in the relative worth of the predictor variables.

☐ Recommended Reading

Allison, P. D. (1999). *Multiple regression—A primer*. Thousand Oaks, CA: Pine Forge Press.

Babyak, M. A. (2004). What you see may not be what you get: A brief, non-technical introduction to overfitting in regression-type models. *Psychosomatic Medicine, 66*, 411–421.

Berger, D. E. (n.d.). *Introduction to multiple regression*. Retrieved November 3, 2007, from http://wise.cgu.edu/downloads/Regression.doc.

Currie, I., & Korabinski, A. (1984). Some comments on bivariate regression. *The Statistician, 33*(3), 283–293.

Friedman, L., & Wall, M. (2005). Graphical views of suppression and multicollinearity in multiple linear regression. *American Statistician, 59*(2), 127–136.

Henard, D. H. (1998). *Suppressor variable effects: Toward understanding an elusive data dynamic*. Paper presented at the annual meeting of the Southwest Educational Research Association, Houston, TX.

Ip, E. H. S. (2000). Visualizing multiple regression. *Journal of Statistics Education, 9(1)*. Retrieved November 3, 2007, from http://www.amstat.org/publications/jsc/v9n1/ip.html.

Krus, D. J., & Wilkinson, S. M. (1986). Demonstration of properties of a suppressor variable. *Behavior Research Methods, Instruments, and Computers, 18*, 21–24.

Meehl, P. E. (1945). A simple algebraic development of Horst's suppressor variables. *American Journal of Psychology, 58*(4), 550–554.

Osborne, J., & Elaine, W. (2002). Four assumptions of multiple regression that researchers should always test. *Practical Assessment, Research & Evaluation, 8*(2). Retrieved May 27, 2007, from http://PAREonline.net/getvn.asp?v=8&n=2

Pickering, A. (2005). Comparing correlations and regressions. Retrieved November 6, 2007, from http://homepages.gold.ac.uk/aphome/correlnotes.doc.

Shieh, G. (2006). Suppression situations in multiple linear regression. *Educational & Psychological Measurement, 66*(3), 435–447.

Smith, R. L., & Ager, J. (1992). Suppressor variables in multiple regression/correlation. *Educational & Psychological Measurement, 52*(1), 17–29.

Vaughan, T. S., & Berry, K. E. (2005). Using Monte Carlo techniques to demonstrate the meaning and implications of multicollinearity. *Journal of Statistics Education, 13(1)*. Retrieved November 3, 2007, from http://www.amstat.org/publications/jse/v13n1/vaughan.html.

Whitlock, M. (n.d.). Comparing two regression slopes. In *Tests of relationships between numerical variables*. Retrieved November 3, 2007, from http://www.zoology.ubc.ca/~whitlock/bio300/LectureNotes/Regression/Regression.html

Woolley, K. K. (1997). *How variables uncorrelated with the dependent variable can actually make excellent predictors: The important suppressor variable case*. Paper presented at the annual meeting of the Southwest Educational Research Association, Austin, TX.

APPENDIX A: CITATIONS FOR MATERIAL REFERENCED IN THE PREFACE

Batancro, C., Godino, J. D., Vallecillos, A., Green, D. R., & Holmes, P. (1994). Errors and difficulties in understanding elementary statistical concepts. *Journal of Mathematics Education in Science and Technology, 25*(4), 527–547.

Callaert, H. (2002). *Understanding statistical misconceptions*. Paper presented at the 6th International Conference on Teaching Statistics. Retrieved May 2, 2007, from http://www.stat.auckland.ac.nz/~iase/publications/1/10_07_ca.pdf.

Cumming, G., & Thomason, N. (1998). *StatPlay*. Retrieved April 28, 2008, from http://www.latrobe.edu.au/psy/cumming/statplay.html.

Garfield, J. B. (1995). How students learn statistics. *International Statistics Review, 63*, 25–34.

Liu, T., Kinshuk, D., Wang, S., Lin, Y., Lin, O., & Chang, M. (2007). The effects of students' cognitive styles upon applying computer multimedia to change statistical misconceptions. In G. Richards (Ed.), *Proceedings of World Conference on E-Learning in Corporate, Government, Healthcare, and Higher Education 2007* (pp. 6242–6245). Chesapeake, VA: AACE.

Mevareck, Z. R. (1983). A deep structure model of students' statistical misconceptions. *Educational Studies in Mathematics, 14*, 415–429.

Misconception. In *Oxford English Dictionary*. Oxford University Press. Retrieved May 2, 2008, from http://www.oed.com.

Morris, E. (2001). The design and evaluation of Link: A computer-based learning system for correlation. *British Journal of Educational Technology, 32*(1), 39–52.

APPENDIX B: REFERENCES FOR QUOTATIONS PRESENTED IN THE SECTIONS ENTITLED "EVIDENCE THAT THIS MISCONCEPTION EXISTS"

1.1 Measures of Central Tendency

(1) Karlik, S. J. (2002, July 9). Exploring and summarizing radiologic data. In *Fundamentals of clinical research for radiologists*. Retrieved October 25, 2007, from http://www.ajronline.org/cgi/content/full/180/1/47.

(2) Benbow, D. W., Elshennawy, A. K., & Walker, H. F. (2003). *The certified quality technician handbook*. Milwaukee, WI: American Society for Quality Press, p. 25.

(3) U.S. Department of State: Office of English Language Programs. (n.d.). *Statistics and research design: Essential concepts for working teachers*. Retrieved November 5, 2007, from http://exchanges.state.gov/forum/vols/vol39/no3/p36.htm.

1.2 The Mean of Means

(1) Lann, A., & Falk, R. (2005). A closer look at a relatively neglected mean. *Teaching Statistics*, 27(3), 79.

(2) Leavy, A., & O'Loughlin, N. (2006). Preservice teachers' understanding of the mean: Moving beyond the arithmetic average. *Journal of Mathematics Teacher Education*, 9, 53–90, pp. 53, 71.

1.3   The Mode's Location

(1) Burt, J. E., & Barber, G. M. (1996). *Elementary statistics for geographers* (2nd ed., p. 43). New York: Guilford Press, p. 43.
(2) Mason, J. (2004). *Concepts in dental public health* (p. 237). London: Lippincott, Williams & Wilkins.
(3) Back, M. (2003). *Statistics in HCI* (slide 21). Retrieved August 23, 2007, from http://www.eecs.berkeley.edu/Research/Projects/CS/io/courses/cs160/fall2003/lectures_files/Statistics_in_HCI.ppt#21.

1.4   The Standard Deviation

(1) Cramer, C., & Howitt, D. (2004). *The Sage dictionary of statistics*. Thousand Oaks, CA: Sage.
(2) *Antarctic explorers*. Retrieved November 2, 2007, from http://tea.armadaproject.org/geelan/10.17.1997.html.

2.1   The Shape of the Normal Curve

(1) Coon, D. (2005). *Psychology: A modular approach to mind and behavior* (10th ed., p. 681). Belmont, CA: Thomson Wadsworth.
(2) Kaps, M., & Lamberson, W. R. (2004). *Biostatistics for animal science* Oxfordshire, UK: CABI Publishing, p. 37.
(3) Lauer, P. A. (2004). *A policy-maker's primer on educational research*. Mid-continent Research for Education and Learning and the Education Commission of the states. Retrieved June 22, 2007, from http://www.ecs.org/html/educationIssues/Research/primer/understandingtutorial.asp.

2.2   Skewed Distributions and Measures of Central Tendency

(1) Levin, J., & Fox, J. A. (2003). *Elementary statistics in social research* (9th ed., p. 85). Boston: Allyn and Bacon.
(2) *Measures of central tendency: Mean, median, & mode*. Retrieved October 30, 2007, from http://simon.cs.vt.edu/SoSci/converted/MMM/activity.html.

2.3   Standard Scores and Normality

(1) Yngve, A., De Bourdeaudhuij, I., Wolf, A., Grjibovski, A., Brug, J., Due, P., Ehrenblad, B., Elmadfa, I., Franchini, B., Klepp, K., Poortvliet, E., Rasmussen, M., Thorsdottir, I., & Rodrigo, C. P. (2007). Differences in prevalence of overweight and stunting in 11-year olds across Europe: The Pro Children Study. *European Journal of Public Health, 1–5,* p. 2. Retrieved November 17, 2007, from http://eurpub.oxfordjournals.org/cgi/reprint/ckm099vl.

(2) McCauley, R. J. (2001). *Assessment of language disorders in children* Mahwah, NJ: Lawrence Erlbaum Associates, p. 37.

(3) *Appendix D: Basic measurement and statistics.* (2005). Retrieved on November 1, 2007, from http://www.aapmr.org/zdocs/resident/appendix_ d.pdf.

2.4   Rectangular Distributions and Kurtosis

(1) *Measures of skewness and kurtosis.* (n.d.). Retrieved October 25, 2007, from http://www.itl.nist.gov/div898/handbook/eda/section3/eda35b.htm.

(2) Zijlstra, W. (2004). *Comparing the Student's t and the ANOVA contrast procedure with five alternative procedures.* Retrieved on September 28, 2007, from http://www.ppsw.rug.nl/~kiers/ReportZijlstra.pdf.

3.1   Correlation Coefficients

(1) Nairne, J. S. (2006). *Psychology.* Belmont, CA: Wadsworth, p. 41.

(2) Lewer, R. (2005). *Sheep breeding: Genetic and phenotypic correlations.* State of Western Australia. Retrieved October 25, 2007, from http://www.agric. wa.gov.au/content/AAP/SL/BGH/FN056_1993.PDF.

(3) Carey, G. (2000). *Human genetics for the social sciences.* Thousand Oaks, CA: Sage. Chapter 17, p. 4.

3.2   Correlation and Causality

(1) MacKenzie, D. (2006). Comment posted on Mises.org Weblog. Retrieved October 25, 2007, from http://blog.mises.org/archives/004987.asp.

(2) Tox-ga. (2004). *Correlation does not equate to causation.* Retrieved October 4, 2007, from http://answers.google.com/answers/threadview?id=368317.

(3) Dill, K. (2007). *Professor Tietbohl where are you?* Retrieved November 7, 2007, from http://lowcarbhit.blogspot.com/.

3.3   The Effect of a Single Outlier on *r*

(1) University of Alberta. (n.d.). Brief version of the case study. In *Sex discrimination problem* (chap. 14). Retrieved October 25, 2007, from http://www.stat.ualberta.ca/people/kolacz/stat252/sexmu14.pdf.

(2) Question 14. Retrieved September 26, 2007, from http://www.math.wisc.edu/~meyer/math141/practice2.pdf.

3.4   Relationship Strength and *r*

(1) Hatcher, L. (2003). *Step-by-step basic statistics using SAS: Student guide* Cary, NC: SAS Publishing, p. 295.

(2) Gunder, H., Schott, J., & Turner, J. (2006). *Faith & environmentalism among United Methodists in Appalachia: Investigating Christian environmental ethics & promoting environmental care in the Holston Conference of the United Methodist Church.* Retrieved November 2, 2007, from http://sambuca.umdl.umich.edu:8080/bitstream/2027.42/35329/2/snre4.17.06.pdf.

3.5   The Meaning of *r* = 0

(1) StatPac, Inc. (n.d.). *Correlation and regression.* Retrieved October 25, 2007, from http://www.statpac.com/statistics-calculator/correlation-regression.htm.

(2) Randolph, C. A. (2007). *Correlation explained.* Inver Hills Community College, MN: Inver Grove Heights.

(3) Lab Instructions: El Niño. (n.d.). Retrieved September 8, 2007, from http://www.ldeo.columbia.edu/~martins/climate_water/labs/lab4/labinstr4.html.

(4) United Kingdom Government Social Research Unit. (2007). What do the statistics tell me? Statistical concepts, inference & analysis. *Magenta book: Guidance notes on policy evaluation.* Retrieved on August 8, 2007, from http://www.policyhub.gov.uk/evaluating_policy/magenta_book/chapter4.asp.

4.1   Statistical Indices of Reliability and Validity

(1) Barbarin, O. A. (2007). Mental health screening of preschool children: Validity and reliability of ABLE. *American Journal of Orthopsychiatry, 77*(3), 402–418, 402.

(2) Hides, L., Dawe, S., Young, R. McD., & Kavanagh, D. J. (2006). The reliability and validity of the Severity of Dependence Scale for detecting cannabis dependence in psychosis. *Addiction, 102,* 35–40.

4.2   Interrater Reliability

(1) Goodwin, L. D. (2001). Interrater agreement and reliability. *Measurement in Physical Education and Exercise Science, 5*(1), 13–34, 15.

(2) Stemler, S. E. (2004). A comparison of consensus, consistency, and measurement approaches to estimating interrater reliability. *Practical Assessment, Research & Evaluation, 9*(4). Retrieved November 12, 2007 from http://PAREonline.net/getvn.asp?v=9&n=4.

4.3   Cronbach's Alpha and Unidimensionality

(1) UCLA Academic Technology Services. (n.d.). What does Cronbach's alpha mean? In *SPSS FAQ*. Retrieved October 25, 2007, from http://www.ats. ucla.edu/STAT/SPSS/faq/alpha.html.

(2) Randolph, C. A. (2007). *Correlation explained*. Inver Hills Community College, MN: Inver Grove Heights.

(3) Morelock, L. T. (2007). A primer on classification and examination administration. *The System News, 5*(2), 2. Retrieved November 4, 2007, from http://www.sucss.state.il.us/documents/newsletter/v5i2.pdf.

4.4   Range Restriction and Predictive Validity

(1) Emery, J. L. (2007, February 26). *A report on the predictive validity of the BMAT (2004) for 1st year examination performance on the veterinary medicine course at the University of Cambridge*. Retrieved October 25, 2007, from http://www. bmat.org.uk/downloads/BMAT%202004%20predictive%20validity%20 report%20–%20Cambridge%20vets%20(26-02-07).pdf.

(2) Valencia, R. R., & Suzuki, L. A. (2000). *Intelligence testing and minority students* (p. 91). Thousand Oaks, CA: Sage.

(3) Simon, S. (n.d.). *Correlation coefficients*. Retrieved on June 22, 2007, from http://www.childrens-mercy.org/stats/definitions/correlation.htm.

5.1   The Binomial Distribution and N

(1) Lane, D. M. (2007). Independence (4 of 5). In *Hyperstat online statistics textbook*. Retrieved October 25, 2007, from http://davidmlane.com/ hyperstat/A126335.html.

(2) Tijms, H. C. (2004) *Understanding probability: Chance rules in everyday life* (p. 24). Cambridge, UK: Cambridge University Press.

5.2   A Random Walk With a Perfectly Fair Coin

(1) Norstad, J. (2006, September 1). *Mean reversion, forecasting and market timing.* Retrieved October 25, 2007, from http://homepage.mac.com/j.norstad/finance/rtm-and-forecasting.html.

(2) Meyr, H., & Popken, L. (1980). Phase acquisition statistics for phase-locked loops. *IEEE Transaction on Communications, 28,* 1365–1372.

5.3   Two Goats and a Car

(1) Wu, W. (2005, February 18). *Riddles.* Retrieved October 25, 2007, from http://www.ocf.berkeley.edu/~wwu/riddles/easy.shtml.

(2) Krauss, S. (2003). *Some issues of teaching statistical thinking.* Unpublished Ph.D. dissertation, Fachbereich Erziehungswissenschaft und Psychologie, Freie Universität Berlin, p. 41.

(3) Kaplan, J. J. (2006). *Factors in statistics learning: Developing a dispositional attribution model to describe differences in the development of statistical proficiency* Unpublished doctoral dissertation, University of Texas, Austin, pp. 68–69.

5.4   Identical Birthdays

(1) Dooren, W. V., Bock, D. D., Depaepe, F., Janssen, D., & Verschaffel, L. (2003). The illusion of linearity: Expanding the evidence towards probabilistic reasoning. *Educational Studies in Mathematics, 53*(2), 113–138, p. 118.

(2) *Birthday paradox* (lab). Retrieved October 25, 2007, from http://cs.wellesley.edu/~cs199/lectures/09-birthday.html.

(3) Białynicki-Birula, I., & Białynicki-Birula, I. (2004). *Modeling realit.* Oxford: Oxford University Press, p. 24.

5.5   The Sum of an Infinite Number of Numbers

(1) Bagni, G. T. (2005). Infinite series from history to mathematics education. *International Journal for Mathematics Teaching and Learning.* Retrieved October 25, 2007, from http://www.cimt.plymouth.ac.uk/journal/bagni.pdf.

(2) *Zeno's paradox and other musings.* (n.d.). Retrieved October 19, 2007, from http://www.fastcoder.net/~thumper/info/zeno/.

5.6   Being Diagnosed With a Rare Disease

(1) Paulus, J. A. (1994). Counting on dyscalculia—The unreliability of health statistics. *Discover, 15*(3), 30–36.

(2) Shaughnessy, J. M. (2006). Research in probability and statistics: Reflections and directions. In Grouws, D. A. (Ed.), *Handbook of research on mathematics teaching and learning* (p. 474). Reston, VA: National Council of Teachers of Mathematics.

(3) Tijms, H. C. (2004). *Understanding probability: Chance rules in everyday life* (p. 222). Cambridge, UK: Cambridge University Press.

5.7   Risk Ratios and Odds Ratios

(1) Holcomb, W. L., Chaiworapongsa, T., Luke, D. A., & Burgdorf, K. D. (2001). An odd measure of risk: Use and misuse of the odds ratio. *Obstetrics & Gynecology, 98*, 685–688, 686.

(2) Newman, T. B., & Kohn, M. A. (2007). *Quantifying treatment effects using randomized blind trials* (chap. 9). Retrieved November 10, 2007, from http://209.85.165.104/search?q=cache:0dj4zOv-IrkJ:rds.epi-ucsf.org/ticr/syllabus/courses/4/2007/11/01/Lecture/readings/9_Quantifying TreatmentEffects.doc+%22Mistaking+the+odds+ratio+for+a+risk+ratio%22&hl=en&ct=clnk&cd=1&gl=us.

(3) Feinstein, A. R. (2001). *Principles of medical statistics* (p. 338). London: CRC Press.

6.1   The Character of Random Samples

(1) Canadian Public Service Agency (2000, October 18). *Demographic analysis of the Federal Public Service workforce—Basic statistics.* Retrieved October 25, 2007, from http://www.psagency-agencefp.gc.ca/hr-rh/psds-dfps/dafps_basic_stat1_e.asp#H.

(2) *Sampling* (chap. 19, slides 6 and 23). Retrieved October 16, 2007, from http://www.stat.washington.edu/handcock/220/handouts/Chapter19.pdf

(3) Woodbury, G. (n.d.). *Sample and population.* Retrieved November 14, 2007, from http://infinity.cos.edu/faculty/woodbury/Stats/Tutorial/Data_Pop_Samp.htm.

6.2   Random Replacements When Sampling

(1) Wallen, N. E., & Fraenkel, J. R. (2001). *Educational research* (2nd ed., p. 118). Mahwah, NJ: Lawrence Erlbaum Associates.

(2) Pita, D. D., Ellison, M. L., Farkas, M., and Bleecker, T. (2001). Exploring personal assistance services for people with psychiatric disabilities: Need, policy, and practice. *Journal of Disability Policy Studies, 12,* 2–9, 6.

(3) Sherraden, M., McBride, A. M., Johnson, E., Hanson, S., Ssewamala, F. M., & Shanks, T. R. (2005). *Saving in low-income households: Evidence from interviews with participants in the American Dream Demonstration.* Center for Social Development, Washington University in Saint Louis, p. 5.

6.3   Precision and the Sampling Fraction

(1) Sarker, R. A., Newton, C. S., & Abbass, H. A. (2002). *Heuristic and optimization for knowledge discovery*...Hershey, PA: IGI Publishing, p. 125.

(2) Baldwin, J. A. *Statistical considerations for agroforestry studies.* USDA General Services Technical Report PSW-GTR-140. Retrieved September 18, 2007, from http://www.fs.fed.us/psw/publications/documents/psw_gtr140/psw_gtr140_baldwin.pdf.

(2) Finkelstein, M., &. Levin, B. A. (2001). *Statistics for lawyers* (2nd ed., p. 261). New York: Springer, p. 261.

6.4   Matched Samples

(1) Edgar, J. C., Keller, J., Heller, W., & Miller, G. A. (2007). Psychophysiology in research on psychopathology. In Cacioppo, J. T., Tassinary, L. G., & Berntson, G. G. (Eds.), *Handbook of psychophysiology.* Cambridge, UK: Cambridge University Press, p. 677.

(2) Slavin, R. E., & Lake, C. (2007). *Effective programs in elementary mathematics: A best-evidence synthesis* (pp. 6, 32). Retrieved September 18, 2008 from http://www.bestevidence.org/_images/word_docs/eff_prog_elem_math_v1.2.pdf.

(3) Weeks, D. L. (2007). The regression effect as a neglected source of bias in nonrandomized intervention trials and systematic reviews of observational studies. *Evaluation & the Health Professions, 30*(3), 254–265, 254.

6.5   Finite Versus Infinite Populations

Yu, C. H. (n.d.). *Misconceived relationships among sample, sampling distribution, and population.* Retrieved October 25, 2007, from http://www.creative-wisdom.com/computer/sas/parametric.html.

7.1   Interpreting a Confidence Interval

(1) Hayward Medical Communications. (2007). *What are confidence intervals?* Retrieved October 25, 2007, from http://www.jr2.ox.ac.uk/bandolier/ painres/download/whatis/What_are_Conf_Inter.pdf.

(2) Glenberg, A. M. (1996). *Data: An introduction to statistical reasoning.* Mahwah, NJ: Lawrence Erlbaum Associates, p. 205.

7.2   Overlapping Confidence Intervals

(1) DiStefano, D., Fidler, F., & Cummingm G. (2005). Effect size estimates and confidence intervals: An alternative focus for the presentation and interpretation of ecological data. In Burk, R. A. (Ed.), *New trends in ecology research* (pp. 71–102). New York: Nova Science Publishers.

(2) Walshe, T., & Wintle, B. (2006). *Guidelines for communicating performance against standards in forest management.* Victoria, Australia: Forest and Wood Products Research and Development Corporation.

(3) Novak, B. (2007). *Ethnic-specific health needs assessment for Pacific People in Counties Manukau* (p. 5). Manukau, New Zealand: Counties Manukau District Health Board.

7.3   The Mean ± the Standard Error

MacRae, A. F. (2002). Experimental evidence that the maize activator (Ac) transposase can act on a non-transposable element promoter to repress reporter gene expression in transient plant assays. *Genetica, 115,* 289–309, 297.

7.4   Confidence Intervals and Replication

(1) Cumming, G., & Maillardet, R. (2006). Confidence intervals and replication: Where will the next mean fall? *Psychological Methods, 11,* 217–227, 218.

(2) Kaye, D. H., & Freedman, D. A. (2000). Reference guide on statistics. *Reference manual on scientific evidence* (2nd ed.), Federal Judicial Center, pp. 83–178, p. 119.

8.1   Alpha and Type I Error Risk

(1) *Testing hypotheses.* (2006). Retrieved on November 9, 2007, from http:// www.nsiassi.de/mathe/Statistics2/is_3_scr.pdf.

(2) Easton, V. J., & McCall, J. H. (n.d.) *Statistics glossary: Hypothesis testing.* Retrieved September 23, 2007, from http://www.stats.gla.ac.uk/steps/glossary/ hypothesis_testing.html.

(3) Kazmier, L. J. (2004). *Business statistics.* New York: McGraw-Hill, p. 86.

8.2   The Null Hypothesis

(1) Healey, J. F. (2005). *Statistics: A tool for social research* (7th ed.,). Belmont, CA: Thomson Wadsworth, p. 198.

(2) Palmer, E. L., & Thompson-Schill, S. L. (2001). *How to prepare for the GRE in psychology* (5th ed., p. 191). Barrons.

(3) *Inference in practice.* Retrieved November 4, 2007, from http://files.ilovemath. org/uploads/administrator/1.

8.3   Disproving H_o

(1) James Cook University. (n.d.). JCU study skills online: Statistical tests. Retrieved October 4, 2007, from http://www.jcu.edu.au/studying/services/ studyskills/scientific/tests.html.

(2) Caruso, J. C. (n.d.). *Converting research questions into statistical hypotheses.* Retrieved October 26, 2007, from http://www.diss-stat.com/files/converting. pdf.

(3) Vowler, S. (2007). Interpreting data—Assessing study results and reports. *Hospital Pharmacist, 14,* 47–51, 48.

8.4   The Meaning of *p*

(1) Sheldon, L. K. (2007). *Quick look nursing: Oxygenation.* Sudbury, MA: Jones and Bartlett, p. 317.

(2) Connor, J. T. (2004). The value of a *p*-valueless paper. *American Journal of Gastroenterology, 99,* 1638–1640, 1639.

(3) *Tools for teaching and assessing statistical inference.* (n.d.). Retrieved October 26, 2007, from the University of Minnesota Web site: http://www.tc.umn. edu/~delma001/stat_tools/tools_p_value.htm#MISCONCEPTIONS.

8.5   Directionality and Tails

(1) Powers, B. A., & Knapp, T. R. (2006). *Dictionary of nursing theory and research* New York: Springer, p. 174.
(2) Wills, G. B., Heath, I., Crowder, R. M., & Hall, W. (1999). *User evaluation of an industrial hypermedia application* (chap. 2, sect. 2.4.1.1). Retrieved on November 14, 2007, from http://eprints.ccs.soton.ac.uk/821/2/html/section2.htm.
(3) Singh, K. (2007). *Quantitative social research methods* Thousand Oaks, CA: Sage, p. 156.

8.6   The Relationship Between Alpha and Beta Errors

(1) *Hypothesis testing.* Retrieved October 3, 2007, from http://academic.umf. maine.edu/~hardys/372/hypotesthandout.htm.
(2) PowerPoint presentation to accompany Berenson, M. L., Levine, D. M., & Krehbiel, T. C. (2003). *Basic business statistics* (slide 14, chap. 9). Prentice Hall.
(3) Ganter, P. (n.d.). *Comparing two independent samples.* Retrieved October 15, 2007, from http://www.tnstate.edu/ganter/BIO%20311%20Ch%20 7%202Sample.html.

9.1   Correlated *t*-Tests

Pearson Education. (n.d.). *If my study adopts a within subjects design, in which repeated measures are taken on a single sample, why is this not a correlation study?* Retrieved October 26, 2007, from http://wps.pearsoned.co.uk/ema_uk_ he_mcqueen_resmeth_1/0,11662,2970120-content,00.html.

9.2   The Difference Between Two Means If $p < .0001$.

(1) Gliner, J. A., Leach, N. L., & Morgan, G. A. (2002). Problems with null hypothesis significance testing (NHST): What do the textbooks say? *Journal of Experimental Education, 71*, 83–92, 85.
(2) Nickerson, R. S. (2000). Null hypothesis significance testing: A review of an old and continuing controversy. *Psychological Methods, 5*, 241–301, p. 246.
(3) Kotrlik, J. W., & Williams, H. A. (2003). The incorporation of effect size in information technology, learning, and performance research. *Information Technology, Learning, and Performance Journal, 21*(1), 1–7, 2–3.

9.3   The Robustness of a *t*-Test When $n_1 = n_2$

(1) Gass, S. M., & Torres, M. J. A. (2005). Attention when? An investigation of the ordering effect of input and interaction. *Studies in Second Language Acquisition, 27*(1), 1–31, 26.

(2) Dawson, B., & Trapp, R. G. (2004). *Basic & clinical biostatistics.* New York: McGraw-Hill Professional, p. 139.

(3) Ulrich, R. (2005). Electronic message posted to Sci.Stat.Math newsgroup. Retrieved November 3, 2007, from http://sci.tech-archive.net/Archive/sci.stat.math/2005-11/msg00014.html.

10.1   Pairwise Comparisons

(1) Ministry of Social Development, New Zealand. (2006). *Work, family and parenting study: Research findings.* Retrieved October 26, 2007, from http://www.msd.govt.nz/documents/work-areas/csre/work-family-parenting-report.doc.

(2) Scott, I., & Mazhindu, D. (2005). *Statistics for health care professionals.* Thousand Oaks, CA: Sage, p. 132.

(3) *Oneway analysis of variance.* Retrieved October 19, 2007, from http://www.valpo.edu/psych/SPSS/FINAL%20WORD/HTML/Chapter%2013.htm.

10.2   The Cause of a Significant Interaction

(1) Amitay, S., Ahissar, M., & Nelken, I. (2002). Auditory processing deficits in reading disabled adults. *Journal of the Association for Research in Otolaryngology, 3,* 302–320.

(2) Kopek, D. M., & Suarez, A. (2004). *Can applied ABA be used in desert turfgrass management?* University of Arizona College of Agriculture 2004 Turfgrass and Ornamental Research Report. Retrieved July 22, 2007, from http://cals.arizona.edu/pubs/crops/az1359/az13593b3.pdf.

10.3   Equal Covariate Means in ANCOVA

Patterson, P. K. (2006). *Effect of study abroad on intercultural sensitivity.* Unpublished doctoral dissertation, University of Missouri, Columbia, p. 54.

11.1   Statistical Significance Versus Practical Significance

(1) Gliner, J. A., Leech, N. L., & Morgan, G. A. (2002). Problems with null hypothesis significance testing (NHST): What do the textbooks say? *Journal of Experimental Education, 71*, 83–92, 86.

(2) Perry, F. L. (2005). *Research in applied linguisitics: Becoming a discerning consumer* (p. 169). London: Routledge.

(3) Armstrong, J. S. (2001). *Principles of forecasting: A handbook for researchers and practitioners* (p. 462). New York: Springer.

11.2   A Priori and Post Hoc Power

(1) Hoenig, J. M., & Heisey, D. M. (2001). The abuse of power: The pervasive fallacy of power calculations for data analysis. *The American Statistician, 55*, 19–24, 19.

(2) Baguley, T. (2004). Understanding statistical power in the context of applied research. *Applied Ergonomics, 35*, 73–80, 75.

(3) Simon, S. (2005). *Post hoc power is never justified*. Retrieved October 8, 2007, from http://www.childrens-mercy.org/stats/wcblog2005/PostHocPower.asp.

11.3   Eta Squared and Partial Eta Squared

(1) Bibby, P. (2003). *C82MST* [Lecture notes]. Statistical Methods 2, University of Nottingham, UK. Retrieved October 14, 2007, from http://www.psychology.nottingham.ac.uk/staff/pal/stats/C82MST/C82MST%20Lecture%205.ppt#24.

(2) Breaugh, J. A. (2003). Effect size estimation: Factors to consider and mistakes to avoid. *Journal of Management, 29*, 79–97, 89.

(3) Administrator. (2007). *Eta squared or partial eta squared?* Retrieved August 25, 2007, from http://www.readybb.com/egss/viewtopic.php?t=13&start=0.

12.1   Comparing Two *r*'s; Comparing Two *b*'s

(1) Ulrich, R. (2002). Message posted on the Edstat discussion board. Retrieved September 18, 2007, from http://www.mail-archive.com/edstat@lists.ncsu.edu/msg00553.html.

(2) Retrieved on October 31, 2007, from http://courses.unt.edu/yeatts/Classes%20taught%20in%20past/6200-Multivariate%20Stats/Lectures-Tests/Test%202/Chapter%206-regression-correlation-continued.pdf.

12.2 R^2

(1) Harrell, F. E. (2000). Overfitting and R-square [Msg 1]. Message posted to http://www.biostat.wustl.edu/archives/html/s-news/2000–08/msg00044. html.
(2) Babyak, M. (2004). What you see may not be what you get: A brief, nontechnical introduction to overfitting in regression-type models. *Psychosomatic Medicine, 66,* 411–421, 411.
(3) Stevens, J. P. (2002). *Applied multivariate statistics for the behavioral sciences.* Mahwah, NJ: Earlbaum, p. 93.

12.3 Predictor Variables That Are Uncorrelated With *Y*

(1) Walker, D. A. (2003). Suppressor variable(s) importance within a regression model: An example of salary compression from career services. *Journal of College Student Development, 44*(1), 127–133, 127.
(2) Woolley, K. K. (1997). *How variables uncorrelated with the dependent variable can actually make excellent predictors: The important suppressor variable case.* Paper presented at the annual meeting of the Southwest Educational Research Association, Austin, TX.
(3) Paulhus, D. L., Robins, R. W., Trzesniewski, K. H., & Tracy, J. L. (2004). Two replicable suppressor situations in personality research. *Multivariate Behavioral Research, 39,* 303–328, 323.

12.4 Beta Weights

(1) Vaillant, G. E. (1995). *The natural history of alcoholism revisited* (p. 93). Cambridge, MA: Harvard University Press.
(2) Lee, J. H. (2007). *Asian American perceived racism: Acculturation, racial identity, social context, and sociopolitical awareness as predictors of Asian American perceived racism.* Unpublished master's thesis, Georgia State University, Atlanta, pp. 61, 69.

SUBJECT INDEX

AUTHOR INDEX